Making extensive use of previously unpublished material, this book gives an unprecedented view of the Waterloo Campaign from the viewpoint of a single regiment. It reveals the preparations that preceded the battle, the role of the regiment in the battle, and the long months spent in France after Paris fell, until the regiment finally returned home in December 1815. An Order Book for the year, and letters and diaries of several officers, shed light on the internal life of the regiment and their – occasionally humorous – social life.

Dr David Blackmore is the author of several books, including the acclaimed *Destructive and Formidable*, an account of British Infantry firepower from 1642 to 1765. He is also well known for his work on the English Civil Wars. He was formerly the Registrar of the Royal Armouries, is a reenactor of over 45 years experience, a keen horseman, and a Fellow of the Society of Antiquaries.

In memory of my mother, Doreen Blackmore, who always encouraged
1930–2018

So Bloody a Day

The 16th Light Dragoons in the Waterloo Campaign

David J. Blackmore

Helion & Company Limited

Helion & Company Limited
Unit 8 Amherst Business Centre
Budbrooke Road
Warwick
CV34 5WE
England
Tel. 01926 499 619
Email: info@helion.co.uk
Website: www.helion.co.uk
Twitter: @helionbooks
Visit our blog http://blog.helion.co.uk/

Published by Helion & Company 2019
Designed and typeset by Mary Woolley (www.battlefield-design.co.uk)
Cover designed by Paul Hewitt, Battlefield Design (www.battlefield-design.co.uk)

ISBN 978-1-912866-66-3

British Library Cataloguing-in-Publication Data.
A catalogue record for this book is available from the British Library.

For details of other military history titles published by Helion & Company Limited contact the above address or visit our website: http://www.helion.co.uk.

We always welcome receiving book proposals from prospective authors.

Contents

List of Plates and Maps

Introduction

This is not a narrative of the Battle of Waterloo; it is rather the story of one regiment's experiences in the battle, the campaign, and its aftermath. It is the battle as seen from the viewpoint of the men of that regiment, and as such some famous incidents pass unremarked. It is also the story of their preparations for the campaign, and their experiences as part of the army of occupation, right up until their return to England in December 1815. Regrettably, there are no voices from the ranks, but, unusually, three of the officers whose writings contribute to this book were in the same troop: Captain William Tomkinson, Lieutenant John Luard, and Cornet William Beckwith.

Captain Tomkinson's diary covers not only the Waterloo campaign, but also his service with the 16th in the Peninsular War. In the chapter dealing with the 16th in the Peninsula, I have used Tomkinson's diary as edited by his son.[1] Where possible, quotes have been checked against the original diary, but there is a gap in the original from 20 March 1810 to 30 March 1812. Additionally, place names have been updated with their modern spelling; where the names are incomplete or have changed completely, the complete or new name is also given. It is important to be aware of the 16th's experiences before 1815: those made them the effective regiment that they were, which is something that probably contributed to their relatively low casualties at Waterloo. Indeed, Tomkinson suggests as much. The Waterloo account is a new transcription from the diary. The order book used here is that of Captain Tomkinson's Troop and is previously unpublished. This is full of a wealth of information concerning training, uniforms, and equipment. Both the diary and the order book are in the Cheshire Record Office and are reproduced with the permission of Cheshire Archives & Local Studies.

The letters, diary, Waterloo journal, portrait of Lieutenant John Luard, and his sketch of Eu, appear by kind permission of the Luard Family and have been made available from the Luard Family Archive. Luard wrote both a Waterloo diary and a Waterloo journal, the latter written some years later.[2] I owe a debt of gratitude to The Venerable Clive Cohen for obtaining access to these and the permission to publish them.

1 James Tomkinson (ed.) and Lieutenant Colonel William Tomkinson, *The Diary of a Cavalry Officer in the Peninsular War and Waterloo Campaign, 1809–1815* (Frederick Muller: London, 1971).

2 Clive Cohen (2016) 'John Luard'. Email (30 November 2016).

The letter of Cornet Beckwith, also of Tomkinson's Troop, is held by the regimental museum of the Queen's Royal Lancers at Thoresby Hall in Nottinghamshire, and I am grateful to Captain Mick Holtby for his help and permission to publish. I am equally grateful to the Auckland War Memorial Museum for the splendid portrait of Quartermaster John Harrison.

The portraits of William Tomkinson and Clement Swetenham are in private collections, and I am grateful to their owners for permission to publish them. Anthony Jacques kindly gave permission to publish Clement Swetenham's letter. Thanks are also due to Jeremy Swetenham, a descendant of Captain Clement Swetenham, for his help with that. The letter of Lieutenant Harris, of Swetenham's Troop is also in a private collection, and I am grateful to Richard Foden for permission to publish it. The portrait and sword of Cornet Polhill are still with the descendants of his sister; he never married, and I am grateful to William Acton for making it possible for photographs of them to appear. The family also donated Cornet Polhill's uniform to the Royal United Services Institute, and from there it was transferred to the National Army Museum. The images of the uniform are reproduced courtesy of the Council of the National Army Museum. Thanks are also due to Oonagh Drage and Tennants auctioneers for help with Cornet Beckwith's pistol.

Letters from the regiment's officers to Siborne are not included, as they are readily available, but they will be quoted from in the commentary on the battle itself.

Transcribing this original material has provided some difficulties. The order book was particularly challenging, being a day-by-day recording of orders in a number of different hands of differing degrees of legibility. Matters have not been helped by the phonetic versions of place names and some places having changed their names completely. As with the diary, where possible, I have corrected the spelling of place names. Where there is uncertainty, or the name has simply been completed, this appears in brackets, thus: *Bellegely [Bellignies?]* or *Boussoit [sur Haine]*. Otherwise the original spelling in the manuscripts has been retained. Illegible words are indicated by *[...]* and sheer guesswork by *[?]*. All errors are mine.

Finally, my thanks are also due to Dr Andrew Bamford and Dr Jacqueline Reiter of Helion, and Janet McKay.

1

The 16th in the Peninsula

The year 1808 saw Wellington defeat the French at Vimeiro, despite not being the senior British officer present.[1] That was Sir Harry Burrard, who arrived on the eve of the battle from Britain as one of a number of officers, all senior to Wellington, dispatched to the Peninsula. He, however, wisely allowed Wellington to get on with it. Soon after that Sir Hew Dalrymple arrived, who was senior to Burrard; he then assumed command. Following the defeat of the French at Vimeiro, Burrard and Dalrymple concluded the controversial Convention of Cintra with the French, which they insisted Wellington sign, under the terms of which the French evacuated Portugal. This did not go down well in London and all three commanders – Wellington, Burrard and Dalrymple – were recalled to face an inquiry into the Convention, leaving Sir John Moore in command. Later in the year came the disastrous Corunna campaign that resulted in the defeat of Sir John Moore's army and the death of its commander. It was not until early 1809 that Wellington was sent back to Portugal as commander-in-chief.

In early 1809 the 16th was in Devon, based in Exeter with squadrons at Taunton and Tiverton, when it was informed that it was going to the Peninsula. On 7 April the regiment sailed from Falmouth and disembarked in Portugal on 16 April.[2] Thus the regiment was in Portugal six days before Wellington.

It was commanded by Lieutenant Colonel the Honourable George Anson, and amongst its officers were many who would go on to fight at Waterloo, including Lieutenant (as he was then) William Tomkinson. In addition to Tomkinson's diary, the other main source for the 16th in the Peninsular War are the journals and letters of Captain Cocks, who was killed at the siege of Burgos in October 1812, having just gained promotion into the 79th Foot.[3]

1 At that time, Wellington was just Sir Arthur Wellesley. As the main subject of this book is the Waterloo campaign, by the time of which he had become the Duke of Wellington, he will be referred to throughout as Wellington.

2 Colonel Henry Graham, *History of the 16th, the Queen's, Light Dragoons (Lancers), 1759 to 1912* (Devizes: George Simpson, 1912), p.23.

3 Julia V. Page, *Intelligence Officer in the Peninsula* (Tunbridge Wells: Spellmount, 1986).

By May the 16th had been brigaded with the 14th Light Dragoons in the brigade commanded by Sir Stapleton Cotton, and was at Coimbra with the army under the command of Wellington. The French, under Marshal Soult, were at Oporto. On 9 April the regiment had its first experience of bivouacking. As Tomkinson wrote:

> This was an event much thought of, and every officer was employed in bringing into use the various inventions recommended in England for such occasions, many of which were found useless; and, again many essentials had been left behind, from a determination to face the campaign with the fewest number of comforts, whereby many requisites were omitted which were now found indispensable. But we were young soldiers, had listened to every suggestion, and can only learn by experience.[4]

The following day saw the 16th's first engagement of the Peninsular War, and their first charge, in which two squadrons successfully drove off four French squadrons.

> Here we found four squadrons of French light cavalry formed, for the purpose of covering the retreat of their main body, consisting of two regiments. There were two squadrons in advance [of the enemy's], with the other two in support. The 16th passed a small ravine, and on forming moved to the brow of a small hill, from the top of which, about two hundred yards distant, on an easy declivity, the two squadrons were formed. The squadron I belonged to, and another of the 16th, were the two in advance. These were the two which charged. The instant we saw the enemy from the top of the hill, the word was given. The men set up an huzzah, and advanced to the charge. The enemy fired a volley at us when about fifty yards from them, and then went about, setting off as hard as they could ride, we pursuing, cutting at them, and making all the prisoners in our power. Their other two squadrons in support went about, and the whole retired in no small confusion. The affair was more like a skirmish at a field day than an affair with an enemy.[5]

A less successful action followed on 11 May, in which Tomkinson was severely wounded and subsequently sent home to recover, resulting in a gap in his account from then until he re-joined the regiment in mid-April 1810.[6]

On 12 May 1809, however, Wellington crossed the River Douro, the result of which was the withdrawal of the French to Spain. This brilliantly executed river crossing was primarily an infantry affair. The 16th appears to have played no part at all. Wellington pursued the French through Salamonde, where Soult's rear-guard was attacked and driven off, until they reached Montalegre and the border with Spain. Further pursuit being unnecessary, Wellington returned to Oporto, the 16th marching back to Coimbra.

4 Tomkinson (ed.), *Diary of a Cavalry Officer*, p.3.
5 Tomkinson (ed.), *Diary of a Cavalry Officer*, pp.5
6 Tomkinson (ed.), *Diary of a Cavalry Officer*, pp.8-10

Wellington's next major engagement was the battle of Talavera, fought over 27 and 28 July 1809. Although the 16th suffered some casualties from artillery fire, they were not engaged. The battle was, however, a very hard-fought one; as Cocks wrote to his father, 'so bloody an action has seldom been fought.'[7] The only cavalry charge was made by Anson's brigade, the 23rd Light Dragoons, and the 1st Hussars of the King's German Legion.[8] The 23rd failed to see a dry river bed, into which they galloped. In the ensuing melee they suffered so badly that they were subsequently shipped back to Britain to rebuild the shattered regiment. They saw no further action until Waterloo. The 1st had advanced less precipitately, and although they too came across the river bed, they did not suffer so badly. Following the battle, Wellington was unable to agree a plan with Spanish General Cuesta, who commanded the Spanish army at Talavera. A gradual retreat followed and by early September Wellington had made his headquarters at Badajoz, while the 16th found themselves quartered in Vila Viçosa. That area was soon found to be particularly unhealthy. At one point, 19 of the regiment's officers were ill and Assistant Surgeon Healde died in hospital at Estremos. Consequently the regiment moved to Abrantes in Estremadura, a small town on the Tagus.[9]

In April 1810 Tomkinson re-joined the regiment, finding the regiment's headquarters and one squadron at Santa Comba Dão, with the rest in adjacent villages. He was sent to Friexedas to look after the regiment's horse that were out to grass. The 16th was then brigaded with the 1st Hussars, King's German Legion, the brigade being commanded by Major General Anson. On 28 April Tomkinson was posted to Captain Cocks' B Troop, thus beginning a relationship that would last until Cocks left the regiment, when Tomkinson succeeded to command of that same troop, which he commanded until he left for Britain in September 1813.[10]

William Tomkinson. (Private Collection)

7 Page, *Intelligence Officer*, p.37.
8 Anson had been promoted to major general and given a brigade. The 16th was then commanded by Lieutenant Colonel Clement Archer.
9 Graham, *History of the 16th*, p.32.
10 Tomkinson (ed.), *Diary of a Cavalry Officer*, pp.21–22.

In June, the brigade was acting in support of Crauford's Light Division between the Agueda and Coa rivers, providing a line of pickets and outposts in front of Gallegos, facing the French (now under Marshal Masséna) who were besieging Cuidad Rodrigo to the east. Despite their presence in the major battles of the Peninsula, it was this sort of work that was the meat and drink of light cavalry. Tomkinson gave a clear description of the situation and the routine involved.

> Piquets of infantry and cavalry occupied the line of the Azaba from the right as far as Carpio, to its junction with the Agueda, and on that river at the ford of Molleno de Floris. General Crawford's headquarters with his infantry were in Gallegos [de Argañán]; the *Caçadores* encamped on the hill on the right of Gallegos, opposite Carpio [de Azaba]. Two squadrons of the 16th, with one of the Hussars, in Gallegos; the other detached to Villa de Puerca [now Villar de Argañán], a league to the left, watching the passes of Barba de Puerca [Puerto Seguro], and the others up to our chain of posts.
>
> From the Azaba to Gallegos is one short league, and two from that river to Cuidad Rodrigo. The enemy have about 8,000 men over the Agueda, which makes us particularly on the alert. We never unsaddle excepting in the evening, merely to clean the horses; and at night the men sleep in their appointments, with their bridle reins in their hands, ready to turn out in an instant. At two in the morning, the whole turn out and remain on their alarm ground until the piquets relieved, come in, and all is quiet.[11]
>
> The 16th, this day, took their share of the duty. The three squadrons found four officer's piquets along the chain of posts. Right piquet at Carpio Ford, an officer, serjeant, and two corporals, and eighteen men supported by infantry at night.
>
> The Mill Ford, an officer and eighteen, sergeant and corporal.
>
> Marialba Bridge: the same, with infantry.
>
> Molleno de Floris (on the Agueda), an officer and twelve of cavalry, with an officer and twenty of infantry.[12]

Tomkinson's first experience of picket duty came on 29 June, and was not without incident, an alarm being caused by an enemy general out for a ride. As Tomkinson commented, it 'may be a pleasant ride for them, though if they would not move their troops it would save us much unnecessary trouble.'[13] On 4 July Tomkinson was in charge of the picket at Marialba Bridge when the French crossed in strength. What followed was a running fight as two squadrons of the 16th and one of the 1st KGL Hussars retired back thorough Gallegos and towards La Almeda. A stand was made briefly at a brook just behind Gallegos, but this position was outflanked. Tomkinson wrote:

11 Tomkinson (ed.), *Diary of a Cavalry Officer*, p.25.
12 Tomkinson (ed.), *Diary of a Cavalry Officer*, p.26.
13 Tomkinson (ed.), *Diary of a Cavalry Officer*, pp.26–27.

> For the last half-mile we were obliged to gallop, with the French dragoons close at our heels, and formed in rear of the infantry, which was drawn up in line in front of the village of La Almeda, and received the enemy with a volley which completely checked them ...[14]

Cocks praised the German Hussars:

> The Hussars behaved particularly well. It would be unfair not to bear unqualified testimony to their courage, zeal and knowledge of their duty. They have not such good seats as English dragoons but their horses are under better command and, I think, better taken care of ...[15]

On the night of 10 July Major General Craufurd assembled a force consisting of two squadrons of the 16th, three of the 14th, and one of the 1st Hussars and marched towards Villa de Puerca. By dawn the force was concealed in a hollow just outside the village. Craufurd rode forward alone to reconnoitre, and when he returned the force advanced in open column of divisions. The advance was delayed by a defile and the enemy alerted. The 1st Hussars' squadron was leading and charged a square of French infantry, but failed to break it. The 16th were sent after some cavalry near Barquilla to the north, and captured two officers and 30 dragoons. Meanwhile the 14th, led by their commander, Lieutenant Colonel Talbot, charged the infantry, in which attack Talbot was killed. A squadron each of the 14th and the 1st Hussars then appeared unexpectedly and were mistaken for French cavalry. In all the confusion, the French infantry withdrew. Tomkinson wrote that 'never was a business so badly managed.'[16] Cocks also pulled no punches in attributing responsibility for the affair. He wrote that:

> ... things were ill-managed. General Crauford [*sic*] appeared to have forgot his own arrangements and our own squadrons were repeatedly pointed out to us as enemies.
>
> On the whole it was very mortifying that an affair, ably planned and favourably carried on to the moment of action should, in the end, turn out so ill through a too great precipitancy in the execution.[17]

Cuidad Rodrigo fell to the French on 10 July and on 24 July Craufurd was attacked and the Light Division was driven back across the Coa after some hard fighting. Subsequently the French besieged Almeida while Craufurd retired to join Wellington at Busaco. In the retreat the 16th suffered badly, with three officers wounded. However, Tomkinson and Cocks were on detached duty, watching to see which way the French would advance. By late July they

14 Tomkinson (ed.), *Diary of a Cavalry Officer*, p.29.
15 Page, *Intelligence Officer*, p.62.
16 Tomkinson (ed.), *Diary of a Cavalry Officer*, p.31.
17 Page, *Intelligence Officer*, pp.64–65.

were encamped at the Convent of Nossa Senhora do Monte, on a hill overlooking Cerdeira. This was their base for a whole month and Tomkinson described it in some detail:

> It was a most excellent camp, the trees affording capital shade: and from the length of time we had been there, each man had a good hut, and the encampment wore the appearance of a small village. We were much safer from any sudden attack; the men and horses both continued healthy from having plenty to eat and something to employ themselves with. The men got as much rye-bread, mutton, potatoes, and wheat-flour from the adjacent mills as they wanted, and the horses as much rye in the ear and thrashed as they could eat, and now and then some wheat nearly ripe. Cocks and myself had nothing with us but a change of linen, a pot to boil potatoes, and the same to make some coffee in, with a frying pan, which were carried on his led horse. We never wanted for a single article excepting wheat-bread, which failed us occasionally, and with a person not accustomed to rye, it does not agree. We could always march in five minutes, never slept out of out clothes, and never enjoyed better health; half-past two in the morning was the hour we got up.[18]

Tomkinson re-joined the main body of the 16th on 5 September at Mesquitela; Cocks continued his patrols as Wellington retreated, finally re-joining the regiment on the ridge at Busaco. On 25 September the regiment was at the northern end of the ridge of Busaco, the regimental headquarters in Moita and Cocks's troop in Vale da Mó. The battle of Busaco was fought on 27 September, but the 16th and the rest of the cavalry took no part.

Wellington was now retiring towards the Lines of Torres Vedras. These were a series of defensive works constructed from the Atlantic to the River Tagus, and which the French were completely unaware of. During the retreat to the Lines the 16th were involved in a number of rear-guard actions. At Pombal on 5 October the French pressed hard; Captain Murray led his squadron in a number of charges, and Lieutenant Penrice captured a French officer. The brigade retired across the Rio de Manda Nilla [?] covered by Captain Swetenham's squadron. He was hard pressed and wounded in the thigh. Then, on the 8th, there was a sharp skirmish in the streets of Alcoentre, where a troop of horse artillery was nearly captured by French dragoons. As the French 14e Dragons entered the town, driving back Captain Murray's squadron, they were charged in the flank by Cocks's squadron from a side road. Six French dragoons were killed and another 12 captured. On the 9th Captain Linsingen's squadron of the 1st KGL Hussars was attacked by two regiments of French cavalry, forcing him to retreat. Cocks's squadron had formed behind the bridge at Quinta da Torre; he allowed the Hussars past and then charged the French, driving them back across the bridge. Twice Cocks had to charge and Tomkinson wrote of the enemy, the French 3e Hussards: 'I never saw their cavalry behave so well.' He also gave an insight into how the cavalry rode:

18 Tomkinson (ed.), *Diary of a Cavalry Officer*, pp.37–38.

> In retiring the second time I caught my bradoon rein in the appointments of a French Hussar who was dismounted lying on the ground, and cut it just as they were about to make me prisoner. My horse's head was held down to the ground, being caught in his appointments; they were not five yards from me when I cut it. I spurred my horse two or three times in hope he would break it; this he did not, and I was fortunate to catch the rein fair at the first cut, and going through it. I will take care not to go into action with a loose bradoon rein.[19]

The bridle used by the British cavalry at this time was a double one, with two bits, a curb and a bridoon, each with its own set of reins. A modern rider will use both bits and sets of reins together but at that time it was usual for cavalry to ride solely on the curb, the bridoon rein lying loose on the horse's neck. This is something that can be seen in many contemporary images. The other point of interest is just how sharp Tomkinson's sword must have been to slice through the rein in one cut. Even if the rein was pulled taught, it was still a leather strap about half an inch wide and an eighth of an inch thick.

On 10 October the 16th passed within the Lines of Torres Vedras, and on the 11th arrived at Mafra. The 16th was billeted in the stables and cloisters of the great convent.[20] Cocks recorded that:

> We had been almost constantly in the field without even tents, for near four months, and our late, long marches had completely worn our shoes. Two or three days more such would have ruined us by laming every horse …[21]

After 10 days at Mafra for the brigade 'to shoe up and refresh itself,' the brigade was ordered north to Ramahal, the 16th taking up quarters in the adjacent village of Ameal.[22] By mid-November Cocks and his squadron were posted in the town of Óbidos, further to the north. It is a mediaeval town sitting on a hill top that dominates the local area, and it is surrounded by high, mediaeval walls. The presence of a Portuguese garrison meant that the dragoons were not required to stand guard duty.[23]

The squadron marched from Óbidos on 16 November and joined the rest of the brigade at Quinta da Torre, Alcoentre having been abandoned by the French. On the 17th the brigade advanced towards Santerém, Cocks's squadron acting as the advance guard. Just past the village of Almoster the advance was halted and parties sent out in various directions from Cocks's squadron. What followed showed the quality of the men and NCOs of the 16th, and is best described in Tomkinson's words:

19 Tomkinson (ed.), *Diary of a Cavalry Officer*, p.52.
20 Tomkinson (ed.), *Diary of a Cavalry Officer*, p.55.
21 Page, *Intelligence Officer*, p.87.
22 Page, *Intelligence Officer*, p.90.
23 Tomkinson (ed.), *Diary of a Cavalry Officer*, p.58.

On passing the village of Almoster we were ordered to halt, and sent out parties right and left after the plundering parties of the enemy. I went with twelve men to the left, and Captain Cocks with as many nearly in the same direction. I fell in at first with five infantry, with a flock of goats and nine asses. On our coming up they surrendered, and I forwarded them with two men to the brigade. I then fell in with thirteen infantry under a sergeant, escorting two mules with some asses laden with Indian corn. They at first seemed inclined to fire, cocking their muskets; but on our riding up, laid them down without a shot. Captain Cocks took twenty.

Sergeant Liddle of Captain Belli's troop, belonging to Cocks's squadron, was sent from Alcoentre with four men on patrol round by Rio Maior. He fell in with an officer and fifteen French infantry, and having followed them for some way, attacked them, when they all surrendered.

Sergeant Baxter was sent on patrol from the brigade with four men to the left.[24]

He met with an infantry piquet of the enemy's, stationed in a house with their arms piled in front, and got so near unobserved that he thought he might get to the arms before they could take them up. He galloped forward; they had time to turn out, gave him a volley wounding one of his men. It was too late to turn back; he persisted in his charge, rode up to the enemy, who laid down their arms, he killing one man. In all, forty-one men and an officer, which number he marched in. It was a most gallant thing; but though he succeeded, he was not justified in attacking them.

Sergeant Nicholls of Captain Cocks's troop, took sixteen infantry with six men, on the right, – though I think they were glad to find an English party to save them from the peasantry.

Sergeant Blood, of Captain Cocks's troop, was sent on patrol to our front, in the direction of Santarém.[25] He got within the enemy's line of piquets, and was surrounded by a troop of dragoons; he cut his way through them, losing Storer, of Captain Cocks's troop, who was made prisoner.[26] We were ordered to march to Santarem, and, should the enemy have left it, to occupy the town.[27]

After some days of manoeuvring around Santarém things settled down for the winter, save for the interminable rounds of '*petite guerre*' that continued. The 16th's brigade had its headquarters at Sãn João da Ribeira, while the 16th itself was at Malaqueijo, Rio Maior, and Entre Portas (possibly Arruda dos Pisões). When Cocks's squadron arrived Malaqueijo, 'The men had been without bread for three days, and procuring as much wine as they wished in the villages, many got drunk.'[28] In December there was a degree of fraternising between British and French officers, with invitations exchanged to plays, horse races, football, and

24 Baxter was a Troop Sergeant Major at Waterloo, where he was killed.
25 Regimental Sergeant Major at Waterloo.
26 There was a Joshua Storer at Waterloo.
27 Tomkinson (ed.), *Diary of a Cavalry Officer*, pp.59–60.
28 Tomkinson (ed.), *Diary of a Cavalry Officer*, p.62.

dog-hunts. A general order was issued putting a stop to it.[29] Throughout January the 16th continued its outpost work watching the enemy and capturing parties out plundering. On 18 January, his 21st birthday, Tomkinson (with two men) attacked a party of seven men of the French 6e Dragons, and captured one of them and three horses. He received a slight wound to his hand, a share of £64 from the sale of the horses, and a mention in the Cavalry Division Orders.[30]

In March, Masséna began a withdrawal back to Spain, his rear-guard commanded by Marshal Ney. On the 9th the French abandoned Leira; Belli's and Cocks's troops, commanded by Lieutenants Weyland and Tomkinson[31] respectively, captured a picket of a sergeant, two corporals, and 22 men after a long chase near Pombal. This squadron then joined one from the 1st KGL Hussars and together they broke, successively, eight squadrons of French cavalry:

> We passed the defile in our front, and came up in time to join the advanced squadron of the Hussars in their charge. We first broke one squadron of the enemy, drove that that on the second; so on, until the whole eight were altogether in the greatest confusion, when we drove them on their main support. We wounded several, and took a few prisoners, and should have made more, only they were so thick that we could not get into them.[32]

On 11 March the 16th was temporarily brigaded with the 14th Light Dragoons, the 1st KGL Hussars having joined the 1st Royal Dragoons. The regiment was then under the command of Major Pelly, Lieutenant Colonel Archer being ill in Lisbon. Colonel Hawker of the 14th commanded the brigade.[33] This arrangement lasted until the 13th when the 16th re-joined the Hussars and re-formed their brigade under Lieutenant Colonel Arenschildt of the Hussars.[34]

The pursuit of Masséna as he withdrew from Portugal ended on 10 April when the French crossed the Agueda and retired to Salamanca. Wellington now laid siege to Almeida and the 16th was sent back, across the Coa, first to the area around Richioso and then to their old quarters in Gallegos de Argañán.[35]

In early May Masséna resumed the offensive and advanced from Cuidad Rodrigo, meeting Wellington at Fuentes de Oñoro. The battle began on the 3rd with unsuccessful French assaults on the village of Fuentes de Oñoro. The 4th was quiet, with sporadic firing and Masséna reconnoitring Wellington's position, before deciding to try to turn Wellington's right flank on the morning of the 5th. Captain Belli of the 16th with his squadron was on the extreme right with Major Meyers and a squadron of the 1st KGL Hussars. Belli charged

29 Tomkinson (ed.), *Diary of a Cavalry Officer*, p.64.
30 Tomkinson (ed.), *Diary of a Cavalry Officer*, p.69.
31 Cocks was on leave in England following the death of his father: Page, *Intelligence Officer*, p.100. Belli may also have been absent in England: Tomkinson (ed.), *Diary of a Cavalry Officer*, p.101.
32 Tomkinson (ed.), *Diary of a Cavalry Officer*, p.39.
33 Tomkinson (ed.), *Diary of a Cavalry Officer*, p.81.
34 Tomkinson (ed.), *Diary of a Cavalry Officer*, p.83.
35 Tomkinson (ed.), *Diary of a Cavalry Officer*, pp.98–99.

an enemy squadron, said by Tomkinson to be double their strength – although he was not an eyewitness, being in the rear of the army suffering with ague. He did describe the action in his diary, presumably based on the accounts of brother officers who were there:

> He [Major Meyers] waited so long and was so indecisive, and the enemy came up so close, that he ordered the squadron of 16th to charge. The enemy's squadron was about twice their strength, and waited their charge.
>
> This is the only instance I ever met with of two bodies of cavalry coming in opposition, and both standing, as invariably, as I have observed, one or the other runs away.
>
> Our men rode up and began sabring, but were obliged to retire across the defile in confusion, the enemy having brought up more troops to that point. Captain Belli [who had re-joined the regiment from England the day before] was wounded slightly, and taken; Sergeant Taylor, of his own troop, and six men from the squadron, were killed on the spot in attempting to rescue him.[36]

Lieutenant Blake was killed, and Lieutenant Weyland was wounded, both of the 16th; while Captain Krauchenburg of the Hussars and 30 to 40 men from both squadrons were wounded.[37]

Having failed to defeat Wellington, Masséna withdrew towards Salamanca. A few days later Major General Anson took command of the brigade, and on 20 May Tomkinson was fit enough to re-join his squadron, which was back in Gallegos de Argañán.[38] From there the regiment was slowly moved south. On 12 June it was at Nisa, where Tomkinson recorded how they camped:

> The troops got to Nisa just before dark, and the baggage not before 9 or 10. We encamped close to the town, and found abundance of hay on the ground.
>
> In using the word encamped I ought to say bivouacked, as the army had no tents. The men put one blanket on the ground, lay down in their cloaks, and being two together had another blanket to cover them. The officers did the same, and if it rained we got wet.[39]

The regiment joined the army at Arronches on 23 June, where it had withdrawn after giving up the siege of Badajos, which was relieved by Marshal Soult. Throughout July and August the 16th undertook the usual round of marches from one quarter to another patrols to watch the French, and suffering in the summer heat. By early September they were back on the

36 Tomkinson (ed.), *Diary of a Cavalry Officer*, pp.100–01.
37 Page, *Intelligence Officer*, p.103.
38 Tomkinson (ed.), *Diary of a Cavalry Officer*, p.103.
39 Tomkinson (ed.), *Diary of a Cavalry Officer*, p.106.

border with the brigade, now consisting of the 16th and 14th Light Dragoons, distributed in towns and villages from Sexmiro, through Martillán and up to Vilar de la Yuega.[40]

In late September the French advanced from Cuidad Rodrigo, pushing a strong force of cavalry along the road that passed through Carpio de Azaba. On the 25th eight squadrons crossed the Azaba and advanced towards Espeja where the 16th were, along with the 14th. Cocks, now a brevet major, took his squadron and one of the 14th forward and skirmished with the French while the brigade formed. As Cocks was commanding the two squadrons, his own squadron was commanded by Tomkinson. The four leading French squadrons, two of which were Lancers, were charged successively by a squadron of the 14th and then by the squadron of the 14th and three of the 16th. The French were driven back for two miles and across the Azaba. Tomkinson wrote of this action, 'The Lancers looked well and formidable before they were broken and closed to by our men, and then their lances were an encumbrance.'[41]

Up until October each cavalry regiment had fielded four squadrons. This was now reduced to three, and, in the case of the 16th, the troops of Captains MacIntosh and Belli were sent home. This choice was no doubt influenced by Belli being a prisoner of the French. MacIntosh, however, remained and took command of G Troop. In April 1810 Tomkinson noted that troop being commanded by Captain Lygon, but nowhere did he say what happened to him for the command of his troop to have become vacant.[42] It is possible that Lygon returned home with the two troops sent back.

Clement Swetenham. (Private Collection)

In January 1812 Wellington laid siege to Ciudad Rodrigo, which fell on the 19th, and the 16th marched to quarters in and around Coja. Here a number of changes to the organisation of the regiment took place, which are best described in Tomkinson's own words:

> A day after our arrival Captain Swetenham's troop, from the centre squadron, and Captain MacIntosh's troop, from the right, were ordered to occupy San Rosnan. This gave a squadron to Swetenham, who was not entitled

40 Tomkinson (ed.), *Diary of a Cavalry Officer*, p.113.
41 Tomkinson (ed.), *Diary of a Cavalry Officer*, p.115.
42 Tomkinson (ed.), *Diary of a Cavalry Officer*, pp.22, pp.118–19.

> to one, [and] took squadrons from two officers, *viz.*: Captain Murray and Major Cocks, both his senior, and permanently commanding their squadrons in the regiment. Our Colonel is uncle to Swetenham.[43]
>
> Major Stanhope was gazetted out of the 16th to the 17th Light Dragoons as Lieutenant Colonel, in reward for the long campaign he has had in Bond Street since the time he left the 16th in July 1810. Captain Hay got the majority, Lieutenant Persse the troop.[44]

However, Captain Swetenham was not long in command of his squadron, leaving the Peninsula in February to return to the regimental depot. Command of his troop was given to Tomkinson, and formed part of Major Cocks's squadron. 'In consequence of his [Swetenham's] departure I was appointed to the command of his troop, and left Cocks after having been with him for nearly two years. I before refused the command of a troop out of his squadron, and would not have taken this had it been out of the one under his command.'[45]

The siege of Badajoz started on 17 March, the 16th with the rest of their brigade moving first to Vila Viçosa and then to Olivenza. Whilst there Tomkinson penned some comments on cavalry training:

> We do everything so quickly that it is impossible men can understand what they are about. They have enough to do to sit their horse and keep in the ranks, without giving their attention to any sudden order. Before the enemy, except in charging, I never saw troops go beyond a trot, though in some cases it might be required, and therefore in some movements they should be taught to gallop. These are few, such as moving to a flank in open column of divisions or half-squadrons, wheeling into line and charging without a halt. In England I never saw nor heard of cavalry taught to charge, disperse, and form, which, if I only taught a regiment one thing, I think it should be that. To attempt giving men or officers any idea in England of outpost duty was considered absurd, and when they came abroad, they had all this to learn. The fact was, there was no one to teach them. Sir Stapleton Cotton tried, at Woodbridge in Suffolk, with the 14th and 16th Light Dragoons, and got the enemy's *vedettes* and his own looking the same way. There is much to be learnt in service which cannot be done at home, though I do not mean to say nothing can be taught in England.[46]

Badajoz fell on the night of 6 April, while the 16th and the brigade were covering operations to the south around Villafranca de los Barros. On the 11th the regiment marched at 1:00 a.m. for Bienvenida, arriving at dawn. Moving through the town towards Villagarcía de la

43 This is a reference to Lieutenant Colonel Clement Archer, who was at that time in England on sick leave. J. Swetenham (2018) 'Clement's Uncle'. Email (28 October 2018).

44 Tomkinson (ed.), *Diary of a Cavalry Officer*, p.126.

45 Tomkinson (ed.), *Diary of a Cavalry Officer*, p.129.

46 Tomkinson (ed.), *Diary of a Cavalry Officer*, p.135.

Torre, approximately seven or eight miles away, the regiment halted after a couple of miles and dismounted. Ahead of them the 12th and 14th Light Dragoons, who had marched from Usagre, had driven the enemy's *vedettes* off the high ground to the west of Villagarcía just before the 16th came into view, leaving the French unaware of the presence of the 16th. In the rear of the 16th was Major General Le Marchant's brigade of the 5th Dragoon Guards and the 3rd and 4th Dragoons, also unseen by the French. Two squadrons, one each from the 12th and 14th, pushed through Villagarcía and found the main French cavalry force on the far side. This consisted of the 2e Hussards and 17e and 27e Dragons, approximately 2,300 in total. The two squadrons were driven back to the village where they were joined by the rest of the two regiments. The heavy cavalry brigade of Major General Le Marchant, meanwhile, was moving, completely unseen, around the left flank of the French, although the rough terrain mean that only the 5th would get up in time to be engaged. The 16th were also again on the move, and also unseen. The French were completely preoccupied with driving the 12th and 14th into Villagarcía when, more or less simultaneously, the 16th came up on the right flank of the 12th and 14th and the 5th appeared opposite the French left flank:[47]

> At this instant the 16th moved forward over the hills to the right of Villa Garcia, and came into the plain leading to Llerena on the right of the 12th. (The 12th and 14th were to our left.) Major General Le Marchant's brigade moved to our right, passing the hills at the same instant. The enemy had got close to Villa Garcia and the 5th Dragoon Guards from the road bearing away to the right, came down on their left flank, charged at the same time that we advanced, broke five squadrons, throwing the remainder into no small confusion back towards Llerena.
>
> When we came on the top of the hill, there were the 12th and 14th formed on our left, close in front of Villa Garcia. The enemy formed a quarter of a mile from them, and a small stone wall betwixt the 16th (our regiment) and the French. We came down the hill in a trot, took the wall in line, and were in the act of charging when the 5th Dragoon Guards came down on our right, charged, and completely upset the left flank of the enemy, and the 12th, 14th, and 16th advancing at the same moment, the success was complete. The view of the enemy from the top of the hill, the quickness of the advance on the enemy, with the spirit of the men in leaping the wall, and the charge immediately afterwards, was one of the finest things I ever saw.
>
> We pursued, and made some prisoners; and in the place of pushing them on, the enemy were allowed to form in rear of a ditch half-way between Villa Garcia and Llerena. Here we delayed a little, when Sir Stapleton [Cotton] ordered the right and left squadrons, 16th (which had got together), down the road, turning the enemy's left flank. They did not halt one instant. The 12th and 14th advanced at the same time, and charged with three squadrons (12th). We drove them quite close to Llerena, and Cookson, of Captain Cocks's troop was killed in the town. …

47 Ian Fletcher, *Galloping at Everything* (Staplehurst: Spellmount, 1988), pp.159–64.

> We killed about 53 of the enemy in the charge from Villa Garcia of the 5th Dragoon Guards, and in our pursuit to Llerena took one lieutenant colonel, 17th Dragoons, two captains, one lieutenant, 132 rank and file, with the same proportion of horses.
>
> The prisoners were dreadfully cut, and some will not recover. A French dragoon had his head nearer cut off than I ever saw before; it was by a sabre cut at the back of his neck.[48]

Despite the one attempt to stand the French were driven all the way back into Llerena. Captain Cocks described the whole thing as 'a pretty affair' and added: 'I had no personal adventure except that in coming in contact with a French Hussar we rolled over each other. I was on my legs first and with a *coup de sabre* invited him to surrender.'[49]

In May 1812 Captain Cocks transferred to the 79th Foot with the rank of major. He was subsequently killed at the siege of Burgos on the night of 7 October 1812. Such was his standing in the army that his funeral was attended by Wellington and many other senior officers of the army as well as officers of both the 16th and the 79th. Wellington wrote to Marshal Beresford, 'He is on every ground the greatest loss we have yet sustained.'[50]

On 22 July the 16th was present at the Battle of Salamanca, when a charge by Major General Le Marchant's brigade of heavy cavalry resulted in the complete destruction of three French infantry divisions. Le Marchant was killed towards the end of the action, depriving Wellington of one of his best cavalry commanders.[51] Although the 16th and the rest of the brigade marched in support of Le Marchant it was not engaged until the following day during the pursuit of the French:

> The 1st and Light divisions, with Major General Bock's and Anson's brigades, this morning crossed the Tormes in pursuit of the enemy. The two brigades of cavalry did not amount to 800, being so weakened by detaching squadrons during the night. The cavalry came up with their rear-guard, consisting of both cavalry and infantry, near the village of La Serna.[52] We charged the cavalry with two squadrons from the 11th and 16th, which fled, leaving the infantry to its fate. General Bock attacked the infantry with his brigade; rode completely through them in one of the best charges ever made. We took 2,000 prisoners, and followed their rear two leagues farther, when about 1,200 cavalry from the north joined their rear-guard, and covered its retreat to Peñaranda de Bracamonte.[53]

48 Tomkinson (ed.), *Diary of a Cavalry Officer*, pp.149–51.
49 Page, *Intelligence Officer*, p.174.
50 Page, *Intelligence Officer*, p.204.
51 Tomkinson (ed.), *Diary of a Cavalry Officer*, p.189.
52 Tomkinson is mistaken here: La Serna is the hill overlooking the village of Garcihernández. Sir Charles Oman, *A History of the Peninsular War* (London: Greenhill Books, 1996), vol. 5, p.477.
53 Tomkinson (ed.), *Diary of a Cavalry Officer*, p.190.

This was the famous action known as García Hernández, where the King's German Legion heavy cavalry broke two squares of French infantry.[54]

The French were followed as far the Douro River, and the 16th and the rest of the brigade were posted in the area around Tudela. In company with the 6th Division, they stayed on the Douro while Wellington first took Madrid and then returned to lay siege to Burgos. Burgos withstood the siege; Wellington lifted it on 21 October and was forced to retreat in the face of a much superior French force marching to the relief of Burgos. The rear-guard of his army included the 16th.

At this time Tomkinson was taken severely ill and appears not to have been present at the rear-guard actions fought at Venta del Pozo and Villadrigo on 23 October.[55] After holding a river line for three hours the rear-guard was forced to retreat, the 16th making several successful charges against the pursuing French cavalry. A force of *guerrillas* on the left of the British was driven in on the 16th by French Hussars, and in the ensuing melee the 16th suffered badly, with Major Pelly and Lieutenant Baker taken prisoner. The rear-guard was able to take up a new holding position at the bridge at Venta del Pozo.

At this juncture four fresh regiments of French cavalry arrived, and three were sent straight across the bridge, while the fourth looked for a crossing point so it could turn the flank of the British position. There was some confusion in forming the British force, and consequently eight French squadrons were allowed to cross and form before being charged. A massive cavalry melee ensued, but the outcome was decided when two more French squadrons crossed the bridge and took the British cavalry in the flank. By the end of the day the 16th had lost Lieutenant Lockhart, mortally wounded; Captain Murray, severely wounded; and six sergeants and 41 rank and file killed or wounded, in addition to losing Pelly and Baker, and one sergeant and 10 dragoons made prisoner. Seventy-two horses were lost.[56]

Wellington's army continued its retreat and although there were other rear-guard actions, the 16th does not seem to have been involved. By 17 November the French had given up their pursuit of Wellington, and the British army arrived at Ciudad Rodrigo at the end of the month. Tomkinson re-joined the regiment on 1 December when it arrived at Freches on the way to winter quarters on the Mondego River. He wrote: 'Considering the work they have done, both men and horses are by no means in bad order. The regiment on the retreat lost about fifty horses.'[57] By 5 December the 16th had moved further south and was divided between Olivera do Hospital and Covos, Tomkinson and B Troop being in Covos. In late December forage became scarce and there was another move, first to the area around Santa Comba Dão. By February B Troop was quartered in Requeixo with the regiment's headquarters in Esgueira, as the cavalry were forced to move in the constant search for forage.[58] For the officers at least there was occasionally some relief from duty.

54 Oman, *History of the Peninsular War*, vol.5, pp.475–81.
55 Tomkinson (ed.), *Diary of a Cavalry Officer*, p.221.
56 Oman, *A History of the Peninsular War*, vol.6, pp.70–75.
57 Tomkinson (ed.), *Diary of a Cavalry Officer*, p.224.
58 Tomkinson (ed.), *Diary of a Cavalry Officer*, pp.224–25, 228.

On 31 December Tomkinson and Captain Weyland left the regiment for Oporto and some leave: 'The Prince of Orange was in Oporto, which made the place very gay. We remained a fortnight, and returned to the 16th on 15th January, after three days' march.'[59]

On 18 February there were a number of changes in the officers of the regiment. Major Hay became a lieutenant colonel, Captain Murray became a major, and Lieutenant King from the 11th Light Dragoons became a captain, taking over Murray's troop.[60]

Through March and April the 16th moved several times in search of forage, as Tomkinson wrote, on this and supplies in general:

> During our long halt in these quarters, the regiment received regular rations of corn from Coimbra, and was tolerably well supplied with straw or Indian corn straw. The latter is not so good, and a large bulk afford but little nutriment. We were within four leagues of excellent wine, equal, I think, to Lamego (best port wine). We got it at two or three *vintines* a *quartilla*. A *vintine* is three half-pence, and two *quartillas* more than a quart bottle. Three will nearly fill two bottles. I was in a very good house, and the other officers of my troop were in good billets. We got fish in abundance from Aveiro, which the *padre* procured for us. I saved a field of his green barley from being cut, – the only one left in the neighbourhood when we moved on. This I afterwards regretted, as from the price of fish in other places I found he had cheated us considerably. If ever we are again in the neighbourhood, I will accommodate him with half a dozen quiet dragoons.[61]

By 22 May the 16th was in the locality of Bragança, where Wellington was assembling the bulk of his army, and on 26 May the 16th crossed into Spain in the opening moves of a campaign that would culminate in the Battle of Vitoria.[62] Tomkinson's diary at this point is a sequence of marches and picket duty. Typical is Tomkinson's entry for 6 June:

> The brigade moved three leagues to Pedraza [de Campos]. Which the enemy passed yesterday. Their piquets were within two leagues, and two squadrons from the brigade were ordered on duty, under Lieutenant Colonel Ponsonby, to Villa Martin [Villamartin de Campos], a league and a half in advance, and the same from Palencia, in front of which the enemy had their piquets half a league. The squadron of the 12th went up to Nortillio [?] on the right, mine of the 16th remained in Villa Martin.[63]

He also had some observations on the campaign's domestic arrangements:

59 Tomkinson (ed.), *Diary of a Cavalry Officer*, p.229.
60 Tomkinson (ed.), *Diary of a Cavalry Officer*, Appendix 1.
61 Tomkinson (ed.), *Diary of a Cavalry Officer*, p.231.
62 Tomkinson (ed.), *Diary of a Cavalry Officer*, pp.232, 234.
63 Tomkinson (ed.), *Diary of a Cavalry Officer*, p.237.

> From the number of sick last campaign, the infantry are all under canvas, carrying three tents to each company on the horse that was allowed for the camp kettles. The iron camp kettles are exchanged for the tin ones, which are light, and in the proportion of one to six men. They are carried on the top of the knapsack alternately by the men in the mess. The cavalry have no tents; we shall get the oftener into the villages.[64]

In the advance the forage situation improved dramatically:

> From the time of our crossing the Esla up to this period, we have been marching through one continued corn-field. The villages are but thinly scattered over the country, so that it appears a difficulty to find hands to cultivate the crops. The land is of the richest quality, and produces the finest crops with the least labour possible. It is generally wheat, with a fair proportion of barley, and now and then a crop of vetches or clover. The horses fed on green barley nearly the whole march, and got fat. The army has trampled down twenty yards of corn on each side [of] the road (forty in all) by which the several columns have passed. In many places much more, from the baggage going on the side of the columns, and so spreading further into the wheat.
>
> But they must not mind their corn if we get the enemy out of the country.[65]

On 21 June Wellington's army engaged the French around the town of Vitoria. Major General Anson's brigade, the 12th and 16th Light Dragoons, was on the northern flank of the army, with the forces commanded by Sir Thomas Graham. During Graham's advance Tomkinson's squadron was sent to join one of the 12th that was supporting Pack's Portuguese when some French cavalry appeared. He comments:

> I had to go a league[66] at a trot, and before I could get there, their cavalry had retired to the rear of their infantry.
>
> (All marches are made at a walk, and cavalry should never go faster, excepting before an enemy. It is impossible where you have daily a change of forage, and some days none, to keep the horses efficient if you move faster).[67]

Anson's brigade advanced towards Vitoria, crossing the Zadorra River at Gammara Mayor, with Tomkinson's squadron and that of the 12th leading. A mile or so from Vitoria, in a wood, they came across a French force:

64 Tomkinson (ed.), *Diary of a Cavalry Officer*, p.235.
65 Tomkinson (ed.), *Diary of a Cavalry Officer*, p.239.
66 Three miles.
67 Tomkinson (ed.), *Diary of a Cavalry Officer*, p.248.

The enemy collected in the wood a rear-guard of six squadrons and a regiment of infantry, with others scattered as light troops in all directions. With this force they occupied a plain about half a mile across, surrounded with wood and ending in a defile, thus keeping the head of the lane, along which we could alone get at them. The Spanish infantry got into a field of corn and down the lane, and on firing a few shots the enemy moved off, and we pushed on after them. My squadron was in advance, and on arriving on the plain formed immediately and advanced to the charge. All was confusion, all calling 'go on' before the men had time to get in their places. We got half across before I was able to place them in any form, and had we been allowed one minute more in forming, our advance might have been quicker, and made with more regularity.

The enemy had about six squadrons in line, with one a little in advance, consisting of their elite companies. This I charged, broke, and drove on their line, which advancing, I was obliged to retire, having had a good deal of sabring with those I charged and with their support. A squadron of the 12th was in my rear, and in the place of coming up on my flank, followed me, so that they only added to the confusion of retiring by mixing with my men. Captain Wrixon's squadron of the 16th then came to the charge. We were so mixed that I could not get my men out of his way, was obliged to front and make a rally back, and the enemy, seeing the remainder of the brigade coming up, retired through the defile with their cavalry, leaving a square of grenadiers in its mouth. We came close upon them without perceiving they were there, and upon our going about they fired a running volley, which did considerable execution, and then they made off through the defile. (We followed them about a mile, when, night coming on, the pursuit ceased, and we bivouacked on the ground we halted on.) I rode up within a yard of the enemy's infantry; they had their arms on the port, and were as steady as possible, not a man of them attempting to fire till we began to retire. They certainly might have reached myself and many others with their bayonets had they been allowed. I never saw men more steady and exact to the word of command.

I lost in my squadron Lieutenant the Hon. Geo. Thelluson, of the 11th Light Dragoons, who had been attached to the 16th. It was the first time he had ever been engaged, and he was so anxious to distinguish himself that he rode direct into the enemy's ranks.

Corporal Hollinsworth and Foxall of my troop are killed; Waterman and Hollinsworth mortally wounded; Barns and McKewin have lost each an arm; Mendleham, McKee, and Crabtree severely wounded. We always lose the best. The whole, with the exception of the last, are the best men in the troop; I may say, the two killed the best in the regiment. I am minus nine men and nine horses. The other troop of the squadron lost one man killed and two wounded. They were not so much exposed to the infantry fire.[68]

68 Tomkinson (ed.), *Diary of a Cavalry Officer*, pp.250–52.

> Sergeant Blood of my troop, with six men, secured a car-load of dollars, and kept them till night, when the infantry came and plundered his wagon. He brought 6,000 to the regiment.[69]

Following Vitoria, Graham and a force including the 16th were sent to Villa Franca (Ordizia) to try to cut off a French force. Graham's force caught up with the French at Tolosa on 25 June. The 16th played no part in the ensuing action, though Tomkinson wrote a fairly full account. After nightfall, the French withdrew, and Tomkinson's squadron was the first to enter the town. He wrote that the enemy left the town 'half an hour after dark, when we entered and took possession of the town amidst the *vivas* of the inhabitants, they having made up their minds to be well plundered that night had we not succeeded. … I was the first with my squadron to enter after the enemy had lest, and ordered all the people to shut their doors, fearing some parties away from their regiments might avail themselves of the confusion, and plunder.'[70] On 1 July the French withdrew across the frontier into France and the 16th were in Lasarte-Oria, with the 12th in Zubieta.[71]

Wellington now laid siege to San Sebastian, and there being no role for light cavalry, the 16th was once again wandering the Spanish countryside looking for forage for the horses. On 7 July Major General Anson left the brigade to return to England and command passed to Major General Vandeleur. On 25 July Marshal Soult launched an attack into Spain, forcing Wellington to give up the siege. In the days that followed there was a series of actions, generally known as the Battle of the Pyrenées, which resulted in Soult being driven back into France. San Sebastian then fell on 31 August. Meanwhile, from 14 August the 16th was in cantonments, with Tomkinson's squadron in Aia and the other troops nearby. As he put it, 'We remained quiet.'[72]

In early September the 16th moved again, to Azpeitia and Azkoitia, and it was from there, on 22 September that Tomkinson left to go home. On the 28th he got his horse, Bob, on board, and on 13 October, having spent a week in quarantine at Spithead, he disembarked.[73] With Tomkinson's return to England the first-hand accounts of the 16th come to an end until the Waterloo Campaign.

Tomkinson's horse, Bob, had been with him all through the war. Even when he had been severely wounded in 1809 he managed, by good fortune, not to lose him. 'I lost my horse (Bob), and was fortunate in seeing him this day pass through Grijo, having been taken by a commissary from some peasants into whose hands he had fallen.'[74] Bob stayed in the Peninsula while Tomkinson returned to England, and on his return they were reunited, although in the meantime Bob seems to have been somewhat neglected.[75] Following Bob's return to England, Tomkinson's son wrote:

69 Tomkinson (ed.), *Diary of a Cavalry Officer*, p.253.
70 Tomkinson (ed.), *Diary of a Cavalry Officer*, pp.259–60.
71 Tomkinson (ed.), *Diary of a Cavalry Officer*, p.260.
72 Tomkinson (ed.), *Diary of a Cavalry Officer*, p.266.
73 Tomkinson (ed.), *Diary of a Cavalry Officer*, p.272.
74 Tomkinson (ed.), *Diary of a Cavalry Officer*, p.11.
75 Tomkinson (ed.), *Diary of a Cavalry Officer*, p.40.

> Here the military career of 'Bob' came to an end. After five campaigns and an absence of four years and a half, he returned safe and sound to his old home, the servant reporting that he knew his way back to his stable at Dorfold perfectly. He lived for many years to carry his master with the pack of harriers kept by him.[76]

At the battle of the Nivelle, on 10 November, the 16th were on the left of Wellington's army, supporting the infantry of Sir John Hope, whose task was simply to pin the French opposite him by threatening to attack. The following day, however, as Sir John Hope advanced across the Nivelle and towards St Jean-de-Luz, the French were endeavouring to destroy a wooden bridge. Sergeant Malony led an advance party of the 16th in a charge that scattered the French and saved the bridge from complete destruction.[77]

The crossing of the Nive on 13 December 1813 was a hard-fought battle, but restricted almost entirely to the infantry. The 16th's casualties amounted to two officers and eight men wounded.[78] In January 1814 the 16th were with Sir John Hope as he laid siege to Bayonne. Consequently they took no part in the last few actions of the war. Then in mid-April came the news that Napoleon had abdicated and the war was over. The regiment marched through France to Calais and in July embarked for England.

The record of the 16th in the Peninsula was remarkable. They were present at seven major battles, besides many smaller engagements. They lost 309 officers, NCOs, and men, and 1,416 horses. Twenty-three NCOs and men were commended for their conduct in the field, not least Sergeant Major Blood and Sergeant Baxter. It was undoubtedly one of Wellington's best regiments.[79]

76 Tomkinson (ed.), *Diary of a Cavalry Officer*, p.272.
77 Graham, *History of the 16th*, p.55.
78 Graham, *History of the 16th*, p.57.
79 Graham, *History of the 16th*, p.58.

2

Before Waterloo

Tomkinson:

> The 16th Lt Dragoons had been quartered since November 1814 at Hounslow and Hampton Court and at the latter end of March 1815 were called up to the neighbourhood of Westminster Bridge for the purpose of being in readiness for the Riots occasioned by the passing of the Corn Laws. During our stay here, Napoleon entered France from Elba, and had placed himself again on the throne. Immediately on this account arriving in London all disturbance on the Corn Laws ceased, and the 16th returned to Hounslow to prepare for embarkation for the Netherlands.

Luard Journal:

> On March 2d 1815 I was gazetted as a Lieutenant in the 16th Light Dragoons.[1] – when Napoleon Buonaparte escaped from the Isle of Elba, & was received in France, by acclamation of the French Army, it was resolved by the European powers, to oppose him, & England sent a large force to the Continent – all of the officers who belonged to Regiments – under orders for embarkation, left the College[2] & joined their corps – I believe there was not one who return'd to finish his studies, except the late Sir Chs Napier[3] – who was then a half-pay Lieut. Colonel – several of those who join'd their Regiments were kill'd at the Battle of Waterloo. – I left the College, join'd the 16th Dragoons at Hounslow & having provided myself with two horses & every thing necessary for a campaign, was appointed to Captn Tomkinsons Troop

1 By purchase, for £2,000, after a short period on half-pay. Clive Cohen, 'Brothers in war: George (1778–1847) and John (1790–1875) Luard – paths to Waterloo', in Andrew Cormack (ed.), '*... a damned nice thing ... the nearest run thing you ever saw in your life ...*' (London: Society for Army Historical Research, Special Publication No. 17, 2015), p.58.

2 Luard was studying at the Military College in Farnham.

3 Commanded the 5th Foot in the Peninsula and subsequently served in India, where he was responsible for the subjugation of Scind.

– I obtain'd leave of absence to go home, & join at Canterbury – to which place the Regiment was to march, preparatory to embarkation. –

My brother George's Regiment the 18th Hussars – was also under orders –

John Luard, a self-portrait when serving as ADC to Sir Charles Dalbiac, Inspector of Cavalry, in the late 1830s. (Luard Family Archive)

Luard:[4]

Farnham
March 1st 1815

I fear as you observed my Dear Loui[5] that our French Epistles would be most studied Compositions, at least I will answer for ~~myself~~ my own being; so & as I have not at present time for the management of one you must put up with a letter from me in our own <u>Vulgar</u> Language – which if not quite so soft is equaly expressive with any. – Your account of Jenny was exactly what it should be, a progressive state of amendment – but that of Harriet was quite the reverse – however a joint letter from Tom[6] & Bessy from Bath rec'd yesterday – weakens her amendment & she is

4 Luard Family Archive, Letter 405, John Luard to his sister, 1 March 1815.
5 John Luard's sister, Louisa Susannah Ward (1798–1885).
6 *Tom* is Tom Fenton, 2nd Royal North British Dragoons; *Harriet* and *Bessy* (Elizabeth) are his sisters.

I trust now restored to her usual state of salubrity – pray thank her with my love for her very kind few lines at the end of your letter – but I suppose they have taken their departure for Leamington – your opposite [?] H.A.[7] however is I conclude stationary you can therefore – kiss her, give my love to her, give my love to her and thank her for her few lines, wishing her joy at the recovery of her chin – I was happy to learn she & Maria had passed their time so pleasantly at the Nethescales [?][8] – remember me to the latter as well as the little man[.]

I congratulate the Fentons upon having one in their family who can keep a secret. You must in your next tell me how Old Bud likes Leamington, & how long, upon moderate calculation he will like to remain there – Tom has made up his mind to go to France in May – & is trying to persuade Walton[9] who was in the 4th to accompany him –

We had a very gay Ball here on the 24th I danced with all the prettiest Girls in the Room & very near lost my heart to one of those – Bessy informs me she has a new admirer, but as he has but one eye, he is not to be placed on the list my Senior. –

I have not heard from George[10] since he arrived at Canterbury, nor have I written to him, which accounts for it. –

I have been very remiss in not yet having written to Charles but shall possibly this week – I conclude he will not move from Geneva until the latter end of April or beginning of May[.]

Farnham March 8th 1815

Since writing the above my Dear Loui I have had the pleasure of dining with Henry at Mr Lamots on Sunday, dining with my Aunt Spooner at Mrs Vigner on Monday; & yesterday dined at Mr Thursbys. – I also breakfasted with Mr Dickson at the Bedford yesterday morning – who is come to Town on his way to France, to accompany the Dean of Ripons son, but the poor lad is taken ill which detains them in London – Perhaps you think I went to London to head the mob in the cry of 'no Corn Bill' – or to quell a riot. I assure you it was for neither of these purposes –

I was delighted with Mr Thursbys family Emma is a sweet little girl & the rest nice fat good humoured children, Mrs Thursby is better but not yet down – Harvey gave me the latest intelligence of you all – & informed me of the Fentons departure –

Dickson said he would write to Tom today he should be happy of his company to France – Henry as well as my Aunt Spooner are looking very well – Mrs Vigner is a nice old lady – I met 2 curious Sisters of hers there – Miss Alalas [?], or Ahes [?] or some such name – I intended to have seen Miss O'Neal as Mrs Beverly in

7 *H.A.* might be Henrietta Armytage, John's brother Charles's future wife.
8 *Nethescales* is possibly Nethergates, Nottingham.
9 Probably Captain Charles Walton, 4th Dragoons, with whom both John and his brother George served during the Peninsula War.
10 John's brother George was with the 18th Hussars stationed at Canterbury.

the Gamester last night, but I was really afraid of crying too much – I took Pack to Town with me & have made him a present to George – I sent him – I saw old Cazenove – John & his two uncouth sons – I heard from George – & I saw young Pechier [?][11] who I understand brought good tidings of Charles so you see I have seen, learnt & heard a great deal since I commenced this Epistle[.]

I understand we have a few days leave of absence at Easter if the time will admit I shall probably pay George a visit –

George has been dancing with one of the Misses Hammonds & says he has lost his heart –

The Life Guards have more to do in London at present than they had all the while they were abroad – Give my love to Jane[12] & tell her I defy her to tire me by the length of her intended Epistle – I must now drink tea & go to bed being tired by coming on an early Coach this morning – My kind love to my Father Mother Aunt & believe me my Dear Loui

your much attached & affect^t Brother
J. Luard

Mr Thursby desired me to send his Love to you

Tomkinson:

We left Hounslow the first week in April and embarked in two Divisions on the 11th April at Ramsgate and Dover –

Lieut. Colonel Hay commanded the 16th

The Regiment was composed of the following Troops of 55 Horses each – in all six, amounting to 350 Horses –

Brevet Major Belli's Troop –

Captains – Swetenham
Weyland
Buchanan
Tomkinson
King

Captain Weyland's Troop, Buchanan's and mine at Ramsgate, with the Head Quarters of the Regiment. Brevet Major Belli's Troop, Captain Swetenham's and King's at Dover. At nine a.m. on the 11th the Troops at Ramsgate were on board and at eleven the first vessel got to sea. The vessels we embarked in were small Colliers – holding from ten to thirty five Horses each. The Horses were put loose in the hold,

11 *Pechier*: could this be a joke on Fisher?
12 *Jane* is probably Jane Fenton.

and being fine weather we did not lose any from there being no bails. Larger vessels could not have passed the Bar at Ostend and to have fitted them up regularly for Cavalry, it would have required so many and caused so much delay that the passage of any considerable body of Cavalry would have been much retarded –

Luard Journal:

April 11th – I march'd to Ramsgate & embarked with 3 Troops of the 16th. – 3 Troops of the Regiment at the same time embarking at Dover. – on 12th we arrived at Ostend at 2 p.m. – sent our men on shore, to catch the horses, as they swam from the ship, from which they were hoisted overboard & swam on shore. – we mounted & march'd 2 leagues to a small village call'd Ghristiles [Gistel?] – the people exceedingly civil – the next day the remainder of the Regiment form'd & we march'd to Bruges 4 leagues – I was quarter'd with Tomkinsons Troop at a small village call'd St Croix –

Order Book:

Extract of Genr^{l} Orders

Head Quarters Klundert 8th Jan[uary]

N° 4 The number of Horses of every discription for wich officers are allowed to draw Forage is fixd as follows,

Cavalry = Colln^{s}: each eight Horses	Adg^{ts}: 3
Le^{t}. Coll^{s}: 7	Regimental Q^{r} M^{r}: 2
Major: 6	Surgens: 2
Capts: 4	Ass^{t} Surgen }
Subalton: 3	Vet^{y} Surgen }2
Pay Master: 2	Troop Q^{r} M^{r}: 1

N° 6 The Surgens Pay Masters and Adg^{ts} are allowed besides the number opposite the Rank to Draw Forage for one Horse for the purpose of carrying the instruments, Field Medicens & Books belonging to each, The Vet^{y} Surgens and Sarg^{t} Saddlers are also allowed Forage for one Horse for the carrying of Medicines and Tools.

N° 8 An allowance of £25 Stirling will be paid for the purpose of purchasing Bat Horses. The Horse to be purchased as soon as possible and upon being approved of by the Commanding officers of Reg^{ts} they will issue an order upon the commissary Genl for the price as above specified,

Signed E. Barns[13]
M.G. & A.G.

13 Major General Sir Edward Barnes, KCB, Adjutant-General.

Tomkinson:

12th April

The vessel I went in with some of the others arrived at Ostend about nine this morning and at 11 a.m. we began to disembark. We landed the Horses on the sands and at six p.m. we marched to Gistel, a small village six miles from Ostend. Lieut. Luard came with me in the same vessel. Lieutenant Beauchamp had been sent forward to Gistel, and on our arrival Billets were ready for us. The men found Forage in every Stable they went into, and the officers a supper at a small Inn in the Village. Our Quarters were inhabited by hospitable people and we found Beds on going to them for the night, and consequently we could not avoid contrasting the *Pays Bas* with Spain and Portugal, not at all regretting the change –

13th April

That part of the Regiment which came last night to Gistel marched 15 Miles to Bruges. We were put up for the night in the *Chateaux* round the Town, with part in an old Barrack in the Town – my Troop went about Three Miles out, my own quarter was in an excellent *Chateau* – I went to dine with the other officers in Bruges, came to my quarter and went to Bed without the people in the House being aware of it. They waited supper for me to near Midnight, when a servant came into my room, and to his astonishment found me in bed – I marched early the next morning without seeing them, and they expressed their regret to my servant at my going to Bed without supping with them – Whether they expected I should have exacted dinner from them as any officer of their own or any Foreign Army would have done and therefore did not offer too much, and on finding that not to be the system of the British Army, felt ashamed at allowing me to go to the Town for one Dinner – Not that I should have troubled them for we were all delighted at once more getting on service, and were so charmed with the abundance of the country, facility of march and Transport of Baggage, that we had a merry meeting after each days march at some Auberge, where dinner was ordered for all the officers – Champaigne too at 4/- per Bottle was a new thing –

The part of the Regiment which had embarked at Dover marched to Bruges without halting and arrived at 2 a.m. –

14th April

The whole of the Regiment marched 12 Miles to Eeklo – The Men cannot stand the good treatment they receive from the persons on whom they are Billeted and some instances of drunkenness have occurred – The old Peninsula Men know their best chance of good treatment is, by being civil (which at least they attempt in the first instance) and the inhabitants finding them not inclined to give trouble generally repay them by something to drink, which being spirits sometimes overcomes them in a morning –

Luard Journal:

14th [April] we march'd 5 leagues to Eeklo.

Tomkinson:

15th April

The whole of the Regiment marched this day to Ghent and was cantoned outside the Town in small Villages and detached Houses on the road to Brussels – Louis 18th is here and if what his staff state is to be relied upon the accounts from France are very favourable to his cause – Marmont[14] and Victor[15] are with him and if their old Master Napoleon is successful will rather sigh after the share they might have had in his glory –

The Duke of Wellington came to Ghent on the 16th and inspected the works round the Town. There has been a considerable sum expended since last year in repairing the Walls and much more is required before the place can be considered secure from an enemy – The Duke is making the Tour of all the Fortresses on this Frontier, yet he will not I conceive lose many British Soldiers in occupying them. The Garrisons must be found from their own Army as the system of War is too much altered to allow them to be of the consequence which in Marlborough's time was attached to them – Many are in a very ruinous state –

Luard Journal:

15th [April] – march'd 4 leagues to Ghent. An excellent Town & market – Louis 18th in the Town – as well as General Marmont & other French officers, who adhered to the Royal cause.

16th [April] – we halted, the Duke of Wellington arrived & order'd the works round Ghent to be strengthen'd

14 Marmont was made a Marshal of the Empire by Napoleon in 1809 and led the French Army of Portugal in the Peninsular War, most notably against Wellington at the battle of Salamanca, where he was seriously wounded. He surrendered his forces to the Allies in 1814 and remained loyal to Louis XVIII when Napoleon returned from Elba.

15 Victor was made a Marshal of the Empire in 1807 and served in the Peninsula from 1808 to 1812, being beaten by Wellington at Talavera. In 1815, he remained loyal to Louis.

Order Book:

> [O]rder of the Brigade of Lt Dragoons under command of Major Genl Sir J.O. Vandeleur[16]
>
> Oudinard 16th April 1815
>
> Picquets
>
> When the Brigade is assembled The Major Genl will give Orders for the security of the Camp or Quarters.
>
> The Brigade not to dismount till the order is given –
>
> When the Brigade is separated, each officer commanding a Reg^{t}, Squadron or detachment is responsible and will act accordingly to circumstances taking proper precautions to guard against surprise and to [missing word] Informations of the enemy – Officers commanding Reg^{ts} or detachments will always endeavour to communicate with the nearest corps, their flanks and with the Head Quarters of the Brigade.
>
> Patroles
>
> Patroles are made either to communicate with the nearest posts on our flanks; to keep our *fidets*[17] and advance Picquets alert or to give intelligence of the enemy thay are allways to Receive instructions relative to the object – if for the last purpose a person who understands the language of the country is to be sent with them if practicable – Most minute reports are allways to be reguarded from officers and NC Officers commanding Picquets and Patroles and transmitted to the Officers Commanding the Brigade all Intelligence wich may be interest to Corps on our flanks is immediately to be transmitted to them.
>
> Baggage
>
> The Regulations of the army relating to Baggage is shortly to be enforced by Officers commanding Reg^{ts} by any diviation from them. Officers will subject themselves to be frequently separate from their Baggage for several Days besides incurring such reprimand disobedience of Orders may require –
>
> An Officer of the Brigade is allways to be in charge of the Baggage when marching in Brigade and a Troop Sarg^{t} Maj^{r} p^{r} Regiment. The Baggage will be orderd to march in front; in flank; or in rear of Brigade as circumstances may require but the strictest obedience expected – The Forge Carts may be sometimes

16 Major General Sir John Ormsby Vandeleur, KCB.

17 *Vedettes.*

separated from the Reg^{ts} or Squadrons but a mounted Farrier with Tools and nails is allways to march with each Squadron and if possible with each Troop if otherwise the commanding Officer will endever to find a man to act for him each Dragoon is allways to carry a set of spair shoes and a complete set to be kept redy in store on the Forge Carte

Reports

Officers commanding Reg^{ts} will send the following reports to the brigade major with every weekly state:

N^{o} of Horses shod since last report
N^{o} of shoes in mens possession
N^{o} of do in store
N^{o} of sets of nails in do
N^{o} of pds of corn in mens possession
N^{o} of do in store

The corn and ammunition in the mens possession to be inspected by the officers wich is to be reported on the back of the weekly state

Arms and Accoutrements

The Arms and Accoutrements of every discription is to be inspected by the Troop officers at least once a week & kept in perfect repair, which is to be reported every Monday.

Sore Backs

After every march the Troop officers will make a minute inspection and any horses which may have Saddle Gauled[18] ever so slightly will be dismounted till quite well – all dismounted are to be marched regularly in Charge of an Officer or NC Officer as the case may require – The number of sore-backed Horses will be reported to the Brigade Major [damaged] the weekly state agreeable to a form wich [damaged] be given –

March

As soon as the Order to Saddle is given weather by sound of Trumpet or otherwise the Baggage immediately to be packed and loaded it his expected to be peraded on the Ground assigned for it as soon as the Reg^{t} to wich it belongs and immediately

18 *Saddle Gauled* – saddle gall, a raw area of skin caused by the saddle rubbing the horse's back.

to march to the Ground oppiset for the Baggage of the Brigade when it will be reported to the Officer who his to take Charge he will report to the Brigade Major or the Major Gen[l] and receve his order to be permitted to fall out at any other time except in case of necessity when he will regain his place in a gentle trot –

Quarters

On arrival in quarters or bivouac Commanding Officers will detech Off[rs] to reconnite all the rodes as far as may be practicable in all directions and make detail'd report to the Major Genl commanding the Brigade specifying the state of the rodes wether paved or otherwise and the features of the Contrey –

Officers are to keep small Books in which they are to insert the names of the villages which they Patrole.

Advance Guards

The nature of the contrey in which the Army will properbly [*sic*] be employd will require much more precautions then that in which it as lately served. Therefore no body of Troop whatever will march without its advance guard when it his possible for an Enemy to approach its rear a rear-guard will also be employed on ordinary marches a rear will follow the Collumn to prevent stragling it is strongly recommended to all Officers of his Brigade to provide good maps and Glasses

Signed
M. Childers[19]

Tomkinson:

17th April

We marched this day to Oudenarde 17 Miles from Ghent and were cantoned in the villages a league from the Town. The Head Quarters of the Regiment were at Petegem. My Troop at Ooike, one league from Oudenarde on the Bruges road. The men are better off than I ever remember – They receive a pound of Meat a day a pound of Bread and a Pint of Gin to six – In general they give their Rations to the person they are Billeted on, and he finds them in what they require – They are scattered about in Farm Houses, where Hay is in such abundance that many of them do not bring their rations from Oudenarde where they go every third day to receive them –

The 11th and 12th Light Dragoons are in the neighbourhood of Oudenarde, and with the 16th form a Brigade under Major General Sir John Vandeleur KCB – The

19 Major Michael Childers, 11th Light Dragoons, Brigade Major.

Duke of Wellington took Oudenarde on his way round the Fortresses and saw the Brigade out near the Town. He expressed himself pleased with its appearance and the Men on hearing what he said expressed their satisfaction by cheering at again finding themselves under their old commander –

My Farm House and the village of Ooike is situated on the position the French held at the Battle of Oudenarde, when attacked by Marlborough in 1709. Part of his Troops passed the Scheldt below the Town. Seven Battalions of the Enemy were taken in the village of Eine. Marshal Vendome commanded the French under the young Duke of Burgundy, – Vendome made one disposition of the Army which the Duke altered just before the attack. Oudenarde was in possession of Marlbro' – When Marlborough was advancing to attack the French, they moved forward from the position they had taken up and attacked him on his left. Marlbro' directed the movements on the left, placing two thirds of his Army with all the British on the right under Prince Eugene. His success was in the end complete; He estimated the enemy's loss at 20,000 Men –

The Country is very rich and almost entirely arable – From the abundance we find in every place an Army must be able with management to subsist for a length of time in one place, without magazines – In any movement for a short space of time I am convinced it might march to any point entirely depending on the resources of the country –

We hear very little information to be relied on from France, and the present disposition of the Troops appears more like a distribution for Winter Quarters; than of an approaching Campaign. It is generally supposed we shall wait the arrival of the Russians and Austrians, and then commence a forward movement. The Prussians are closing upon our left and will have their out Posts in the neighbourhood of Charleroi on the Meuse.

Luard Journal:

17[th April] we march'd 5 leagues to the neighbourhood of Oudenarde – Head Quarters at Petegem – I was at Ooike – the country between Ostend & Ghent perfectly flat, intersected with Canals & ditches – the inhabitants remarkably civil & very clean in their houses.

The country about Oudenarde not unlike England. – the River Scheldt divides the Town of Oudenarde, which is fortified – the high roads paved, the cross roads neglected & bad.

18th [April] – the Regiment inspected by General Vandeleur.

19th [April] Halt.

20th [April] – our Brigade consisting of the 11th 12th & 16th – was reviewed by the Duke of Wellington – as well as the 54th Regt which garrison'd Oudenarde. –

Order Book:

R[egimental] O[rders] Petegem 20th April 1815

The Brigade Standing Orders of the 16th Instant to be strictly complied with by every individual –

The Officers Commanding at each Quarter will send out an officer to recounite [*sic*, reconnoitre] all roads, and reports to be sent in to the Commanding Officer for the information of the Major Genl agreeable to the Brigade standing orders under the Head of Quarters

The Troops to be imeadetly compleated to two sets of spair Horse shoes and nails one of which is to be in posion of the Dragoon and the other set to be carried in the Forge Carte –

The Troop States to be sent in future to the Adgent on the following days vis 7th 14th 24th and the last day in each month agreeable to a form deliverd and no state or return to be sent in without the sig^{n} of an officer of the Troop the Non Comis^{d} Officers to be found in memorandum books –

A Return of Dismounted men in each Troop to be sent in this afternoon stating opposite each name wether batmen to whome or dismounted for wont of Horses

RO Petegem 26th Apr 1815

A Regim^{t} Court Martial to assemble at H^{d} Quarters tomorrow morn^{g} at 11 o'clock for ye trial of all Prisoners brought before it

President Brevet Maj^{r} Belli

Lt Osten}		{ Lt Wheeler
Crichton}	Members	{L^{t} Lloyd
	All Evidences to attend	

RO Petegem 27th Apr 1815

The Regim^{t} to assemble in watering order tomorrow morning at Head Q^{rs} at 11 o'clock

The whole of ye Farriers to attend

Each Farrier to have a proper Cat O-Nine Tails

RO Petegem 28th April 1815

Any Officer wishing to draw their Pay from ye Regimental Agents from ye 25th Ins^{t} are requested to send in their names to ye Regimental Paymaster before ye 1st May next –

RO Petegem 29th April 1815

Officers Commanding Troops will make an Inspection of ye mens Necessaries tomorrow at ye most convenient hour, and ye deficiencies (if any) to be immediately replaced – after which ye mens accounts to be closed up to ye 24th inst, & ye balances paid to ye men – a list of Debts and Credits to be given in to ye Adjutant after settling –

'Necessaries' was the name given to those items of kit and equipment that the individual soldier paid for by means of stoppages from his pay. They including items of clothing as well cleaning materials and shaving kit. See the list of 'Necessaries to be carried' given out on 7th June. Other kit was either 'Clothing', paid for by the regiment's colonel, or 'Appointments', issued at public expense and including – in the case of cavalry – saddlery, sword, sword belt and *sabretache*, carbine belt, cloak, boots, and spurs.[20]

RO Petegem 30th April 1815

A Regimental Ct Martial to assemble tomorrow morning at 11 o'clock at the adjutants Quarters for the trial of all prisoners brought before it.

	President $Capt^n$ Swetenham	
Lt Osten}		{ Lt Wheeler
Lt Beaucham}	Members	{ " Richardson
	All Evidence to attend	

Notwithstanding the orders of yesterday the balance due to the NCOs and privates up to y^e 24th April is not to be paid to them until further orders

Luard Journal:

April 21st – 22d – 23d 24th 25th – 26th 27th 28th 29th & 30th Halt. – on the 23d the 10th Hussars pass'd thro Oudenarde – on the 24th – the 18th Hussars pass'd & I saw my brother George – the 91st Reg^t arrived at Oudenarde.

May 1st at 11 am received an order to march immediately to Ninove. March'd thro Geraardsbergen [Grammont] 6 leagues, Lord Hill's[21] head quarters, & did not arrive at Ninove till 10 p.m. – & found we were quarterd a league back, & did not get into our quarters till midnight dispersed in farm houses, all over the country – near the village of Denderwindeke – the country between Oudenarde & Grammont

20 Anon., *Regulation for the Provision of Clothing, Necessaries, and Appointments, for Corps of Cavalry, dated 17th August 1812* (London, 1812).

21 Lieutenant General Lord Hill.

beautifully cultivated & wooded – the 11th Dragoons at Neigem & Meerbeke – the 12th at Waarbeke – head quarters of the Brigade at Meerbeke – part of the 7th Hussars at Ninove – head quarters of the cavalry, Lord Uxbridge.[22]

Tomkinson:

May 1st [the date given in the diary is 8th, which must be an error as he describes the regiment moving to Denderwindeke]

An order came this day for the Brigade to march – We moved about 12 and passed Geraardsbergen in the evening not arriving at our Quarters at Denderwindeke until Midnight. From receiving the order to march immediately, we fancied it was some movement towards the enemy or at least a concentration of the Army previous to taking the Field. We were cantoned around Denderwindeke as in the neighbourhood of Oudenarde, the Men in the Farm Houses and abundantly supplied –

On going round their Quarters I did not find this to be the case, there are more Troops in this neighbourhood and many of them are in cottages, but those in the Farm Houses are as well supplied as in the last Quarter – Head Quarters of the Army are at Brussels with a considerable force of Troops in the immediate vicinity.

Lord Hill with a Corps is at Geraardsbergen and the Earl of Uxbridge commanding the Cavalry is at Ninove. –

The Guards are at Enghien, and there is a Brigade (if not two) of Troops of King of the Netherlands at Nivelle. Sir Thomas Picton[23] with a Division of British Infantry is in the neighbourhood of Waterloo, and from the general disposition of the Army I should say it was the Dukes intention to cover Brussels on either road the enemy advance on, and at the same time not his intention to attack until the other powers come up – We hear of their advance though it is said they cannot be so forward in six weeks as to admit of a forward movement on our part.

The Duke de Berri[24] is I believe at Hal – He claims rations from the British Army, and is said to receive an allowance *per diem* for ten or twelve Horses, which he profits from; by only keeping a couple.

Order Book:

RO 2nd May 1815

A Subaltern officer from each Troop will be sent out early in the morning to Requinite[25] the roads and [...] in their vicinity & a report to be sent in to the Commanding Officer for the information of the Major General agreeable to the Brigade standing orders.

22 Lieutenant General The Earl of Uxbridge, GCB, Commander of the British and Hanoverian Cavalry.
23 Lieutenant General Sir Thomas Picton, GCB.
24 Nephew of Louis XVIII and the commander of the small French Royalist army.
25 *Reconnoitre*: one of several spellings of this term.

The Troop Officers will be in future cantoned with their Troop & not on any account to change their billets out of their cantonments.

Officers Commanding Troops will report this evening to the Commanding Officer how long it will take to assemble their Troops

The sore-backed horses will Parade this afternoon as follows, *viz.*

Those of Cap$^{t.}$ Weylands Squadron at 4 o'clock in their cantonments & the remainder to assemble at Head Quarters this afternoon at 1/2 past 5 for this inspection of the Vet^{y} Surgeon –

Asst surgeon Evans to be attached to Capt. Weylands Squadron at Laitliengen [?]

B[rigade] O[rders] Meerbeke 2nd May 1815

Off^{rs} Commanding Regiments will send out Off^{rs} to reconnoitre ye Country in their vicinity tomorrow, they will report the state of ye roads ye nature of the country its produce in Forage as near as can be ascertained and the capacity of each village and commune containing Troops, also what villages are occupied by Troops or not –

The 11th dragns will take the destination of Lonsbecke [?] & St Martin [Sint-Martens-Lierde?] – The 16th Dns Luffeunghind [?] Lubecke [?] & Casteres [?] –

Luard Journal:

2d 3d 4th [May] – Halt.

Order Book:

RO Denderwindeke 3rd May 1815

The Brigade Standing Orders of the 30 Ins^{t} to be strictly attended to –

The horses for the conveyance of Camp Kettles to be immediately purchased by Officers Commanding troops and sent to H^{d} Quarters for approval when an order will be issued for the allowance being granted to them agreeable to the Genl

Order 30th April 1815 –

Lieut.G^{l} the Earl of Uxbridge will inspect the Regt^{s} in compleat marching order tomorrow, the hour and place of assembly will be made known to the troops as soon as ascertained –

Correct marching states to be sent in to the Adjt this evening – The horses unfit to be road must be returned present and not in the ranks –

Initially troops had been issued with cast iron camp kettles, but these were replaced with lighter, tin kettles in the Peninsula in 1813 at the ratio of one kettle to six men. During the Waterloo Campaign it was found that two sizes were in use and their allocation was changed accordingly. Twelve-pint kettles were issued at one per six men, and seven-pint kettles for four men.[26] In the cavalry the camp kettles were carried on horses, one horse per troop. Additionally every soldier had a mess tin. See the list of 'Necessaries' under 7th June.

RO 3rd May 1815

The Regiment to assemble tomorrow morn^{g} at 1/2 past 10 o'clock at Head Quarters for ye Inspection of Lt Genl ye Earl of Uxbridge

Those Horses totally unfit to be rode are to be led without Saddles – the remainder will be mounted on the Parade –

The whole of ye men Dismounted to appear in full Dress with side Arms

Cap Lines & Feathers to be worn

The whole of ye Publick Baggage animals to be out –

Cap lines were cords that passed around the shako, or cap, and were fastened to the jacket at the front. Their original purpose was to avoid headgear being lost if it came off, but by 1812 (and the issue of the new uniform for Light Dragoons) they were purely ornamental. On campaign oilskin covers were worn over the shakos and the cap lines left off. The feather is the plume that was worn on the shako.

RO Denderwindeke 4th April [*sic*] 1815

For the Day tomorrow Lt Oston

The Regimental Cort Martial of which Capt. Swetenham was ordered as President in the Reg^{tl} Order of the 30th April will assemble tomorrow morning at H^{d} Quarters at 11 o'clock –

RO^{s} Denderwindeke 4th May 1815

For the Day tomorrow Lt Wheeler

The Regiment to assemble in watering order tomorrow morning at 10 o'clock halfway between hear [*sic*, here] and Capt. Weylands Squadron

The whole of the Farriers to attend

Reconoitring Report of Capn ______________ Troop 16th Light Dns

Names of villages	Distances	No. of troops capable of containing	Roads	Roads passable for artillery	Nature of the Country	Forage	Remarks
From to Maerbeck Nyere Neyere Dinderwindicke	 1/2 1/2	 400 360	Paved Clay	If so yes in the column will be sufficient	Hilly Woody Open or Enclosed	Quantity and nature as far as can be ascertained	

26 Lieutenant Colonel John Gurwood (ed.), *The General Orders of Field Marshal the Duke of Wellington, KG* (London: W. Clowes, 1832), p.357.

NB The Column specifying the no of troops a village is capable of containing refers to the first column –

The accompanying forthwith to be adopted in the 2nd Brigade of Cavalry it is desirable that these reports should be accompanied by sketches when practicable – Officers Commanding Regiments will make a General report to the Major General comprising the information of each officer sent to reconnoitre – a copy of which will be kept by the adjutant, the above will only be required on entering new cantonments –

Signed M. Childers

Extract of Cavalry Orders – Ninove 3rd May 1815 –

N°1 Lieut.G[l] the Earl of Exbridge [*sic*] in Announcing that he has been placed in the Command of the Cavalry of this army by field marshall his Grace the Duke of Wellington begs leave to state the high sense he Entertains of the Honor that is Confered upon him-

N°2 He expects from this Cavalry every thing that Can be Attained by Discipline Bravery and a high sense of Honor –

N°7 At whatever Rate an Orderly may be Instructed to go he must walk his Horse from the Entrance of the Town to the Quarters occupied by the officer to whom the Dispatch is addressed on his arrival there he will Instantly Dismount and remain so until ordered to return to his post –

N°8 No orderly is on any account to be Dispatched unless he perfectly understands the Duty he is going upon the Road he is to take must be clearly pointed out and on the Cover of the dispatch must be legibly written the hour of departure and the rate of march with the name of the place he goes from and to. All of which must be read and fully explained to those orderlies who cannot read –

N°9 For the conveying of Private Letters or messages no orderly Dragoon is ever to be Employed –

N°10 It is desirable that the Ranks should at all times be as strong as possible and Mounted Dragoons should not be allowed to lead Baggage Animals or Camp Kettle Mules –

Signed
J. Elly Col.
A.A.G.[27]

27 Colonel Sir John Elley, KCB, Royal Horse Guards, Assistant Adjutant General.

RO Denderwindeke 6 May 1815

For the day tomorrow Lt Crichton –

An orderly officer of the 16th Light Dns will attend at the A.A. Gen^ls Cavalry Head Quarters 12 o'clock tomorrow to take orders for the Brigade he will provide himself with pen ink and paper for the above purpose –

Signed
M. Childers
M.B.

For the above Duty Lieut.Crichton

The whole of the orderly serjeants quartered out of the village will sleep at the Serj^t Majors untill further orders.

Whenever a man is ordered for duty the orderly Serj^t is to parade him and see him to the Serj^t Majors

When an order is sent to a troop the first Serj^t the Dragoon delivers it to whether orderly Serj^t or not he is to see the order put in execution

Each Dragoon previous to his being sent as an orderly to Head Quarters or any other place is to have the name of the Head Quarters of the Brigade Regiem^nt and Troop given to him in writing and also to know where the officers of his troop are quartered

RO Denderwindeke 7th April [*sic*] 1815

For the day tomorrow Lt Nepean

The Troops to Parade in the Convent yard tomorrow after noon at 1 o'clock for inspection of health –

RO Denderwindeke 9th April [*sic*] 1815

For the day tomorrow Lt Luard

The Reg^t to assemble in watering order tomorrow morning at H^d Q^rs with saddles & bigg [?] Bitts ~~Saddles~~ blankets only to be worn the sore-backed Horses to be lead in watering order –

'Bigg' may be a corruption of 'bridoon', the name given to one of the two bits on a cavalry bridle, the other being a curb bit, each with its own pair of reins. The curb is a much stronger bit, giving more control over the horse and was the bit invariably used in battle. The bridoon, the same as a modern day snaffle, is much gentler in its action and was used when less severe control was required.

RO Denderwindeke 10th April [*sic*] 1815

For the day tomorrow Cornet Hay
The Troops to be out in watering order tomorrow morning at 10 o'clock
Riding Drill for the third class at 1/2 past 8 o'clock –

The Regulations of the 12th Light Dragoons, published in 1813, instructs the riding master to divide recruits into classes, according to ability, for the purposes of instruction.[28] It would appear that something like this was operating in the 16th. If the Third Class are, apparently, the most in need of instruction, it would suggest that the First and Second Classes were recruit and novice riders, and left at the depot. Classes were also used in teaching the sword exercise. In this case the First Class were taught on foot, the Second Class on horseback, and the Third Class practised combat techniques and what today would be called skill at arms, all at speed.
Luard Journal:

On the 10th [May] the 7th Hussars moved from Ninove & 11th Dragoons from Meerbeke & Neigem – the Life Guards occupied their quarters.

Order book:

RO Denderwindeke 11th May 1815

For the day tomorrow L[t] Osten riding drills for the 3rd Classes of each Troop at this place tomorrow morning at 7 o'clock –
Watering order for the remainder at the same time foot Parade with side arms for the whole in stable dress at 5 in afternoon

Luard Journal:

11th May George dined with us.

Order book:

RO Denderwindeke 12th May 1815

For the day tomorrow L[t] Wheeler
The Classes of G & H Troops that rode yesterday to be out in riding school order tomorrow morning at 7 o'clock and those at this place at 1/2 past 7 o'clock
Watering order for the remainder at 7 o'clock

28 Major General Robert Browne, *Regulations and Orders Observed in His Majesty's 12th or Prince of Wales's Regiment of Light Dragoons* (London: W. Clowes, 1813), p.40.

RO Denderwindeke 13th May 1815

For the day tomorrow Lt Crichton –

A Regimental Cort Martial to assemble at Hd Qrs tomorrow morning at 11 o'clock for the trial of all prisoners brought before it –

President Captn Weyland

Lt Crichton} { Lt Luard
Cnt Beckwith} Members { Cornet Hay

All Evidence to attend –

The Troop to be out in watering order tomorrow morning at 10 o'clock –

Denderwindeke 13th [14th] May 1815

For the day tomorrow Lt Nepean –

The Regt to assemble in Marching Order tomorrow morning at 11 o'clock half way between this place & Zandbergen the sore-backed Horses to be led in watering order – Cap Cases[29] to be worn and the Jackets to be Blue Facings[30] outwards –

memd each man to have two Bundles of Hay[31] tied up and on no account to be used previous to a march

Camp Kettle Horses to be on the parade tomorrow morning –

Memo Clarks of Troops to be over at Capt. Waylands Quarters tomorrow morning at 4 o'clock and to take a man with them

RO Denderwindeke 15th May 1815

For the day tomorrow Lt Luard

Watering order tomorrow morning at 7 o'clock

A Regimental Cort Martial to assemble tomorrow morning at 11 o'clock at Hd Qrs for the trial of all prisoners brought before it –

29 Waterproof covers for the shakos, referred to here as caps, but in the *Regulations for the Provision of Clothing, Necessaries and Appointments for Corps of Cavalry*, August 1812, as '*Chacos*'.

30 The uniform jackets adopted by the Light Dragoons following the issue of the 1812 warrant were double-breasted, with lapels in the facing colour of the regiment; in the case of the 16th, this was scarlet. However, the jacket lapel could be buttoned across so that the scarlet was hidden and only the blue of the jacket on the reverse of the lapel showed.

31 The standing orders of the 12th Light Dragoons for 1813 stated that the dragoons were 'to practice making up long forage trusses of 300 pounds, and riding upon them. The hay carried by the regiment in marching order is always to be spun when time admits, but, whether spun or not, is to be carried in bundles of equal weight, in front of the dragoon's knee.' The reference to trusses of 300 pounds may be a printing error; 30 pounds is more likely. Browne, *Regulations and Orders*, p.20.

President Captn Buchanan

Lt Osten} { Lt Lloyd

Lt Nepean} Members { Cornet Polhill

All evidence to attend –

Clarks of Troops to be at H^{d} Q^{rs} tomorrow morning at 11 o'clock with receipts of quarters for Canterbury Dover &&

BO Zandbergen 14 May 1815

Off^{rs} Commanding Regiments will Report to the Brigade Maj^{r}, for the information of the Maj^{r} Genl if they have provided Camp Kettle & Forge Cart Horses and if they have not they will state the Impediment that has Prevented them –

Off^{rs} Commanding Regt^{s} will be Plaised to Order a minute Inspection to be made once a Day by there Farriers – in Order to gard against Glanders & the similar Inspection by the Veter^{n} Surgeon as often as Sircumstances will admit

Glanders is a highly infectious disease affecting horses, mules, and donkeys. It leads to coughing and fever, followed by septicaemia and death. When discovered the usual course of action was to shoot the infected animal. In the Peninsula a General Order of 17 November 1810 stated: 'The cavalry and horses of the army must not be put into any stables or places, which have been occupied by the enemy, without very carefully cleansing and washing the mangers etc., to take every precaution against glanders.'[32]

RO Denderwindeke 16th May 1815

For the Day tomorrow morning Cornet Beckwith

The Reg^{t} to assemble tomorrow morning in Exercising Order at 8 o'clock on the same ground on which they assembled yesterday – Sore-back Horses to be led to the field in Watering Order

Denderwindeke 17th May 1815

For the Day tomorrow Cornet Hay

The Troops to Parade for Forraging tomorrow morning at 6 o'clock for three Days Hay the Orderly Officer to attend

32 Gurwood, *General Orders*, p.254.

RO Denderwindeke 18th May 1815

For the Day tomorrow Lt Osten

The Commanding Officer having observed that a number of Saddle Trees brought to the Tradesmen to be Repaired have been destroyed by Neglect of the Dragoons – and not by Fair Wear – In Future any Repairs occasioned by neglect will be charged to the Dragoon and the Tree Maker will Report to the Adjt for the Information of the Commanding Officer when a saddle is brought to him under such circumstances previous to its being repaired –

The above Order to be read to the men –

Corpl Webb[33] of H Troop is reduced to the Ranks for Drunkenness on Duty from this Day inclusive

The Regt to assemble in Exercising Order tomorrow morning at 8 o'clock on the same ground as yesterday Sore-Backed Horses only to be left in –

Luard Journal:

On the 18 May – I got a few days leave of absence & went with Capt. Swetenham & Cornet Hay to Brussels about 14 miles – Lord Wellingtons head quarters.

Order Book:

RO Denderwindeke 19th May 1815

For the day tomorrow Lieut. Wheeler –

The 3rd classes of each Troop to assemble in ye same Order and on ye same Ground as this Day, at seven o'clock tomorrow morning –

Luard Journal:

19th [May] we went to Antwerp – 12 leagues, a flat well cultivated country thro which we pass'd, Vilvoorde & Malines [Mechelen] in our route – we were much pleased with Antwerp – strongly fortified – with magnificent Basins capable of holding 15 of the largest ships of the line – the Cathedral a fine building and had some of Reuben's best paintings, which Buonaparte sent to Paris. – every thing dear – CoteRhone [Cote de Rhone] 7 francs a Bottle – at night we return'd to Brussels

33 Subsequently killed at Waterloo.

Order Book:

RO Denderwindeke 20th May 1815

For the Day tomorrow Lt Crichton

The troops to assemble to Morrow Morning at 8 o'clock on the same ground as the last day in Exercising order

Luard Journal:

20th visited the Gallery of Paintings – thought the modern paintings better than the ancient ones, return'd in the evening to Denderwindeke – heard from my mother.

Order Book:

RO Denderwindick 21st May 1815

For y^{e} Day tomorrow Lt Nepean

The Troops to be out in watering order tomorrow morn^{g} at 7 o'clock

Luard Diary:

21st [May] Wrote to Louisa

Order Book:

RO Denderwindick 22nd May 1815

For y^{e} Day tomorrow – Lieu$^{t.}$ Luard

Riding Drills for y^{e} 3rd Classes of each Troop tomorrow morning at 7 o'clock on y^{e} same ground as before –

Ninove 22nd May 1815

Genl Cavalry Orders

N°1 Major Genl y^{e} Honble Sir Wm Ponsonby & Major Genl Lord Edward Somersets Brigades will Assemble in Marching Order (without Forge Carts or Batt Horses) at 1/4 past 11 o'clock a.m. on Wednesday next ye 24th on ye Common near Hoeldenghim [Heldergem?]–

N°2 Each Regim^{t} will form Close Collumn of half-Squadrons, Right in Front, at ye Point of ye Common where they respectively enter

Signed J. Elley Col
D.A.G.

A squadron was made up of two troops, combined and then equally divided, so a half-squadron did not necessarily equate exactly to a troop. In an open column of half-squadrons a gap was maintained between the half-squadrons sufficient to allow the squadron to form line by a wheel to the left or right – that is, the gap was equal to the length of each half-squadron.[34] In a close column of half-squadrons, the interval between the ranks and the half-squadrons was only half a horse's length. Obviously this could not be formed in the same way as an open column, that is by a simple 90° wheel by the half-squadrons. Instead, the half-squadron that was to lead remained stationary while the others wheeled an eighth of a wheel, approximately 11°. While the half-squadron that was to lead stood fast, the others wheeled 90° by threes in the same direction. This manoeuvre turned a line two deep into a column six wide, but, crucially, of the same length as the line. These columns then moved until they were behind the leading half-squadron and wheeled by threes back into their original line. To deploy from close column into line, the lead half-squadron halted and stood fast while the following half-squadrons wheeled by threes, marched out from behind the lead half-squadron, wheeled by threes back into line when opposite their position in the line, and then marched forward until in line with the leading half-squadron.[35] Right in front meant that the right hand half-squadron would lead.

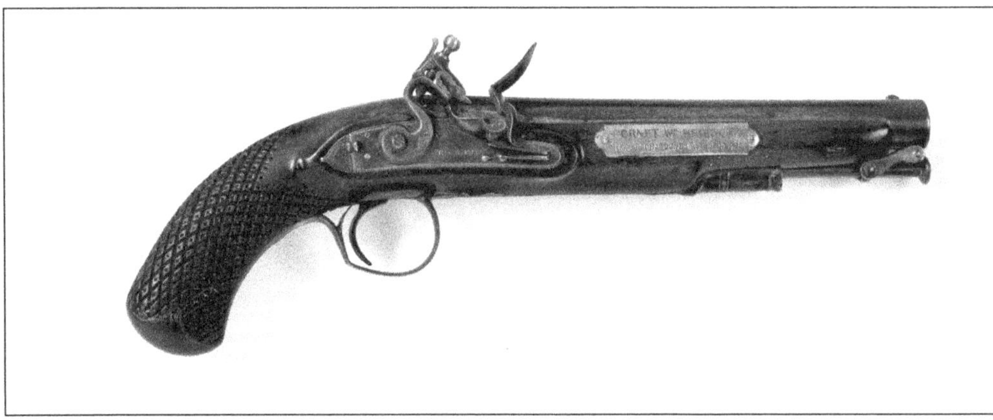

Pistol carried by Cornet Beckwith at Waterloo. The jaws of the cock are modern. (Tennants Auctioneers)

RO Denderwindeke 23rd May 1815

For the Day tomorrow Cornet Beckwith

The Troops to Assemble for muster tomorrow morn^{g} in Exercising Order at 8 o'clock on ye new ground between Head Quarters & ye Cantonments of ye 12th L Drag^{ns} –

The sore-Backed Horses to be led in Watering Order

34 Anon., *Instructions and Regulations for the Formations and Movements of the Cavalry* (London: War Office, 1796), pp.2, 86–99.

35 Anon., *Instructions and Regulations* (1796), pp.143–65.

RO Denderwindeke 24th May 1815

Watering Order with Saddle tomorrow $Morn^{g}$ at 8 o'clock
Foot Parade for Drill with Side Arms at 4 o'clock in the Afternoon
For the Day tomorrow Cornet Hay

RO Denderwindeke 25th May 1815

For the Day tomorrow Lt Osten
The Regiment to Assemble tomorrow morning in Exercising Order at 8 o'clock on y^{e} same Ground as Yesterday – The whole of y^{e} Subaltern Officers only to attend

25th May 1815

R[egimental]A[fter]O[rders]
Notwithstanding y^{e} Orders of this Day y^{e} $Regim^{t}$ will assemble in Exercising Order with Pouch Belts tomorrow $Morn^{g}$ at 1/4 before 9 o'clock on the Exercising Ground near Schendelbeke –
The Troops at this Place will be ready to march off at 1/2 past 6 o'clock –
Captain Weylands Squadron will be in Readiness to join y^{e} Troops from Head Quarters at 7 o'clock
Sick and Lame Horses to be left in and the Ammunition to be left at y^{e} mens Quarters, Pack'd up in y^{e} mens veleeces[36] –

RO Denderwindeke 26th May 1815

For the Day tomorrow $Lieu^{t.}$ Wheeler
The Troops to be out in Watering Order tomorrow morning at 7 o'clock –
Assistant surgeon Evans will Inspect the Troops at Head Quarters tomorrow at 12 o'clock, & Assistant Surgeon Mc Mullock the Troops at Zandbergen at the same hour

G[eneral]O[rders] H^{d} Q^{rs} Brussels 19th May 1815
Officers are not to be permitted to quit their Regiments for y^{e} purpose of appearing before a medical board without a previous application being made to y^{e} $Adjut^{t}$ General & y^{e} Commander of y^{e} Forces leave obtaind – A Certificate of y^{e} Officers Case signed by y^{e} Surgeon of y^{e} $Regim^{t}$ to which he belongs must accompany y^{e} application, and directions will be given to y^{e} Inspector of Hospitals to assemble a

36 This is a reference to the valise, the tubular saddle bag carried behind the saddle. The implication is that the valise was not carried in Exercising Order, which would serve to lessen the load on the horses slightly.

Medical Board accordingly – Without such Directions, no Officer is to be Examin'd by a Medical Board –

G[eneral]C[avalry]O[rders] Ninove 25th May 1815

Lieut. Genl ye Earl of Uxbridge calls ye attention of ye Cavalry to ye General Principles & Rules laid down for its movement, & particularly to ye following Points –

1st – The strictest silence must be preserved in ye Ranks whether at a Review, or during Exercise, & still more in presence of an Enemy, no voice should be heard, but for words of Command which should be given loud & Distinct –

2nd – Genl Officers, & Officers Commanding Regts, should with ye greatest quickness, correct all errors & particularly those of Intervals within their Corps, but they can make no change to effect ye Regt or Brigade upon their flank–

3rd – In manoeuvre no greater Interval is allowed between Regiments than those between Squadrons, In a line of Parade & in Marching in Column with open Ranks, a small additional space may be taken for ye Trumpeters

4th – In Column of Parade as well as in Column of Manoeuvre wheeling Distance must be accurately observed from front Rank to Front Rank. It invariably happens that ye rear Rank takes too much Interval – The NC Officers must be particularly Caution'd upon this Head –

Wheeling distance, from the front rank of a half-squadron to the front rank of the following half-squadron, had to be exactly the frontage of the following half-squadron so that there would be no gap in the centre of the squadron when the half-squadrons wheeled into line. If the gap was too small, or the rear rank of the leading half-squadron was too far behind its front rank, then there was a danger of the following half-squadron colliding with it when wheeling.[37]

5th – The Trumpet is used only as a preparatory Caution & ye Word of Command for execution follow Immediately –

The Trumpet must not be partially used, it is meant for ye whole Body, not for a part of it only, & therefore when a movement is to be made, by a part of ye Line Only; it must be directed by word of Command, distinctly calling to attention by its name ye Squadron, Regimt, or Brigade that is to move, for it is obvious that the Trumpet partially used might set in motion ye whole Line

6th – The Lieut. Genl Earnestly entreats ye attention of every on to ye above Points, & generally to ye Principles & Rules for all movements – He well knows that he may expect from ye Cavalry he has ye high honor to Command, every thing that bravery can Effect, he further asks to have it in his Power to manoeuvre with it to advantage –

37 Anon., *Instructions and Regulations* (1796), pp.21–22.

Important movements with large masses can only be Executed with great success by ye means of quickness & precision, & to accomplish this, much individual attention, activity & intelligence is absolutely necessary

Sign'd, J. Ellis[38]
D.A.G.

RO Denderwindeke 27th May 1815

For ye Day tomorrow Lt Crichton

The Reg^{t} to parade in Watering Order in its cantonments tomorrow morning, when Officers Commanding Troops will read to their men ye Cavalry Genl Order of ye 25th Inst and a strict attention to them is expected from every Individual –

Private Wm Mitchell of H Troop is appointed Corp^{l} in ye same until further orders, *vice* Webb reduc'd to ye Ranks for Drunkenness & Unsoldierlike conduct –[39]

The above Appointment to take date for 25th May Inclusive

Luard Diary:

27th [May] heard from my Mother date 21st

Order Book:

RO Denderwindeke 28th May 1815

For the Day to Morrow Lt Nepean

The Troops to assemble in Marching order to Morrow Morning at 1/2 past 9 o'clock on the same Ground on which the Regt assembled on the 26th Ins^{t}

The troops at Head Quarters will be ready to march off at 1/4 before 8 o'clock & Cap^{n} Weylands Squadron will join the troops from this place on their arrival at Zandbergen

The Nose bags Forage cords & Corn to be left in – The men to appear with their Cap lines, Feathers & Red facings outwards –

The Sick Lame & Sore-Back'd horses of the troops at H^{d} Q^{rs} to parade in rear of the troops in Watering order -

38 Colonel Sir John Elley, KCB, Royal Horse Guards, Deputy Adjutant General.
39 Webb was killed at Waterloo.

Luard Journal and Diary:

> 29th May the whole of the British cavalry were reviewed by the Duke of Wellington – consisting of the 1st & 2d Life Guards, the Horseguards Blue, 1st Drag^{n} Guards – 1st 2d & 6th Dragoons – 7th 10th 15th & 18th Hussars. – the 11th 12th 13th 16th & 23d Light Dragoons & 6 Troops of Horse Artillery including a Rocket Brigade – amounting to about 6,400 Cavalry – exclusive of Artillery

Order Book:

RO Denderwindeke 29th May 1815

For the Day tomorrow Lt Luard
The Troop to be out in watering order tomorrow morning at 7 o'clock

GCO Ninove 30th May 1815

N°1 Lieu$^{t.}$ General The Earl of Uxbridge has the pleasure to announce to the Cavalry & Royal Horse Artillery the universal satisfaction that was given by the Review Yesterday

N°2 He is charged by Field Marshal The Duke of Wellington to express his every approbation –

N°3 The admiration of all the distinguished Foreigners present was general and unqualified

Sign'd J. Ellis
D.A.G.

RO Denderwindeke 30th May 1815

For the Day tomorrow Lieu$^{t.}$ Beckwith
Watering order at 7 o'clock tomorrow morning
Foot parade at 4 p.m. with side Arms –

RO Denderwindeke 31st May 1815

For the Day tomorrow Corn^{t} Hay

The Regt to assemble in Exercising order tomorrow morn^{g} at 8 o'clock without Pouch Belts on the ground near the village occupied by the 12th Lt Dragoons –

The Sore-Back'd Horses to be led to the Field in watering order, Farriers to attend –

RAO Notwithstanding the RO of this Day the Reg^{t} to assemble in exercising order tomorrow morning at 7 o'c^{k} on the Meadow near Schendelbeke (without Pouch Belts)

The Horses unfit for the Ranks only to be left in –
The Troops at this place to march off at 1/2 past 5 –

Denderwindeke 1st June 1815

For the Day tomorrow Lt Osten
The whole of the Serj^{ts} to be out in Riding School order tomorrow Morning at 7 o'clock on the Exercising Ground – and the Regiment to assemble in watering order on the same ground at 9 o'clock Farriers to attend

BO Zandbergen 2nd June 1815

The 11th & 16 Light Dragoons will assemble for Exercise tomorrow morning at 7 o'clock on the ground near Schendelbeke – The Troop Serjants Major, Privates & the Camp Kettle animals as directed by the GCO of the 31st May will assemble at the Head Quarters of the Brigade at 9 o'clock a.m. In consequence they are not expected to be in the field.

RO Denderwindeke 2nd June 1815

For the Day tomorrow Lt Wheeler
In compliance with the above BO the Regt to assemble in the same order and on the same ground as last day – The troops at head Quarters to march off at a Quarter past 5 o'clock – The Camp Kettle Horse the Troop Serjeant Majors &c to be at Zandbergen by 9 o'clock tomorrow morning –

RO Denderwindeke 3rd June 1815

For the Day tomorrow Lt Crichton
The Troops to be out in watering order tomorrow morning at 7 o'clock

RO Denderwindeke 4th June 1815

For the Day tomorrow Lt Nepean
The whole of the Sore-Backed Horses of the Regiment to assemble in watering order at H^{d} Q^{rs} tomorrow morning at 11 o'clock –
Foot Parade with Side Arms at each quarter at 1/2 past 4 in the afternoon

Extract of G O H^{d} Quarters Brussels 3rd June 1815

N°5 So much benefit was felt during the late War particular by soldiers of the Army from the system then adopted of paying them every day that the Commander of the Forces has determined to adopt it again –

N°6 Accordingly he desires that the Ballances which shall appear to be due on the face of the accompts to the 24th of May last of each Serjeant, Trumpeter, Rank & File shall be paid to him by daily subsistence – to the amount of his daily subsistence –

N°7 The Paymasters of Regts are in future to send in their Estimates for the months Pay for their Regiments on the 12th of the month so that the Warrants may be sign'd and an issue may be made upon them by the 25th of each month –

N°8 They will thus be provided with the means to issue to the Captains of Companies the Daily subsistence of their men which after the Ballances due on the 24th of the month will have been paid as above ordered in Number Sixth – is to be paid entered [?] every day –

N°9 In case any soldier should now be in Debt or should at any time hereafter require Necessaries the Captain is to make arrangements for the stopping the payment of his Daily Subsistence till the Debt will be Discharg'd all the Necessaries will be paid for

N°10 The Paymasters of Regiments are to wait on the Paymaster Genl to receive their balances due on their several estimates to the 24 May –

N°11 The Ballances will be paid in Dutch Ducats at the rate of Eleven *Francs* and Forty *Centimes* or nine shillings and sixpence each –

N°12 The 12th Light Dragoons are to be in Major Genl Sir J.O. Vandeleurs Brigade –

N°13 the 23rd Light Dragoons are to be in Major General Sir Wm Dawnburghs [von Dornburg] Brigade

N°14 The 13th Light Dragoons are to be in Col. Sir Fredrick Arentschildts Brigade –

Sign'd E. Barnes
A.G.

BO Zandbergen 5th June 1815

The Major Genl will inspect the Camp Kettle and Publick Baggage Animals loaded at the Hd Quarters of the Brigade at 10 o'clock a.m. on the 7th Instant a Dragoon from each Regiment in Marching Order carrying Articles as described by the Earl of Uxbridge on the 3rd Instant will Parade at the same time.

Signed M. Childers
M.B.

RO Denderwindeke 6th June 1815

For the Day tomorrow Cn^t Beckwith

The Paymaster will pay to the officers & troops to morrow morning at 12 o'clock the subsistence to the 24th May last –

An inspection of Necessaries to take place to morrow at the most convenient hour and the men to be immediately compleated with such Articles as may be wanting after which the accompts of the NC Officers trumpeters & Privates are to be closed up to the 24th May 1815 and the Ballances paid to them Daily agreeable to G O 3rd of June 1815 –

The Camp Kettle and Publick Animals namely Surgeons Paymasters Adjutants Veterinary Surgeons and Seg^t Sadlers Loaded will Parade to morrow morning at 9 o'clock in the Convent Yard and from thence they will proceed to Zandbergen for the Inspection of Major Genl Sir J.O. Vandeleur agreeable to the B.O. 5th Instant.

The Troop Serjeant Majors to attend

The troops to be out in Watering Order tomorrow morning at 7 o'clock

RO Denderwindeke 7th June 1815

For the Day tomorrow Cornet Hay

The Troops to parade in Watering order tomorrow morning at 7 o'clock – Foot Parade with side Arms in Stable Dress at 1/2 past 4 p.m. for Drill –

Mem.

The Clerks of Troops to Pay into the hands of the Hospital Serjeant 3d *Per Diem* for each man in Hospital Commencing on the 8th *Ultimo*

By Order of
Surgeon Robinson

It is requested to pay a week }
In advance previous to a }
Man going into Hospital }

C.G.O.

N°1 the great movements in the field of large bodies of cavalry are generally made in column of divisions and at a trot this pace has never been accurately defined –

It is obvious that if every horse is to go at a trot it is the slowest trotter of the whole column that will determine the pace – and this would be too slow – Lieu^t. Genl the Earl of Uxbridge directs that the movements of the trot shall be invariably at the rate of at least 9 miles an hour & it will be very advantageous that Off^rs & NC Off^rs leading divisions should know the pace with accuracy –

N°2 The Necessarys in future to be in the possession of each Heavy & Light Dragoon & Hussar are to be in strict conformity to the articles inumerated in the following list –[40]

N°3	In Wear	In the Velise
Stable Jacket		1
Overalls Strapd	1	
Trowsers		1
Flannel Drawers discretionary		1
Flannel Waistcoat do		1
Foraging Cap		1
Breeches Slings	1	
Shirts	1	1
Stockings or socks	1	1
Shoes		1
Shoe clasps or strings		1
Sash	1	
Stock & clasps	1	
Brushes		2
Razor		1
Shaving Brush & Soap		1
Hair Comb		1
Turn screw worm & picker each in wear		
Main Comb & Sponge		1
Black Ball		1
Curry comb & brush discretionary		
Gloves	1	
Oil Pan		1
Mess Tin	1	

The Canteens & haversack must be carried on the mans back on the left side The Canteen strap must be shortened so as to place the Canteen well up under the left arm

The Mess Can to be fastened to the middle baggage strap by the Heavy Cavalry; by the Light as heretofore –

'Strapd' refers to reinforcing down the inside of the leg of the overalls. According to the Clothing Warrant of 1812 this could be 'strapped with leather when necessary at the discretion of the Com'ing Officer.' In a number of contemporary images it is clear that

40 This would appear to be the list of articles referred to in the Brigade Order of 5 June.

this strapping was often of the same cloth as the overalls. In the two known contemporary images of men of the 16th in 1815 there is no indication of leather strapping.[41] The D-shaped mess can is visible in exactly the position described for heavy cavalry in Denis Dighton's painting of Sergeant Ewart of the 2nd Royal North British Dragoons (The Scots Greys) taking a French colour at Waterloo.[42] The 2nd were, of course, heavy cavalry. The method of carrying the mess can for light cavalry remains a mystery, the only hint being in an undated note in the 16th's Order Book: 'No wallets to be worn or bags of any description, Corn Sacks the exception, Water Buckets to be carried on the off side tins & nose bags on the near side.'

Luard Journal:

> June 7th received 24 ducats from the paymaster, worth 9s/6 each £11.8.

Luard Diary:

> June 7th – Rec[d] from Paymaster 24 Ducats at 9/6 each being £11:8–
> Capt[n] Barra being sick I took the Duty of Adjutant –.

Joseph Barra is listed on the Waterloo Roll as a lieutenant. He was promoted to captain on 29 July 1815 *vice* Captain John Buchanan, who was killed at Waterloo. Curiously, this premature promotion appears in Luard's contemporaneous diary, rather then his later journal. It is, of course, possible that Barra's promotion was pending and known about.[43]

Order Book:

> BO Zandbergen 8th June 1815
>
> A Detachment Court Martial according to the following Detail will assemble at the Quarters of the Major of Brigade to morrow morning at 11 o'clock for the trial of such prisoners as may be brought before it

Detail	Captains	Subalterns
11th Lt Dragoons	1	2
16th Lt Dragoons		2
Total	1	4

41 Anon., *Regulation for the Provision of Clothing*, p.7. One image is by J.B. Rubens, *Bibliothèque Royale de Belgique*; the other is by Raffet, after Norblin, *Bibliothèque Nationale de France*.

42 Denis Dighton, 'The Battle of Waterloo: The Charge of the Second Brigade of Cavalry', Royal Collection, RCIN 404825.

43 Tomkinson (ed.) *Diary of a Cavalry Officer*, Appendix 1.

Officers Commanding Regiments will be pleased to Caution all Officers Particularly those who had Half-squadrons and Divisions in the field to make themselves acquainted with the rate of pace as Directed by the Earl of Uxbridge in the Cavalry orders of the 6th Instant

290 yards in a minute is the pace required

RO Denderwindeke 8th June 1815

The troops to be out in Riding School order to morrow morning at 10 o'clock on the Exercising Ground near the village occupied by the 12th L^{t} D^{gs}

Horses unfit for the Ranks only to be left in –

Clerks of Troops to be at H^{d} Quarters with the accounts books to morrow at 12 o'clock –

Officers for the Detachment court Martial have been directed in the BO of this Day

Lt Osten
Lt Wheeler

RO Denderwindeke 9th June 1815

For the day tomorrow Lieu$^{t.}$ Wheeler

Subaltern Officers are Trooped as follows & to join their respective Troops on the Arrival of those from England.

Major Bellis Troop	[C]	Lieu^{ts} Wheeler, Crichton & McDougall
Cap Swetenham "	[D]	L^{ts} Osten, Harris & Cornet Hay
Cap$^{t.}$ Weylands "	[H]	L^{ts} Beauchamp & Richardson
Cap$^{t.}$ Buchanans "	[G]	Lt Baker, Cnts Nugent & Polhill
Cap$^{t.}$ Tomkinson "	[A]	L^{ts} Swinfen Luard & Ct Beckwith
Cap$^{t.}$ Kings "	[F]	L^{ts} Lloyd Nepean & Moncton

Major Murray to be stationed at Gautlingen [?] Clerks of Troops will make the necessary arrangements for Quarters for the above Officers this day –

The circular Letter dated 5th June 1815 Relative to soldiers whose period of service has expired to be red to the men at the first Parade

G & H Troops will form the right squadron, D & F the Centre, A & C the left Squ^{n} until further orders

Circular, Head Qrs Bruxells

5th June 1815

Sir

I am directed by the Commander of the Forces to acquaint you that his Grace deems it expedient under existing circumstances to exercise the power vested in him of retaining in His Majestys Service soldiers whose period of service has expired or may hereafter expire for six months beyond the period for which they were enlisted & in conformity with their engagements has expired in their attestations –

To the Officer Commandg
16 L Dgns

I have the Honor
[?]
Sign'd
E. Barnes
A.G.

Memorandum Zandbergen 9th June 1815

Major General Sir J.O. Vandeleur's Brigade. 13th and 23rd Lt Dns in marching order without Forge Carts or Baggage to be in the Medow near Schendelbeke to-morrow morning at 10 o'clock

Signd Uxbridge
Lieut. General

RO Continued Denderwindeke 9th June 1815

The Regiment to assemble in marching order without Forage or Corn tomorrow morning at 10 o'clock on the exercising Ground near Schendelbeke agreeable to the memorandum the Horses unfit for the Ranks to be out in watering order and the men leading such horses to appear in their stable dress Caps to be worn cov'd and the Jackets Blue facings outwards. The Troops at this place to march off at 1/4 past eight – Correct marching states from each Troop to be given in this evening to the Adjutant and the Horses led in watering order to be returned Present and not in the Ranks in the marching states

RO Denderwindeke, 10th June 1815

For the Day tomorrow Lt Crichton

The undermentioned men & Horses from the Depot England are Troop'd as follows *vizt*

Thos Ratcliffe to D	Ja$^{s.}$ Lang to C
McBride to D	Jno Tiley to C
Rich^{d} savage to F	Jas. Oates to H
Jno Maidmant to G	Richd Pendleton to H
And one horse to A Troop	

The above men & horses to take Date for the of June 1815 inclusive[44]

Memo; Corp^{l} Shooter of C Troop & one man of Capt. Buchanan's Troop will relieve Corp^{l} Floyd and Private Thomas Dent at Attre and to Parade tomorrow morning at Head Quarters at 5 o'clock for that purpose – the Troops to be out in watering order at 7 o'clock tomorrow morning.

RO Denderwindeke June 11th 1815

For the Day tomorrow Le^{t} Lloyd

A Regm^{t} Cort Marshall to be assembled to morrow morning at 11 o'clock Trial of all Prisoners to be brought before it

	Present Cap$^{t.}$ King	
Lieu$^{t.}$ Swinfen}		{ Lt Baker
Lieu$^{t.}$ Harris}	Members	{ Lt Monkton
	All evidence to attend	

Assistant surgeon Evans as Rec^{d} Orders from Commander of forces leve to Return to England in Consquence of giving in Resignation any clame against him will be given in on or before tomorrow evening as after that period as none will be attended to

Troop to be in rediness tomorrow morning to turn out in watering order at 8 o'clock

RMO 12th June 1815

The Court Martial orderd to assemble this morning will not sit until tomorrow morning at ye same hour & place –

BO St Burge [Zandbergen] 12 June 1815

The 16th Lt Dragoons to Parade for Regimental Exercise at 8 o'clock tomorrow morning on the usual ground near Schendelbeke

Sign^{d} J.O. Vande^{lr}
M.G.

44 The date is omitted in the order book.

RO Dana^th [Denderwindeke] 15[45] June 1815

For the [day] tomorrow
Lt W Nepean

The Regt to assemble tomorrow morning agreeable to the BO at 8 o'clock
The Troops from this Place to march off at 1/4 past 6 o'clock

Gen CO Ninove 12th June 1815

N°1 the Swords of every Reg^t of Cavalry are to be Ground & Pointed according to ye Pattern received by ye Troop Serj^t Majors & men assembled this Day at Cavalry Head Quarters –[46]

N°2 This Order to be carried into Execution without loss of time –

RO Denderwindeke 13th June 1815

Watering Order tomorrow morn^g at 7 o'clock –

For ye Day tomorrow Lieu^t. Luard

The Command^g Officer desires that ye Officers Command^g squadrons will see that ye Officers of their respective Squadrons marches to & from ye Field in their proper places –

The Officers first & second chargers will parade tomorrow at 1 o'clock for ye Command^g Officers Inspection at Head Quarters & ye whole of ye sore-Back'd Horses at ye same time –

The following charges having been received at ye Depot for ye repairs of Arms of ye undermentioned Troops –

The Pay Master will charge ye same in ye Troop abstract and ye sum total to be remitted to ye Acting Pay Master at ye Depot – *viz*

	£ –	s –	d
Captain Tomkinsons Troop		11	
Brevet Maj^r Bellis	3	7	17½
Captn Swetenham	1	19	7½
Captn Kings	2	14	6
Captn Buchanans	1	9	1½
Captn Weylands	2	2	10½
	£12	14	3

45 This would appear to be an error and should be the 12th. These Regimental Orders are in the same hand as the Brigade Orders for the 12th.

46 This must be the order that resulted in some heavy cavalry sabres having a spear point rather than the original hatchet point. It would seem, from surviving sabres, to have been applied to only a few light cavalry sabres.

Foot Parade with Side Arms at 4 o'clock in ye afternoon

RO Denderwindeke 14th June 1815

For ye Day tomorrow Cornet Beckwith

The Troops to be out in Watering Order tomorrow morn^{g} at 7 o'clock –

Foot Parade with Side Arms in Stable Dress at 4 p.m. for Drill

Clerks of Troops to be at H^{d} Quarters tomorrow at 12 o'clock, & to bring with them a correct list of Debt & Credits y^{e} 24th April 1815 – they will also bring the Troop Legers –

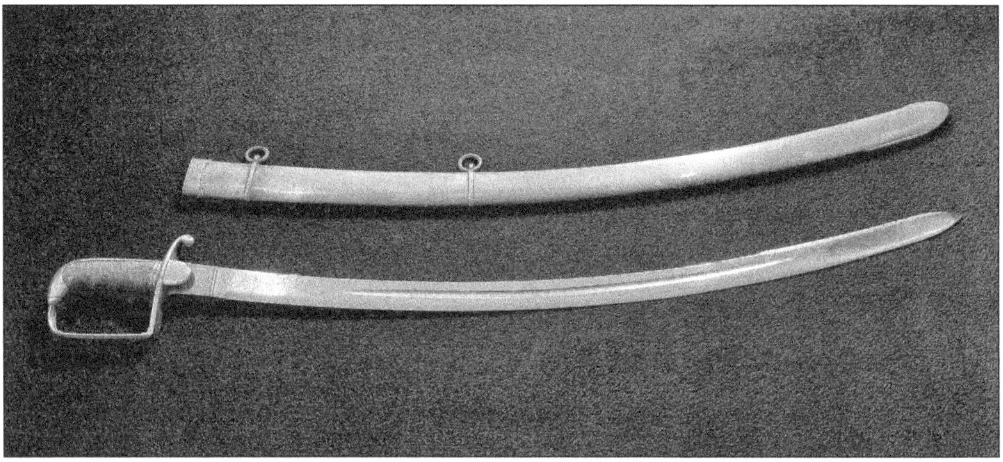

Sabre carried at Waterloo by William Polhill (Polhill Collection)

BO Zandbergen 15th June 1815

Letters for England are to be sent to the Brigade Majors office on Sunday & Wednesday

Signed M. Childers
M^{r} of Brigade

BO Zandbergen 15th June 1815

The Brigade to be on the Meadow near Schendelbeke at the following hours and to exercise Regimentally

11th Lt Drag^{s} at 7 & 16th Light Dragoons at 8 and 12th Light Dragoons at 9 o'clock

Signed M. Childers
M.B.

RO Denderwindeke 15th June 1815

For the Day tomorrow C^{t} Hay

The Regt will assemble in Exercising Order to morrow morning at 8 o'clock agreeable to BO

The troops at this place to march off at 1/4 past six o'clock

3

16 and 17 June

Tomkinson:

June 16th

My Brother Henry who had come out from England (about a week) 7th he arrived at my quarters was impatient at the idle life we were leading in our Quarters and was anxious to go and see the Country in our front and visit some of the Towns occupied by the Prussians, for the purpose of seeing their Troops and the Towns they occupied. Soon after day light my servant came into my room saying there had arrived an order to march directly, and that the whole Army was moving. We were ignorant of the cause and heard rumours that it was occasioned by an attack the enemy had made on the Prussian out Posts – We marched about five moving on the Enghien road. On our arrival at Enghien we found that the Guards had left it, and it was said we were to remain in its neighbourhood for the purpose of watching the road from Enghien to Mons – We halted for a considerable time near the Town waiting for orders – when we moved on towards Braine le Comte. This we passed and in about a mile on the other side and I think about two p.m. we began to hear some firing beyond Nivelles on which we were moving – When within about a mile of Nivelles an order came for us to proceed on without delay, the enemy having made an attack on our Troops beyond Nivelles. We threw away the bundles of forage (hay) we were carrying; passed Nivelles at a trot proceeding on towards Quatre Bras; with the least possible delay. The firing continued, the cannonade was sharp and on our getting nearer musketry and in a heavy fire was distinctly heard. We met several wounded, who told us the enemy had made an attack and had been repulsed.

The Earl of Uxbridge commands the Cavalry. I do not know what his orders were yet it appeared to me no decided point was given for our Brigade to move to. Had the Brigadier in the first instance received an order to march on Nivelles and proceeded directly there, we should have been up in time to have acted and though our numbers would have been much inferior to the enemy force yet it was very desirable to have Cavalry and however few considerable advantage would have resulted from it. We should have been the only Brigade up and had to contend with a force very much our superior. We most likely should have suffered greatly. From the obstinate manner the ground was contested by being held by such an inferior force on our part, it was evident the object was a great one, and we of course should have come in for the same fate which fell to the lot of the Infantry; in being opposed to a superior force, but which in Cavalry would have been greater to one brigade than the force of the enemy's Infantry was to ours –

From Lord Uxbridge being an Hussar it was said he would bring them forward on every occasion and therefore a subject of regret on our part that the Brigade should have missed a chance in which we alone could have been employed –

On approaching Les Quatre Bras we formed in line advancing to the point the two roads intersect each other when we brought forward our left Shoulders advancing on the enemy. They had discontinued their attack being repulsed at all points; and we only moved forward under a slight cannonade for the purpose of showing ourselves and to prevent any small party of our Infantry being molested when withdrawing for the night. The enemy did not show any inclination and all was quiet, excepting a chance shot occasionally from the sentries. It appeared that the first Division under Lieut. Genl Cooke had occupied a wood to the right hand in advance of Quatre Bras, where a Brigade of Guards under Genl Maitland (2nd and 3rd Battalions of the 1st Regiment) had been sharply engaged repulsing every attack – The 5th Division under old Picton had arrived from Waterloo in the nick of the moment, and advanced to take up a position on the left of the wood – Here they were repeatedly attacked and more than once charged by the *Cuirassier* of the Guards. In going over the ground we saw several cuirasses lying scattered about. Some of them had been carried away by the infantry and used for frying their meat, the Baggage being in the rear and nothing to cook with then up with the Regiments – They were attacked very suddenly and had to form in square without loss of time in the standing corn. The enemy attacked most gallantly but were received so coolly and in such order, it was impossible to succeed unless they had ridden the Guards down by main force. A thing never heard of. The infantry either break before the cavalry come close up or they drive them back with their fire – It is an awful thing for infantry to see a body of Cavalry riding at them full Gallop – The Men in the square frequently begin to shuffle and so make some unsteadiness. This causes them to neglect their fire, the cavalry seeing them waver, have an inducement for riding close up and in all probability succeed in getting into the square when all is over. When once broken the infantry of course have no chance. If steady it is almost impossible to succeed against infantry, yet I should always be cautious having seen the best of Troops more afraid of Cavalry than any other force, if in command of infantry attacked by Cavalry – The 28th, 42nd, 79th and 92nd Regiments (The three last Highland) are named by Lord Wellington as having distinguished themselves. The 79th infantry had more to do than the others and was said particularly to have distinguished itself – Of all Troops to resist Cavalry when great steadiness, coolness and obedience to orders is required I should select the Scotch. In out Post duty or any service where quickness is required and immediate advantage to be taken of any sudden change I do not think they are equal to others –

We remained on the ground we had halted on until after dark and then retired for the night to [the] rear of Quatre Bras, having Piquets in out front. Napoleon is in command of the French Army. He has only the Duke to beat that he may say success has attended him with every General in Europe. It is an anxious time.

Through the whole of the evening and after dark we heard a very considerable fire on our left in the direction of Sombreffe – This was an attack of Napoleon's on the Prussian Army, in which he employed his whole force with the exception of the 1st & 2nd Corps & these attacked us at Quatre Bras. Ney conducted the attack on us, which from the numbers he brought and the hurried manner our Troops came up, and obliged to occupy the first ground which presented itself, he had a fair chance of success. The French Troops behaved well. The attack on the Prussians was very decided. The enemy more than once attempted carrying the villages of St Amand and Ligny which Blucher occupied and in which for some time they failed. Blucher at one time was nearly taken, his Horse was killed. He was said to be saved by a charge of his Cavalry – Fresh Troops and in greater numbers were brought down when the French succeeded in occupying these posts but not so as to oblige the Prussians to abandon their position. They however after repeated attacks succeeded in driving the Prussians from the two villages of St Amand and Ligny and Blucher not being joined by his 4th Corp from Liege (under Bulow) he retired in the night and on the 17th on Wavre –

From six until dark the different Corps of the British Army continued to arrive at Quatre Bras, and before midnight I think the whole was assembled. We Bivouaced as we could find ground. I slept on a Door with my Brother Henry. It was the first time he had ever been in bivouac or out all night sleeping in the open Air. I rather think I slept better than the Amateur. At day light our men were discharging their Muskets when he bridled his Horse thinking it was an attack on our Troops. The point where we passed the night was close to the main road and near a house with a well near the road. Our Brigade close to Quatre Bras in rear of the infantry. The night was fine but considerable inconvenience in a scarcity of water there being no running stream or other water near where we were and the Wells exhausted before our arrival. I attempted to get water at a well but found so many Belgians it was impossible. A Cellar of wine had been plundered by them and I came in time to witness the conclusion [of] a contest between two parties for the last Barrel in it.

From the scattered position of the Troops and their manner of moving on Quatre Bras much has been said of the Duke of Wellington allowing himself to be surprised. From the force the Prussians had in front and around Quatre Bras I do not conceive he was much called upon to watch in any force that point in the line which the two Armies had occupied and as there was a considerable extent of country on the right by which the enemy might move on Brussels he was obliged to protect the frontier on that side. He heard of the attack on the Prussians at Charleroi on the 15th and immediately (I believe) sent an order for the Guards from Enghien to move on Nivelle and an order for the whole Army to hold itself in readiness to march.

Major Gen[l] Alten stationed at Mons sent one or two reports of the advance of the enemy and conceiving from all he could collect it was with a view to attack with their whole force, he sent off his Aide de Camp with another report worded more decidedly. He arrived at Brussels about 3 a.m. on the morning of the 16th and going to the Duke's House requested to see him. He was shown into his room where the duke was lying down in his Clothes. He told him all he had heard and delivered his letter. The Duke said – 'Then it is your opinion it is their intention to attack us?' He replied it was his opinion they would. The Duke then said 'Ride up immediately to Waterloo where you will find Sir Thomas Picton with his Division and order him to turn the Troops out immediately.' He did so and in five minutes after he arrived the duke himself rode up and directed the Troops to move on Quatre Bras –

I had this from the ADC – From this I think it appears that the Duke did not think they would attack and therefore he possibly might not pay that attention to the reports on the 15th which they required – yet again it would not be prudent to move his whole force to one point on every demonstration of the enemy.

Something has been said of the Head Quarters at Brussels thinking so little of the enemy's advance that they were at a Ball and considerable delay occasioned in consequence – If an Army receives information at night which requires an immediate move of Troops, it is of great consequence to have the Quarter Master General and other staff officers collected; in the place of having to seek and assemble them over a large town – There was considerable time saved by this and no objection to attending a Ball 20 miles from an enemy –

Luard Journal:

June 16th – Capt. Barra being sick I was appointed to act as adjutant.

We march'd at 7 a.m. – we were just turning out for a field day when an order arrived from head quarters to march immediately – we pass'd thro Braine le Comte – & Enghien – soon after leaving Braine le Comte we heard cannonading on our right, we proceeded thro Nivelles & order'd to trot – about 2 leagues from Nivelles we saw the French & our Troops engaged – Soult having attack'd Blucher, Lord Wellington moved a force to his assistance, which was vigorously attack'd by the French but repulsed with great loss, & we held our ground; their Currassiers charged frequently but unsuccessfully & were fearfully slaughterd – when nearly dark on our side the Duke of Brunswick was kill'd & our troops suffer'd much, the Guards in particular – the 16th Drags did not reach the ground in time to act – I was sent to the front with Colonel Hay – & was order'd to return & wheel the Regiment into line but it was too late & we bivouac'd, near the village of Quatre Bras – I slept in a cabbage garden.

Luard Diary:

June 16th Marched at 7am thro' Enghien – 2 leagues thro' Brain Le Comte We heard soon after Cannonading to our right. We proceeded thro' Nivelles & were ordered to Trot – 2 leagues from Nivelles, we saw the Enemy and our Troops engaged – Soult having attacked, Blucher Lord W– moved to his assistance – by which he attacked him vigorously but was repulsed with great loss & we Kept our Ground – their *Curassiers* [*Cuirassiers*] charged frequently – but without success – The Duke of Brunswick was killed & our army suffered much – the Guards in particular – Our Regt could not get to the Ground in time to act. – encamped near the village of Quatre Bras.

Tomkinson:

17th June

We heard early this morning from Colonel Ponsonby that that the Prussians had retired & that we were to do the same

I always applied to him for any news from Head Quarters & he told me himself – He regretted that we were obliged to retire.

The Duke rode up at day light to Quatre Bras – we soon heard that in consequence of the attack made on the Prussians last night they had retired on Wavre and that we were likewise to retire to a position in our rear for the purpose of covering Brussels. The infantry withdrew quietly leaving the Cavalry to cover their retreat.

We remained on the ground we passed the night on until about two p.m. when in consequence of the enemy showing some Cavalry we turned out forming in three lines to the left and rear of Quatre Bras.

Nothing can show more clearly the result of the affairs of yesterday, than the late hour at which the enemy attempted a forward movement. They did not move a man in pursuit of either the Prussians or English until late in the day, and not until all (excepting the rear-guard) had withdrawn. Had either of the affairs proved successful they would have attempted a forward movement against the beaten opponent at daylight – they were successful against the Prussians because they obliged them to abandon their position. Two more successes tho' will ruin their Army – They suffered greatly.

Both affairs ought to teach them that great judgement and good conduct in their Troops will be requisite to ensure success – and in case of a reverse on their part, they have not their usual resource of averting the evil by a suspension of hostilities or profiting in any way by intrigue.

Blucher is exasperated and the Duke determined. They act together with cordiality.

The two Brigades of Hussars were formed by Lord Uxbridge in the first line – the Light Dragoons (Sir J.O. Vandeleur's Brigade) in the second and the Heavy Cavalry in support some distance in the rear – The intention of Lord Uxbridge was to keep the Hussars in front, to take advantage of any favourable chance, and on the enemy advancing in such force as to oblige us to retire they were to pass through the second line and for it to cover the retreat.

They came out in column after column and in greater force than I ever recollect seeing together at one point.

There was not time for the Hussars to pass through our Brigade the enemy were so close upon them, and had we not got off with the least possible delay, the Hussars and our Brigade would have been in one confused heap. We had learnt the necessity of making way for those in front when we and they were retiring from acting in the narrow roads of Portugal & the retreat being ordered we fortunately made way for the front line as we were ordered to do.

I saw the French Cavalry when moving out of their Bivouac and thought from their numbers we must either bring all our force to oppose them and keep our ground, or that if a retreat was determined on, the sooner we moved the more prudent. They advanced in very large bodies and Lord Uxbridge soon saw that so far from having any chance afforded of charging, that he had nothing left but to get his Troops away without the least delay – We in the second line were ordered away immediately and retired leaving Genappe to our left (in retiring) – The first line got away without much loss retiring with the Heavy Cavalry on Genappe, but had not time allowed it to retire through the second line as first intended. The Infantry being all clear and the enemy showing so large a force of cavalry we ought not to have waited so long, Retreat being our object the more easily it was effected the more prudent it would have been.

Lord Uxbridge having all the Cavalry under him and detached from the Infantry was aware of the opportunity of distinguishing himself, could he bring about a successful affair. It is a chance few can resist and in their anxiety not to lose the opportunity, are frequently led into errors, which causes a Head of an Army to distrust them on any future occasion. They are opportunities desired by all Officers and those serving in the particular Corps and Regiments engaged, they are more spoken of in an Army than the General Actions in which all bear a part, from a desire on those employed to make the most of their own exertions and from an inclination in those not engaged to be acquainted with what they had not an opportunity of seeing, and but too often with an intention of finding some error to distract from the credit of the affair –

I think the result to the Duke must be that Lord Uxbridge is too young a soldier to be much relied on with a separate command, from a feeling that he will risk too much in a desire to do something –

This was the error Crawford [*sic*] fell into with the Light Division in 1810 on passing the Coa and I think Lord W. was not much inclined to trust him again with a distinct command –

The conduct of Lord Hill (when Sir Rowland) was quite the reverse, through the whole of his operations distinct from the Duke, when employed south of the Tagus. His orders were to watch the enemy's force opposed to him, he never engaged but when obliged and lost so many chances in bringing on petty affairs that the men called his Division the Observing Division.

At Genappe the enemy came up with the rear and pushing on into the village. Lord Uxbridge ordered the 7th Hussars to attack a Regt of French Lancers – The enemy were formed across the street and in this position were charged by the 7th. The men rode up most gallantly and attempted to drive them back, cutting at them with their sabres, the enemy holding their Lances before their Horses – The men of the 7th from all I could hear behaved well but were obliged to retire unsuccessful. The French then advanced out of the Village when the 1st Life Guards were brought down and charged. They advanced most Gallantly and the enemy ran away before the Life Guards got up to them – they were from what I could learn within about 100 yards when the enemy went about, and though the French were awed by their appearance and ran away before they came near them, yet the charge was entirely attributed to the superior strength of the Life Guards and weight in riding down the enemy – Nothing could be better done than the charge, yet I much question had the Life Guards attacked in the situation the 7th attempted if they would have succeeded – The 7th was Lord Uxbridge's own Regiment and an opportunity desired by him for distinguishing them – He selected the first that offered fancying he had only to allow them to come in contact with the enemy and that the result must be to their credit. I have seen the same thing frequently occur, that those Regiments which a General wishes to bring forward are either placed where they do nothing, or get into action under unfortunate circumstances, losing many men without gaining much credit –

We retired to the rear of the position the Army was about to occupy and Bivouac'd for the night about a mile and a half in rear of Ter la Haye and half a mile in the rear of our position – During our retreat from Quatre Bras we had been exposed to the heaviest rain I was ever out on, and in consequence not a dry thread throughout the Army.

From the appearance of the Weather everyone was desirous of obtaining Wood to keep up a fire. One of our Dragoons came out of the Village of Waterloo with a Clock on his Back. An officer from a distance and behind him (Lt Luard) called to know what his object was in bringing it. The Dragoon replied (not knowing who spoke to him) that 'if you will – come to our troop you shall soon see what I will do with it. I'll make the Beggar tick.' So far from making him tick he prevented his ever striking another tick by setting the Clock on the fire and making a Chimney of him – (On revisiting the field of battle more than forty years later, my father, on telling this story to his party, was importuned by a Belgian peasant for compensation, on the ground that the clock belonged to his family – Note by James Tomkinson in original edition)

It eased a little at night fall but it as it became dark again commenced and rained incessantly through the night – The country was entirely arable land, and fancying a clover root (nearly fit to eat) would be dryer to lie down upon than either standing Wheat or Fallow we selected it as the best spot we could find – With the Horses moving about to get their backs to the rain and the men walking to feed them and light fires, the clover soon disappeared and the whole space occupied by the 16th became one complete puddle – It was knee deep at day light – I lay down in my Cloke and having been up at 2 a.m. on the morning of the 17th and occupied through the whole of the day I slept for two or three hours –

Luard Journal:

June 17th moved into position at 7 a.m. our infantry retired – we remained on our ground the Cavalry form'd in 3 lines till about 4 o'clock, the French push'd on a large force of Cavalry & commenced a cannonade, we retired & encamp'd near Waterloo in rear of a position our army had taken up on Mount St Jean. – there was an affair of Cavalry today the 7th Hussars & part of the Life Guards were engaged & Capt. Hodges of 7th Hussars was kill'd – the French advanced & our artillery open'd on them when they halted & the two armies bivouac'd in front & in sight of each other. – it rain'd hard with thunder & lightening – the noise of the thunder & the cannonade of artillery & the lightening & flash of guns was awful – it ceased at dark but it rain'd heavily during the night. – we bivouac'd in a clover field.

Luard Diary:

June 17th Moved up in position at 7 o'clock – soon after our Infantry retired – at 4 p.m. the Enemy pushed on a large force of Cavalry & commenced a cannonade, – we retired – & encamped near Waterloo in rear of a position our Army occupied on Mount St Jean in front of Waterloo.

The enemy advanced and our Artillery opened upon them when they halted – & the two Armies encamped in sight of each other –

4

Waterloo, 18 June

The movements of the 16th and the rest of Major General Vandeleur's brigade can be followed with some degree of certainty as a considerable amount of detail can be extracted from the various accounts and the letters gathered by Major General Siborne. A summary of those movements, with an analysis of how the movements were made, is given before the eyewitness accounts continue.

Vandeleur's brigade passed thc night of 17 June bivouacked to the rear of Lieutenant General Picton's division. At 9:00 a.m. the regiments mounted and moved to take up a position at almost the extreme left of the Allied line; only Major General Vivian's hussar brigade was to their left. By 11:00 a.m. the brigade was in position on the brow of the ridge. The three regiments were formed side by side, each in a close column of squadrons, the left squadron in front, then the centre squadron and the right squadron at the rear.[1] In this formation the gap between each squadron was only a horse's length.[2] Each squadron would have been approximately 60 metres wide. When formed in line, a space equal to a third of the frontage of a squadron – in this case approximately 20 metres – separated the squadrons. The same distance was used to separate regiments.[3] Thus Vandeleur's brigade occupied a frontage of approximately 220 metres. Allowing a depth of three metres for each rank and the spaces between the squadrons, the depth was only some 24 metres. The formation with the left squadrons leading indicates that it was expected that any deployment into line was to be by extending to the right, each squadron moving to take its place to the right of the squadron in front. Of course, this would not be possible with the regiments in columns only 20 metres apart, indicating an expectation that they would move from their position before deploying into line. The expectation of moving is supported by Vandeleur's statement that he received an order from the Earl of Uxbridge 'to engage the Enemy whenever they could do so with advantage without waiting for orders'.[4]

1 Major General H.T. Siborne, *Waterloo Letters* (London: Greenhill Books, 1993), p.114.
2 Anon., *Instructions and Regulations for the Formations and Movements of the Cavalry* (London: War Office, 1799 3rd Edition), p.141 (first published in 1796).
3 Anon., *Instructions and Regulations* (1812), p.11.
4 Siborne, *Waterloo Letters*, p.105.

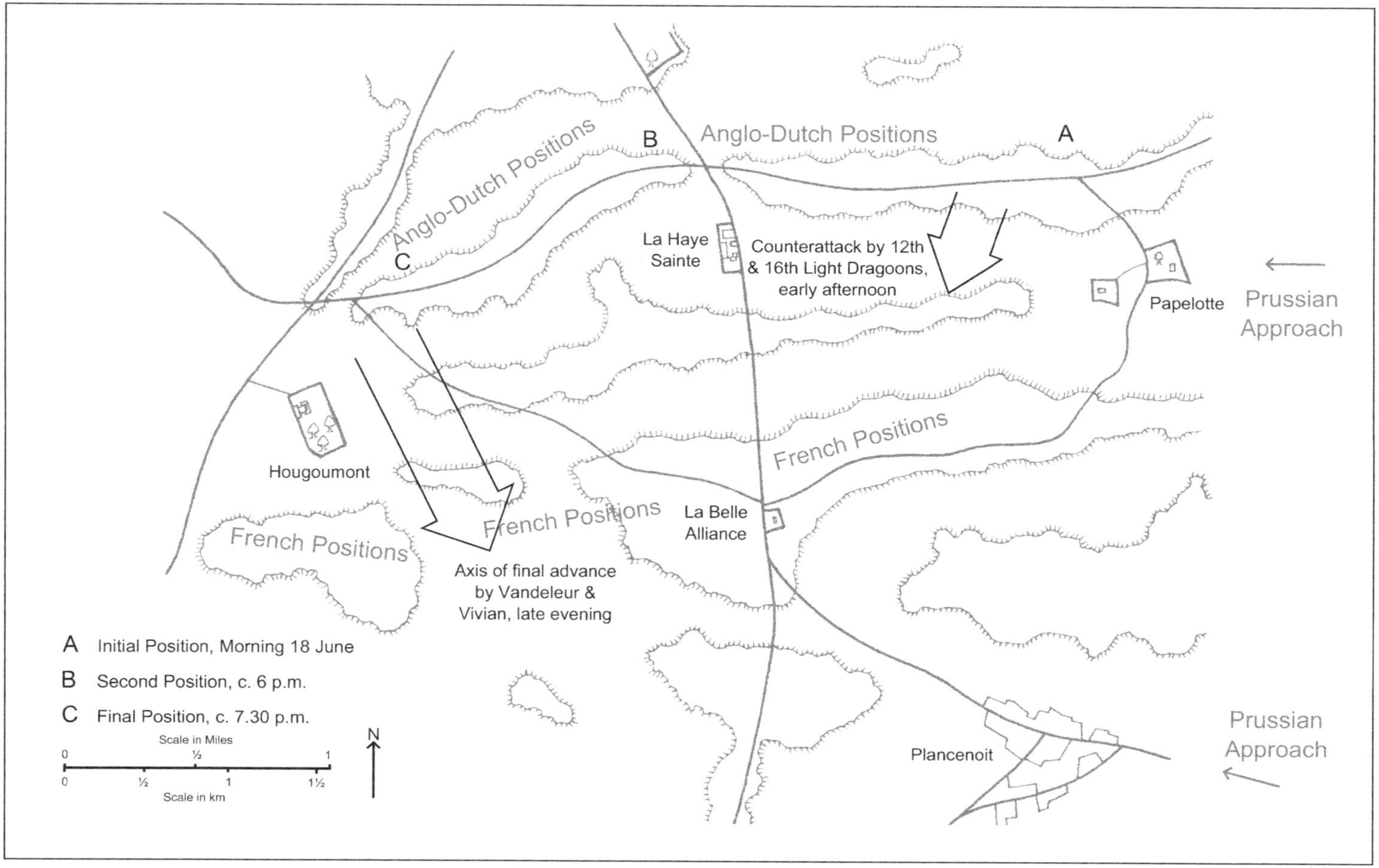

Movements of Vandeleur's 4th Cavalry Brigade at Waterloo

Although initially drawn up to the brow of the ridge it was found that the brigade was within range of the French artillery; consequently the brigade was moved back from the ridge, and then dismounted. Even so, some casualties were taken, and when some officers of the 16th walked to the brow of the hill, leading their horses they attracted enemy fire, and an exploding shell killed Captain Swetenham's horse.[5]

Following the order from Uxbridge about engaging without waiting for orders, Vandeleur received what he later wrote was the second of only two orders that he received prior to the brigade's first charge. This was to close to the infantry to the brigade's right, which had themselves moved to their right.[6] This required the brigade to cross what is referred to in many sources as a ravine, but was, and still is, a sunken lane, lined with hedges. Vandeleur stated that the brigade crossed the ravine, on their right, in column 'with a small front.'[7] Lieutenant Baker of the 16th was more specific, writing that the brigade 'moved forward from their supporting ground in the rear of the extreme left, in column of half-squadrons (or divisions I do not remember which) left in front, the 12th of course leading.'[8] In the light of Vandeleur's comment about a 'small front,' a movement by divisions would seem most likely.

This was not a simple manoeuvre. The 12th were to lead the march to the right, but were on the left of the brigade, and had to change from a close column of squadrons into an open column of divisions to the right. To do this each squadron in turn first had to march forwards to get clear of the other regiments in the brigade. Having done so it had to break down into divisions, or quarters of a squadron.[9] To do this, each squadron had to halt and then each of its four divisions would simultaneously wheel in the direction that it was going to march, in this case to the right, thus forming a column, and march off.[10] To re-form the line required each division to wheel to the left. In order to do this, however, it was essential that the left flank of each division marched in alignment with the one in front, and maintained a distance from it exactly equal to its own front. If this was not done the resultant line could have gaps in it or divisions could overlap, preventing the squadron from forming quickly. The commander of each squadron rode on the left flank of the column and the regimental commander rode in front of the left flank of the first division to give it its direction.[11] In this manner each of the three regiments became a column of 12 divisions, the 12th leading, followed by the 16th, and the 11th bringing up the rear.

The brigade crossed the ravine to its right and this took some time, which resulted in the 11th being left a little behind and subsequently kept in reserve by Vandeleur.[12] According to Luard the column separated once across the ravine, with the 12th moving to the left and

5 Siborne, *Waterloo Letters,* p.120; private collection, letter of Captain Clement Swetenham to his mother, 19 June 1815.
6 Siborne, *Waterloo Letters,* p.105.
7 Siborne, *Waterloo Letters,* p.105.
8 Gareth Glover (ed.), *Letters from the Battle of Waterloo* (London: Greenhill Books, 2004), p.78.
9 Anon., *Cavalry Regulations*, p.2.
10 Anon., *Cavalry Regulations*, p.21.
11 Anon., *Cavalry Regulations*, p.257.
12 Siborne, *Waterloo Letters*, p.105.

the 16th to the right.[13] This was a move in accordance with the Regulations when it was necessary to bring more than one regiment quickly into line.[14] Vandeleur now became aware of the predicament of Ponsonby's Union Brigade. Following its successful counter-attack against the French infantry assault on the Allied left centre, it had gone too far and was retreating, severely harassed by French cavalry, lancers in particular.[15] The two regiments then passed through the Hanoverian infantry of Colonel Best's brigade.[16] The 12th were ahead of the 16th and formed line first. With the left of a regiment leading it did this by extending to the right. The first four divisions of the column, being the leading squadron, wheeled right until the rear division was opposite where the left flank of the regiment was to be. The four divisions then halted and wheeled to their left, thus re-forming the squadron in line. The following divisions wheeled to pass behind it before halting and wheeling to the left to re-form the squadron in a line. The two squadrons would then advance to dress on the first squadron formed.[17]

In forming a regiment into line, the place of its commander was at the head of the line as it extended; thus Lieutenant Colonel Hay, commanding the 16th, was on the right of the regiment. It was at that moment that he was hit by a musket ball and so badly wounded that he was not expected to live. The effect of this was a loss of coordination between the three squadrons of the regiment. Consequently the left hand squadron attacked in the same general direction as the 12th, while the centre and right hand squadrons charged more to the right.[18] Both regiments, however, were moving obliquely down from the Allied ridge towards the remnants of Ponsonby's Union Brigade, the last of the French infantry and the French lancers pursuing Ponsonby's cavalry. The Scots Greys in particular were suffering badly at the hands of the lancers. On forming line the right flank of the 16th was very close to the retreating cavalry and the pursuing lancers, so Vandeleur ordered the regiments to half wheel their squadrons to the right and charge.[19] It is possible that, in the confusion, only the centre and right squadrons of the 16th fully complied, and they engaged the pursuing French lancers head-on, who they repulsed.[20] The 12th and the left squadron of the 16th dispersed the last of the French infantry and then charged into the flank of the French lancers.[21]

This was not the first time that the 16th Light Dragoons had fought French lancers. The first occasion had been on 25 September 1811, near Azava, in the Peninsular War, and the 16th had come out victors then. Tomkinson wrote of that occasion: 'The Lancers looked well and formidable before they were broken and closed to by our men, and then their

13 Siborne, *Waterloo Letters*, p.120.
14 Anon., *Cavalry Regulations*, pp.200–01.
15 Siborne, *Waterloo Letters*, pp.105, 112–13.
16 Glover, *Letters from Waterloo*, p.78.
17 Anon., *Cavalry Regulations*, pp.256–57.
18 Siborne, *Waterloo Letters*, pp.107, 113; Glover, *Letters from Waterloo*, p.78.
19 Siborne, *Waterloo Letters*, Nos 53 and 51.
20 Cheshire Archives and Local Studies, DTM/67, Diary of William Tomkinson, 18 June 1815.
21 Siborne, *Waterloo Letters*, pp.112–23, esp. pp.114–15 and p.121.

lances were an encumbrance.'[22] There is no indication in any of the writings of the men of Vandeleur's brigade that they were particularly troubled by the lancers at Waterloo. Indeed the 12th had trained to counter lancers.[23]

The 11th Light Dragoons, meanwhile, had formed line on the brow of the hill to provide support.[24] The 16th had been ordered not to go beyond the bottom of the slope and, now commanded by Major Murray, retired to re-form their line to the right of the 11th.[25] This allowed the survivors of Ponsonby's brigade, the Scots Greys in particular, to reach safety, passing by on both flanks of the 16th. The 12th also fell back on the rest of the brigade.[26] The brigade now sent forward skirmishers, those of the 16th commanded by Lieutenant Baker of G Troop, and retired behind the brow of the hill.[27] At this point Tomkinson commented that the officers of the 16th had trouble keeping the regiment together and preventing the men from breaking up into small parties to attack the French pursuing the retiring heavy cavalry. If they had not done so, they would have been unable to cover the retreat of the retiring cavalry. Two of the three regiments of Ponsonby's brigade had not seen service in the Peninsula, and here the experience of the officers and men of Vandeleur's brigade told in not succumbing to the same temptations that had proved so fatal to the heavy cavalry.

Having re-formed behind the Allied ridge, the brigade was ordered, at about 5:00 p.m., to move to its right, to a position about half way between where it had first formed and the main road between Brussels and Charleroi that ran through the centre of the battlefield. It was soon ordered to move again, crossing the Charleroi road, halting to form with its left flank resting on the road. This was followed by a further move to the right, to the Brussels-to-Nivelles road behind Hougoumont.[28] Here the brigade stood in line with the regiments in their original order, the 12th on the left, the 16th in the centre, and the 11th on the right. The 12th, however, had been reduced to just two squadrons as a result of the casualties that had been received during the first charge against the French infantry and lancers.[29]

When the order to advance was given following the defeat of Napoleon's last attack by the infantry of the Imperial Guard, the brigade advanced to the ridge line and changed from line to column of half-squadrons, left in front, to pass through the Allied infantry.[30] Tomkinson wrote that the ground in front of them to their left was more suitable for deployment back into line than that to their right. This may have been due to the proximity of Hougoumont. With the regiments advancing left in front, they should have deployed by extending to the

22 Cheshire Archives and Local Studies, DTM/67, Diary of William Tomkinson, 18 June 1815.
23 Andrew Bamford, *Gallantry and Discipline* (London: Frontline Books, 2015), pp.103–04.
24 Siborne, *Waterloo Letters*, p.107.
25 Glover, *Letters from Waterloo*, p.78; Graham, *History of the 16th*, p.62; Cheshire Archives and Local Studies, DTM/67, Diary of William Tomkinson, 18 June 1815.
26 Siborne, *Waterloo Letters*, p.107; Cheshire Archives and Local Studies, DTM/67, Diary of William Tomkinson, 18 June 1815.
27 Glover, *Letters from Waterloo*, p.78.
28 Cheshire Archives and Local Studies, DTM/67, Diary of William Tomkinson, 18 June 1815; Siborne, *Waterloo Letters*, p.106.
29 Glover, *Letters from Waterloo*, p.76; Siborne, *Waterloo Letters*, p.115.
30 Cheshire Archives and Local Studies, DTM/67, Diary of William Tomkinson, 18 June 1815; Siborne, *Waterloo Letters*, pp.118, 122.

right.[31] Instead the half-squadrons inclined to their left, moving out from behind the half-squadron in front, and then moving up into line.[32] The effect of this was to reverse the order of the squadrons in each regiment. Thus Tomkinson's left squadron was then on the right of the regiment with what had been the extreme left hand half-squadron on the extreme right. This deployment also reversed the order of the regiments in the brigade; thus the 12th was on the right and the 11th on the left, with the 16th still in the centre.

Vandeleur's Brigade advanced a considerable distance, its last action being a charge across a road that may be the road called the *Chemin du Crucifix*.[33] If so, pursuing a little way to the top of the next rise, the brigade may have finally halted, at about 10:00 p.m., somewhere to the east of Bruyère Madame.[34] Subsequently the brigade withdrew and bivouacked on the edge of a wood, near the observatory.[35]

Order Book:

> RO Mont St Jean 18th June 1815
>
> Officers Com[g] Troops will call the rolls of their troops at twelve o'clock and six in the evening till further orders and report on the subject to the Com[g] Officer

Tomkinson:

> June 18th, 1815. Battle of Waterloo
>
> The rain had fallen through the night without ceasing, the Army had no Tents consequently there could not be a dry thread left to us – The fires were attempted to be kept up at the commencement of the night, but from the rain and want of fuel not many were continued through the night. All was quiet at day light when the rain ceased. The fires in the 16th were lighted and attempts made to dry our clothes. Occasional showers however fell during the morning, though light in comparison to the rain of the night and preceding day – The enemy had brought a considerable force to the Hills opposite our position, their fires were seen extending for some distance along our front, and it was evident they had moved to the front of our position nearly the whole of their force –
>
> Curious scene which took place betwixt Price a Private in my Troop and myself, when moving from the Bivouac we occupied for the night to the ground appointed for us in the Line –

31 Anon., *Cavalry Regulations*, pp.256–57.

32 Cheshire Archives and Local Studies, DTM/67, Diary of William Tomkinson, 18 June 1815.

33 Cheshire Archives and Local Studies, DTM/67, Diary of William Tomkinson, 18 June 1815; Siborne, *Waterloo Letters*, p.122.

34 Cheshire Archives and Local Studies, DTM/67, Diary of William Tomkinson, 18 June 1815.

35 Cheshire Archives and Local Studies, DTM/67, Diary of William Tomkinson, 18 June 1815.

He got off his Horse and ran away to the rear before we were engaged being deranged. He was an old soldier yet not the wisest and had been the shoemaker to the Troop for many years – The men after the day was over did not resent his leaving them knowing the kind of man and his weakness.[36]

At night I had only one man absent excepting killed & wounded with not a man to assist each wounded. The one absent had got away during the advance to plunder, was reported to me by the men and booted by the men on the morning following the Action.

From the march the Army had made yesterday and the hurried manner the position was taken up considerable arrangement of the line was necessary. This commenced soon after day light under the immediate inspection of the Duke of Wellington, and was soon completed. Lord Hill was out the instant it was light and had arranged his own Corps before the Duke arrived.

The position selected was across the Nivelle and Charleroi Roads from Brussels, leading to both those points. The right was thrown back *en potence* to a ravine near Merbe Braine which place was also occupied, and the left extended to the Hamlet of Ter la Haye – There were two Farm Houses immediately below the position, the occupation of which was of the greatest consequence to the holding of the position. Hougoumont in front of that part of the line called the right centre and close to the Nivelle road and La Haye Sainte in front of the left centre – The latter was a single House with a Garden and not affording cover to any great body of Troops.

Hougoumont was more important, the House Garden and Wood in possession of the enemy, would enable them to form any number of men unmolested immediately below the position and admit of their making an instantaneous attack. The 4 Light Companies from the four Battalions of the Guards were posted in the first instance in the Wood in front of the *Chateau* – Some of them retired when attacked with the other Light Troops which with them occupied the Wood, and some took shelter in the House and Garden continuing through the day to assist in its defence – In what proportion I could never learn – The Wood in front of the House was occupied by a Light Battalion of Nassau Troops and one Battalion of the Brunswick contingent. The *Chateau* and Garden were in the first instance only occupied by 3 Companies of the Coldstream. There were afterwards reinforced by four more companies of the same Regiment – The first detachment of 3 Companies was under the command of Lt Col Macdonald and the latter of 4 Companies under Co^l^ Woodford. The Light Troops placed in the Wood would of course retire on the advance of the enemy's columns and there being but three Companies for the defence of so important a place I cannot but conclude the Duke either did not think the enemy would consider it an object, or he himself did not think it of consequence – The first effort made by the enemy was repulsed by the three companies, when finding the point the enemy considered it, the other four Companies were sent to

36 Despite this Price is still listed as receiving his Waterloo medal. The National Archives, MINT 16/112/26.

reinforce them – It was entrusted to too weak a force and would have been carried but for the determined courage of the Troops – I think a great risk was run in the commencement of the Battle –

[At this point in the diary are a number of lists and tables of the Allied troops engaged at Waterloo. As these are neither accurate nor complete and add nothing to the story of the 16th in the battle, they are omitted.]

From the preceding return [omitted] it appears that there were only 17,500 British Infantry in the Field, and allowing for men absent for Baggage &c &c to place the efficient Bayonets in the Field at 700 each Battalion it is accounting for the numbers present. To this number we must add 5,600 of the Kings German Legion in British pay, and having served through the Peninsula Campaigns and always behaved well, we considered them equally efficient with British Infantry – This makes 23,100 effective men – 3 Battalions Nassau Troops of 800 each and 8 Battalions of the Duke of Brunswick also behaved well and must be considered effective amounting to 8,800, making a total –

British	–	17,500
German	–	5,600
Nassau	–	2,400
Brunswick	–	8,800
		31,900 [in fact 34,300, a difference of 2,400, the same as the number of Nassau troops]

The total number of Infantry amounted to 50,300 so that there remains 18,400 of Dutch Line Regiments, *Pays Bas* Line Regiments, and Dutch Militia – of these I believe the answer made by the Spanish General Alava to the Prince of Orange is so nearly the truth that I mention it, to point out the estimation they be considered in for their services on the 18th. Both Gen[l] Alava & the Prince had been for many years together on the Dukes Staff in Spain –

Question from the Prince

'Well Alava, what do you think your Spaniards would have done had they been present on this occasion [?]' –

Answer from Alava –

'Your Highness I do not think they would have run away as your Belgians did, before the first shot was fired.'

They certainly did not behave well and tho' placed in the second line and in many instances under cover of the Hill it was difficult to keep them even in that position. When a man was wounded two or three went away with him to the rear, they took great care of their comrades in going off the field and then commenced plundering in the rear –

Of Cavalry there were 49 Squadrons of British amounting to 5,220 men. Also 16 Squadrons of German Cavalry in British pay and equally efficient, amounting to 1,730 making a total of 6,950. The number of the German Regiments is calculated at their greatest strength and I think overrated. The Cavalry was considered 6,000 which is probably nearer their numbers – The Horses being just from England and at a time of year when they look well, I think they justified the Duke of Wellington stating to Blucher, that he had 6,000 of the finest Cavalry in the World – There were several Regiments of Cavalry of the *Pays Bas* and of Hanoverian – These did not long remain on the Field. In deed some never came up to the Army. They did nothing but plunder the Baggage in the rear. Riding along side of the road cutting at the Bat Men in charge of it, obliging them to abandon their Horses and Baggage both of which they seized – The Bat Men of the 16th drew their swords, and preserved their baggage – The 1st Dragoon Guards lost all their Baggage and the Officers nearly all their Horses – One Officer of the 16th only lost his and that through the negligence of his Servant (Lt Luard was the Officer) –

The position extended as before mentioned from Merbe Braine on the right to Ter La Haye on the left. There was some strong ground near Merbe Braine which protected the right, and a considerable detachment of Troops occupied, or were rather advanced to the neighbourhood of Braine l'Alleud. The approach to Brussels from Mons was likewise protected. Major Genl Sir Charles Colville being stationed with part of the 4th Division and a body of Troops of the *Pays Bas* contingent, near Braine le Chateau. He was not employed; the enemy making no effort on that point, therefore the loss of his detachment and of so old a Soldier as their General is to be regretted.

With regard to the position we held; on our right it is evident for any enemy to attack they must either possess themselves of Hougoumont or make the detour round it – In doing this they must show the force they moved to that point and enable a General holding the position of Waterloo to reinforce his right – They could not make a feint with a small body on that point, as their object would be defeated by our seeing the strength they brought; and nothing but a very large body would cause any fears; and if a large one we could spare men from other parts of our line.

A successful attack on our right would open Brussels to the enemy, but would drive us back on the Prussians at Wavre and so unite the two Armies – An attack on our left had the strong ground in that point to contend with and also some fear of interruption from the Prussians whose situation Napoleon from his Patrols and information ought to be aware of.

From La Haye Sainte to the left was likewise strong and any force attacking at that point, had a very considerable length of plain to cross, exposed to our Artillery and a also a height to ascend on coming in contact with our line –

The Duke was apprehensive of the enemy making an attack on the right and getting betwixt us and the Wood of Soigne.

From the left of the Nivelles road to the Charleroi road was the weakest part of the position, here the Hill was of a gentle declivity, and Hougoumont and La

Haye Sainte in the enemy's possession an attack on that point would be made to advantage. The whole Field was covered with the finest Wheat, the soil was strong and luxuriant, consequently from the rain that had fallen was deep – heavy for the transport and moving of Artillery and difficult for the quick operation of Cavalry – The heavy ground was in favour of our Cavalry from the superiority of Horse and likewise in any charge down the face of the position we had the advantage of moving down Hill, and yet we felt the inconvenience in returning up hill with distressed Horses after a Charge – The difficulty of returning up the Hill with distressed Horses occasioned a great loss in the charges made by the heavy Brigades. The Ground was so deep that numberless Shells burst where they fell and did little or no injury from being buried in the Ground, and many round shot never rose from the place they first struck the ground, instead of hopping for half a mile and doing considerable injury – Many lives on both sides were saved from this circumstance. The Corn was laid quite flat, both on the ground held by our own Troops and before and in rear of the position. The piquets being posted for the night and the men going from place, soon altered the appearance of the Country. In front of the left there was some grass, as likewise on the rising ground near Ter La Haye and again beyond that on the line the Prussians advanced.

From the late hour the enemy had moved in pursuit of us yesterday, it was clear they could not close up their Army for a very early attack and it was past eleven before they assembled. Napoleon directed the operations from a small Hill near the Farm of Rossomme – not far from the *Chaussée*.

The French Army amounted to 78,000 men including from 12 to 15,000 Cavalry – Calculated at 66,000 Infantry & 12,000 Cavalry – This did not include the 3rd *Corps d'Armée* under Grouchy which was detached to observe the Prussians and moved on Wavre – Their strength was said to be 30,000 –

The First *Corps d'Armée* under *Comte* d'Erlon (Drouet) was stationed on the right – Its right extended towards Souhain, its left rested on La Belle Alliance –

2nd *Corps d'Armée*, Lieut. Genl *Comte* Reille. The right was on La Belle Alliance, the left opposite to Hougoumont.

6th *Corps d'Armée*, Lt Genl *Comte* Lobau was in reserve at the commencement of the Action; behind the right wing. The Division of the young Guard was also stationed in rear of the second corps –

The two Divisions of the old Guard were likewise stationed in rear of the second Corps.

Artillery	1st *Corps d'Armée* – including the reserve	80 pieces
	2nd --------------------------------------	60
	6th --------------------------------------	30
	A further reserve of --------------------	40
		210

We took 150 pieces (The Prussians 60) and there was probably a considerable reserve not employed – Possibly the last 40 might not have got into Action – In addition to the Generals named at the head of Corps Jerome Bonaparte directed the operations of a large force of possibly one Corps and a Division of the Guard. He was employed on their left. Marshal Ney had a similar command and directed the operations on the right. I believe he led the old Guard in the last attack – The Cavalry was disposed through their line, a large force being on the right of La Belle Alliance. Their heavy Cavalry and Lancers were fine and being principally opposed to us, we had not an opportunity of ascertaining the state of the remainder – The Infantry of their Guard was good, but those taken in the charge of our 2nd Brigade of Cavalry and being Troops of their line were not good.

Small young Soldiers –

At about half past eleven they began an attack on Hougoumont with the advance of their Corps under Jerome Bonaparte – whilst their light Troops attacked and carried Papelotte on our left, which was not intended to be held – The attack on Hougoumont was very sharp – The wood in front of the *Chateau* was carried by the enemy after considerable loss, and more than a common resistance on our part from light Troops holding a Wood in front of a position. The enemy proceeded to attack the *Chateau* and Garden in which they failed and retired unsuccessful – The defence as well as the attack was gallant –

We (11th, 12th & 16th Light Dragoons) moved from our Bivouac about eleven and were stationed on the left of the line, below the Hill occupied by the Infantry. The 6th Brigade of Cavalry was stationed further on our left[37] – The 2nd Brigade on our right near the Charleroi road, possibly half way to that from the situation we occupied. The 1st Brigade was immediately on the other side that road with its left on it. The 3rd Brigade a little farther to the right and 5th Brigade on the right again of the 3rd – We moved to the ground assigned for our Brigade, and all being quiet on our point dismounted – We had not been long on our ground before the cannonade opened and became general along the whole line.

Lieut. Col. Ponsonby, myself and some others, my Brother Henry was of this party, rode out in front to see what was going on, and standing together near a hedge attracted a few of the enemy's round shot. The enemy's fire was directed against our whole line and we lost a few Horses in the Brigade whilst dismounted. Having for some time remained in this position during the attack on Hougoumont on the right, we were ordered to mount and moved in front of the position to check the enemy's Cavalry in pursuit of the 2nd Brigade of Cavalry, which had charged in advance of the position and was on its return to our line – It appeared that the enemy with the 2nd and 3rd Division of their 1st Corps under Count d'Erlon had moved to the attack of the left Centre of our position. They advanced in good order

37 Major General Sir Hussey Vivian's Brigade: 10th Hussars, 18th Hussars, and 1st King's German Legion Hussars.

coming close up to our line. At this moment they were attacked by the 5th Division with the Bayonet under Lt General Sir Thomas Picton and driven back on their support in confusion – To repulse this attack the second Brigade moved to the charge – It consisted of 1st (Royal) Dragoons, 2nd Dragoons (Scotch Greys), 6th Dragoons Inniskillen – It was one of the finest charges ever seen.

We were told very early in the Day that a Corps of Prussians were on their march to join us. Being on the left we were constantly looking out for them. Not knowing by what line they would come I rode forward to see if there was any road along the valley in our front and leading up to the left. This was near Ter La Haye –

About 4 p.m. we saw a column advance out of a Wood beyond Frichermont, and anxiously waited to ascertain by the fire, whether it was a Corps joining the enemy or the expected Prussians – They had Artillery with their advance and ere long we saw them forming to their front and their guns open against the enemy –

Such a reinforcement during an Action was an occurrence, compared to former days in the Peninsula where everything centred in the British Army, that it appeared decision of the fate of the Day.

On going over the ground the following morning I saw where two lines of Infantry had laid down their Arms, whose position was accurately marked from the regularity the muskets were placed in. After their success they continued to advance and moved forward in scattered parties up to the reserve of the enemy, and to the top nearly of the heights held by them. In this scattered state they were attacked by a heavy Brigade of Cavalry belonging to the First Corps of the enemy and one of Lancers – They were obliged to retreat and on our moving out in front of the left of the position were seen riding back to our line in parties of 20 and 30 followed by the enemy, whose Horses were not blown and suffering greatly from theirs being scarcely able to move –

In moving to support them we had to cross a deep lane which broke us and occasioned some confusion, we however got forward as quick as possible, charged and repulsed a body of Lancers in pursuit of a party of the Scotch Greys. Lieu$^{t.}$ Colonel Hay com^{g} 16th L Dragoons was shot through the body. The shot entered his back coming out in front – It was at the time supposed he could not live – he has recovered. I think he was shot by our own Infantry firing to check the enemy and not perceiving our advance to charge. There is little doubt of it – The 12th on our left attacked and dispersed a considerable body of the enemy, and by being on our left and not much delayed with the lane got in advance. We supported them having joined immediately after our charge and by forming line (with the 11th) presented a front which enabled the 12th to retire with safety as likewise all the men of the 2nd Brigade that had retreated on this point. We had some difficulty in preventing the men of the 16th from attacking in small bodies after the charge those parties of the enemy which had pursued the 2nd Brigade, had they done this we should have got into the same scrape, at least, we could not have covered the retreat of the others, but must have retired to form ourselves – The loss of the second Brigade was immense, and the more to be regretted for had they halted after completely routing the enemy's Troops (making the attack) their loss would have been trifling and the Brigade remained efficient for the rest of the Day – What with men lost and others gone to the rear in care of the wounded, and many absent from not knowing where to assemble and other causes, there does not remain efficient above a Squadron –

In repulsing this attack we had the misfortune to lose three excellent officers – Sir Thomas Picton who was shot at the Head of his Division leading them to his favourite and decisive attack with the Bayonet. He is a great loss – a person in whom the Troops have the greatest confidence and of such experience and knowledge in his profession as to be of the greatest loss to the Army. Through the whole of the Peninsula War he had been at the head of his 3rd Division. No Division ever more distinguished itself – Had he survived this day he must have been raised to the Peerage and in the titles conferred at the peace of 1814 (the conclusion of the Spanish War) he said that had his Patent been in a Fortress with those of the others then considered, he certainly stood before most of the others – I can only exempt Lord Hill –

Sir William Ponsonby was killed at the head of his brigade. He had led them to the charge and his horse being shot (or he dismounted) was killed by one of the Lancers. Perhaps in the confusion no report is very much to be relied on, but the one I have named was the only mention I ever heard of the manner he fell. He had commanded the 5th Dragoons [sic - 5th Dragoon Guards] for three campaigns in the Peninsula and had been in command of the Brigade in which they served for a considerable part of that time. He was very much esteemed by those under him and regretted both as a Gentleman and an Officer.

The third was L[t] Colonel Ponsonby of the 12th who fell into the enemy's hands desperately wounded having his Horse killed in the charge our Brigade made to cover the retreat of the 2nd Brigade – He was very much wounded and remained in the enemy's hands through the day – His loss as a Cavalry Officer would be great and in any future War where he has an opportunity of commanding a body of Cavalry it will appear he is one of the best Officers in the service.

A French Lancer thrust his Lance into him when on the ground saying – '*Tu n'est pas encore mort, coquin.*' He recovered and told a very discreditable tale of the conduct of a French Lancer when he lay on the ground. The fellow came up and said 'You are not yet dead, villain' and ran the Lance into his body – An Infantry Man rested his Musket on him firing from behind him; lying down. After a short time he went away put a knapsack under his head saying the day was ours –

The cannonade continued along the line though the Day – Whenever the enemy made an attack they covered it with all the Artillery they could thunder at us and we again worked their columns in advancing with every Gun we could bring against them. One Brigade of Guns was firing at a Brigade of the enemy's which had got their range and annoyed them. They were ordered by the Duke not to fire at the enemy's Guns but direct all shot against their columns – We might run a chance of losing the position for a severe attack of one of their columns, but could not by their cannonade. The manner their columns were cut up in making the attack was extraordinary and the excellence of practice in Artillery was never exceeded. The enemy fired a great deal at times I thought rather wildly –

During this attack the enemy had attempted the forcing of La Haye Sainte in which one Brigade of their Infantry was nearly annihilated – This attack was at length supported by a reinforcement from their first Division and a considerable body of *Cuirassiers* under General Kellerman. They moved forward to the attack of La Haye Sainte and from the body of Troops moved against it there appeared an intention of carrying our position on that point. They came so forward that the 1st Brigade of Cavalry Lord Edward Somerset's (Household) were moved to the Charge – they attacked and succeeded against the *Cuirassiers* following up their success in the same imprudent manner as the other heavy Brigade had done after their charge. They suffered very much but not I think to the same extent as the others.

Towards the end of the evening the whole [1st] Brigade did not form above one Squadron. It could not be supposed so few remained over the killed and wounded – The fact was, that the Men did not know where to assemble after the Charge and being the first Action they had ever been in they I suppose fancied that nothing remained for them to attend to after this one attack, and many went in consequence to the rear. There was one Squadron of the 1st Dragoon Guards that not above one or two Men returned – they rode completely into the enemy's reserve and were killed. The enemy I suspect did not spare a single prisoner falling into their hands – It is impossible to suppose a whole Squadron killed without one Man surrendering. In one instance in the first Dragoon Guards one Quarter Master was the only person who returned to give any report of the remainder. I did not hear of above two or three officers taken and spared to return to their Regiments. These came probably under protection of a French officer who saved them –

The building of La Haye Sainte was occupied by the 2nd Light Battalion KGL under Lt Co^{l} Baring. The enemy had attempted to dislodge them from it for some time and on bringing down their reinforcements they surrounded the place and approached so close to our own line that the communication with La Haye Sainte was interrupted and consequently the Battalion occupying it soon became short of Ammunition. The fire they were obliged to keep up to enable them to hold was so great that they were soon under the necessity of sending for more; in attempting which, they found the communication occupied, and it could not be procured. It so happened that the communication with La Haye Sainte was on the side of the Building and not directly in its rear so that the enemy by occupying the ground on that side rendered the approach impossible. There ought to have been a hole broken through the Wall directly in the rear which would have preserved the communication. The Duke said he ought to have ordered this but to use his own expression 'it was impossible for me to think of everything.' The officer stationed in it ought to have seen its necessity and made the communication through the rear. They could not retain the post without ammunition and were obliged to abandon it to the enemy; making the best retreat they could to our line, in doing which they suffered greatly – Their defence had been a gallant, severe, affair; and their numbers by it considerably diminished – The occupation of La Haye Sainte enabled the enemy to form a considerable body of Troops close in its rear and from that position to commence attacks on the Troops in position immediately above the house. These attacks were made at intervals for nearly two hours, they were the most singular daring attempts ever heard of and in many instances appeared like an inclination to sacrifice themselves sooner than survive the loss of the Day – Parties of *Cuirassiers*, from two to three Squadrons and frequently less, occasionally supported by a few Infantry and in many instances without Infantry, rode up to the hill occupied by our Troops – An Officer of *Cuirassiers* rode up to one of our Squares with a detachment of Men. He saw he had no chance of success and by himself alone rode full Gallop against the Square, was shot and killed, our Men and Officers regretted his fate.

Lord Wellington in his dispatch speaking of the Artillery Men mentions them. 'The Artillery and Engineer department were conducted much to my satisfaction by Colonel Sir G Wood and Colonel Smyth' – It was an action in which the Artillery suffered Greatly and particularly distinguished themselves. Repeatedly they had to leave their Guns and take refuge in the squares of Infantry and the instant the French Cavalry turned to the rear, they ran to their Guns firing at them in their retreat – They were too, exposed to the whole fire of the enemy's Guns without being suffered to return their fire. They were directed to fire only at the enemy's Columns – Without meaning any slight to the Engineer department yet in an action such as this, there is nothing for them to be employed in and therefore to couple the Artillery with them is rather passing over their exertions unnoticed and I conceive that if any part deserved to be especially named it was that part of the Artillery placed above La Haye Sainte.

Captain Ramsey [sic - Ramsay] of the Artillery was killed near this point. His head was carried away by a round shot. He had been through the whole of the Peninsula attached to Major Gen[l] Ansons Brigade and was invariably zealous and willing to run every risk to get his guns in action – He rode a couple of six pounders over a hedge & ditch at Vittoria to get them up to act against the enemy's retreating Troops – We all regret him exceedingly.

The Artillery Men at our Guns remained at them to the last moment firing grape on the enemy in which the *Cuirassiers* suffered. Our Infantry got into Squares of Regiments and the French Dragoons came riding amongst them waving their swords and in many instances approaching close to them. They never attempted in any body to attack the Infantry and after remaining on the position for ten minutes or possibly longer, retired again. The instant they turned their backs, the Artillery in the Squares of Infantry ran to their Guns and commenced their fire against them. During the time the enemy were employed in this attack our Guns were in their hands, but without any means on their part of either injuring them or carrying them away – It was the most singular, hardy conduct ever heard of and had such gallantry been properly directed it must have turned to some account. Had it happened immediately after an attack or been once adopted in the zeal of the moment by any officer foiled in his object there might be some excuse, but for such a thing to be continued for any length of time and under officers who had been serving all their lives, is a proceeding quite unaccountable – They made two or three separate attempts to the one just mentioned – All of which ended in the same manner.

The *Cuirassiers* and Imperial Guard were excellent and from the manner they were always pushed forward and the selection made of them through the Army for the two Services, it appears that they alone were considered and that the others were injured by having their best Men taken from them and broken in spirit from being considered inferior. In a small French Pamphlet giving an account of the spirit in the French Army in its advance previous to Waterloo I believe the domineering spirit of the Guard is well and justly described and that the account of their quarrels with the rest of the army is an accurate one.

The action continued through the day, by the enemy making attacks on our position from near La Haye Sainte and by occasional efforts to possess themselves of Hougoumont. In one of these they forced the Doors leading into the Court Yard and were entering the place. They were attacked by the Bayonet and driven back. They attempted to scale the Wall into the Garden, and on inspecting it the following morning I found that three or four French Infantry had so far succeeded, that they had got to the top of the Wall and were there killed, falling into the Garden. The Garden Wall was about seven feet in height. The enemy opened a fire of Shells on the *Chateau* and set it on fire – a considerable part of it was consumed yet by the exertions of the Soldiers the flames were extinguished in sufficient time to admit of its being retained as a post and the enemy repulsed in every attempt they made against it.

In consequence of the arrival of the Prussians to attack the right of the enemy and a further reinforcement of them expected to join us and occupy the left of our position, our Brigade was moved from the left to about half the distance from whence we stood (towards our right) to the Charleroi road. This took place about 5 p.m.. We halted for a short time in this position, marching to it in rear of the Infantry, and occasionally receiving a spent Musket Ball and judged of the Cannonade from the shots which passed over us – They were very frequent for a cannonade which had been continued through so long an attack –

In passing along the line it appeared to have been much cut up and the Troops which in parts held the position were but few and had suffered greatly – From marching under shelter of the Hill we could not distinctly see yet I conceive from all I could learn that many points in the position were but feebly guarded. The opinion I formed was a correct one – The enemy's point of attack for some hours had been La Haye Sainte to which we were moving and to the point in the position opposite to which the Duke had assembled a considerable force – The Foreign Division formed *en potence* on the right of the Army had been brought to near the Charleroi road forming in rear of our line. The Guards were stationed in their front.

After halting a short time in the place I have mentioned we were ordered to the Charleroi road which we passed halting immediately and forming line with the left of the Brigade resting on the road. In our front the Guards held the position. Foreign Battalions were formed in Squares in support of them and our Brigade was placed immediately in rear of the Squares. We had not long arrived in this position before the enemy commenced their desperate effort to carry our position –

They had pushed some Guns close up to La Haye Sainte and from these our Troops suffered considerably by a fire of Grape – They also opened a heavy cannonade of round shot. We were placed just under cover of the Hill.

Whilst in this situation my coverer (Sergeant Flesh) was hit by a spent ball. It struck him on the chest and with such violence he said he was killed. I fancied the Ball had gone through. In a few minutes I saw the Ball drop from under his overalls at his Feet on to the ground and on desiring him to go to the rear he said he should see it out & fell in again. He had not been five minutes in the ranks before another spent ball struck him but not with such violence as the first. He continued with us – The shots coming from the front I was fortunate to escape them both as he was directly behind me – He suffered afterwards from being bled and taking no care of himself.

A Regiment of Cavalry of the *Pays Bas* not liking to remain so close to the Infantry had withdrawn to a greater distance and received many shots which passed over our heads – From the place we stood we could not see what force came up to the attack but from the showers of Musketry which came over our heads and the volleys in our front or rather constant roll of Musketry, we were aware some important attack was attempted by the enemy and that from the situation of our Brigade we were placed to meet and attempt to stop any column which might carry our line. It was a most anxious moment, the Men were perfectly aware of their situation. They gave two or three huzzas and had any column made its appearance I never saw soldiers more ready than the whole of our Brigade then appeared to do their duty. I never saw them evince greater steadiness.

There was a Regiment of the *Pays Bas* in Square. They were not engaged nor suffering much from fire. I may say not in the least cut up whilst I saw them. They were immediately in our front, and fancying the affair rather serious and that if the enemy advanced any farther (as their fears apprehended) they would have to oppose them, they began firing their Muskets in the air and their rear moved a little, intending under the confusion of their fire and smoke to move off. Major Childers 11 L. Dragoons and myself rode up to them, encouraged them, stopped those who had moved the farthest (10 yards perhaps) out of their ranks and whilst they were hesitating whether to retreat or continue with their column, the Duke rode up and encouraged them – He said to us 'That is right, that is right, keep them up.' Childers then brought up his Squadron and by placing it in their rear they continued steady – The Duke rode away again immediately. Had this one Battalion run away at that moment the consequence might have been fatal. The Duke was hurried and rode away very quick –

During this attack we remained stationary and after a short time the fire slackened and we were ordered to advance – We moved to the front in a column of half-Squadrons left in front and on getting to the crown of the hill saw the whole French Army in the greatest confusion and the Infantry which had made the last attack running away down the Hill and over the plain below in the greatest haste and confusion. In our moving to this point we were ignorant of our success and not knowing whether we were going to charge a successful column of the enemy or pursue a beaten one, the extent of our success was a greater surprise and delight to us.

The enemy in this last attack brought up two close Columns of Infantry. One in advance of the other. They came with the first nearly to the top of the Hill and then opened a fire on our line. They did not attempt to deploy into line, standing still holding their ground and firing from their outer ranks – In this position the most advanced column suffered greatly from our Grape and the number of wounded with comrades to assist them going to the rear appeared so great to the second column, that they almost thought those in advance were retiring and giving way, from the many Soldiers who came away to the rear. In this hesitation they were charged by the 52nd and a Battalion of the 95th (Rifles) when they gave way and their retreat became general. I believe some parts of the Guards charged at this time tho' I could never exactly ascertain – I believe not – The 52nd & 95th certainly for I knew an artillery Officer who mentioned their passing through his Guns in their advance – Sir Frederick Adams Brigade, 52nd, 71st & 95th, Co[l] Coulborn [Colborne] 52nd, Colonel Rennel [Reynell] 71st [Lieutenant Colonel Ross] 95th –

This was the last desperate effort in which the Old Guard of Napoleon was employed – This is the system they have gone upon with every other Nation and have succeeded. They move an overawing column or two to one point. It comes up with the greatest regularity, and arriving at close quarters with their opponents they carry so determined an appearance that those hitherto opposed to them, have generally abandoned their positions without being beat out of them – The nearer this column gets to the enemy the greater will be its loss from Grape and a fire of Musquetry concentrated on it, and if the Troops holding the position are inclined to use the Bayonet, they have the advantage in being able to move quick against it, whilst the column must receive the charge from not being able to move at such a quick pace as Troops acting in line. At Waterloo they came nearly to the top of the Hill and there halted. They never attempted to deploy into Line and seemed to consider their very appearance and holding the position they occupied must cause our retreat. On our Infantry charging (52nd & 95th) they set off down the Hill and on our Brigade getting to the point from which we overlooked them they were seen running away on every side in the greatest haste and confusion – Not knowing when we moved to the front which had succeeded, it was a sight I shall never forget.

Before we moved an Officer of the Guards came to us shot in the hip. I put him before one of our dragoons to be taken to the rear – He could not bear the motion of the Horse and was obliged to remain on the field. On moving to the point Colonel

Canning of the Duke's staff lay on the ground. My Troop moved to the spot he was lying on, when he begged we would not ride over him, saying he was the Duke of Wellington's AD Camp. The men opened out and on my asking him if I could assist him or leave a Man with him, he said it was quite useless, that he would not live long, being shot in the body with Grape. I encouraged him, telling him of our success and that a Surgeon would soon arrive on being sent for. He was quite determined not to allow of anything being done and on my mentioning my name and his recollecting me, he begged me to dismount, to take his Sword and Watch to be delivered to his relations. He did not live above a couple of Hours.

The Duke himself gave the orders to the 52nd & 95th to charge and the 71st being the same Brigade and not hearing the order were retiring. Colonel Egerton rode up to Colonel Reynell, telling him the 52nd & 95th were charging and begged him to put his Men about and join them – The 71st were halted, fronted and joined in the charge and this act done at a very important moment. It was a service of consequence – Colonel Egerton was ADC to Lord Hill and was desired by him to get up some Troops to the crest of the Hill. He went to a distinguished Corps commanded by a distinguished Knight but could not induce them to move to the point he requested them to occupy.

Being in a column of half-Squadrons, we were ordered to form line, descend into the plain and pursue the enemy. We did not feel inclined to lose any time and the ground being more favourable for a formation to the left instead of the right (as it ought in regularity to have been) we inclined to our left forming on the left of the left half-Squadron of the 12th which clubbed the Brigade. It was of no consequence as we probably had nothing but to move on in line, attacking the first Troops we met. We were led into the plain by our General between the road to Charleroi and the Observatory and had to open out and pass over many killed and wounded. In retiring from the last attack the enemy had made considerable haste to the rear and not until we were lineable with the Observatory did we receive any fire or perceive any intention of stopping us. They were in complete *déroute* and confusion. On the top of a small hill they at length opened a couple of Guns and fired a few round shot. We continued to advance in a trot and on coming closer to these guns they fired once with Grape which fell about 50 yards short of the Brigade and did not the least damage. The Observatory was situated at the edge of a Wood, and as from the line we were moving on we must leave this in our rear I sent Sergeant Major Greaves of my Troop to see if the enemy had any force in the Wood. He returned and caught us saying they had none, when I rode before the brigade to an eminence (which we were ascending) to see what force the enemy had in our front. From this point I saw a body of Infantry with a Squadron of *Cuirassiers* formed in the valley, close to a by-road which ran at right Angles to the point we were moving on. The Infantry were about 1,000 in Column with about three Companies formed behind a hedge which ran along side of the road in question. I rode back and told General Vandeleur that the enemy had the force I have named and that the left of the 16th and right of the 11th would (as they were then advancing) come in contact with [it]. That the

12th had nothing in their front and if ordered to proceed on to the point and bring forward their right, they would get in their rear and make a considerable number of Prisoners. He took no notice excepting saying 'where are they' – and in a minute the Brigade was on the top of the rising ground, in a gallop the instant they saw the enemy and proceeded to the charge. The enemy's Infantry behind the hedge gave us a volley, and being close at them and the Hedge nothing more than some scattered bushes without a ditch we made a rush and went into their column with their own companies which were stationed in their front, they running away to the Square for shelter – We completely succeeded, many of their Infantry immediately throwing down their Arms and crowding together for safety – Many too ran away up the next rising ground – We were riding in all directions at parties attempting to make their escape, and in many instances had to cut down men who had taken up their arms after having in the first instance laid them down – From the appearance of the enemy lying together for safety they were some yards in height, calling out from the injury of one pressing upon another and from the Horses trampling upon them on their legs – I had rode after a Man who took up his Musket and fired at one of our Men and on his running to his comrades my Horse trod on them. He had only one eye (Cyclops) and trod the heavier from not seeing them – L[t] Beckwith 16th stood still and attempted to catch this Man on his sword, he missed him and nearly ran me through the body. I was following the man in a hand Gallop. Captain Buchanan of the 16th was killed in the midst of their Infantry – After some little delay in seeing they all surrendered we proceeded in pursuit on the enemy's other scattered Troops. It was nearly dark at the time we made the charge and when we moved from the spot it was quite so. We went up the next brow of a hill following the enemy scattered in all directions and on coming to the top the first thing that stopped us were some huts which some of the enemy had constructed and in ignorance of the fate of their Army had occupied them for the night, or some of their Troops had taken shelter in them. I rode into the mouth of one of them, when the Men in it turned out and commenced a fire over the back of the Huts.

L[t] Hay of the 16th was killed in the pursuit – His Horse was found but no search could ever discover him. He probably fell in the corn and was stripped early the next morning by the Peasants.

On hearing the firing on the 18th the peasants for miles round assembled the following morning on the field. They plundered all they could get and in one instance I saw them pulling off a pair of Boots from the legs of a Soldier of the Guards before he was dead – I made the fellow desist and attempted to teach him we did not allow of such proceedings – Colonel Currie ADC to Lord Hill was killed late in the evening. Colonel Egerton was with him and marked the spot through which he found him the next morning – He was stripped and with difficulty distinguished from those around him –

The Men were ordered to stop not knowing in that light what force the enemy might have & the Brigade being scattered we halted and formed. The 16th was the only Regt which came up to the Huts the 11th & 12th being to our right and left and halted rather before. On forming we were told a Reg[t] of French Cavalry was coming up in our rear and a general feeling in the Men to charge them. We were moving for that purpose, but on approaching we found them to be our own Regiment. The 1st Hussars KGL. The old Reg[t] with which the 16th had for such a length of time been Brigaded in Spain. Each happy to discover its error – I rode back and met Sir Hussey Vivian coming up with his Brigade and told him of our being in his front fearing the same might occur again. Sir Hussey told me he had turned the fate of the day by charging with his Brigade – The place he charged was 2 miles out of the position and half an hour after the enemy retired. Here the pursuit ended being ten o clock and the Brigade was ordered to retire.

To know the point we charged on, it is across a road leading from the Nivelle Road to the village of Genappe (I think). On going from the Charleroi road, leaving it at Genappe, to the Nivelle road you leave the Wood we bivouacked in on the right and the point we charged is about a Mile or perhaps not so far from the Wood.

The Ground was covered with Muskets thrown away, Guns, Ammunition Waggons, Tumbrils, Brandy, &c. We came across one of the latter and got as much as the Men required – We retired to the edge of the Wood near the Observatory and not half a Mile from the point we charged the Infantry and there bivouacked for the night. The Wood was full of French Soldiers, who had run to it for safety – Most of them got away during the night. We had gone through a very long day, yet had we proceeded a great many prisoners who got away in the night would have fallen into our hands – From the time our Brigade made the first charge until our moving to the right of the position we had been quiet and dismounted nearly the whole time. We could have pursued through the night but must have gone on without orders.

The Prussians came on the line of the enemy's retreat to Charleroi from our left, and as they came up and proceeded along the road in pursuit of them they greeted us with Cheers and acknowledgements for the stand we had made and assuring us we had no necessity of proceeding as they would march and complete the affair, by following up the enemy through the night. The Officers shook hands with us –

Much has been made of Grouchy not appearing on the 18th in pursuit of the Prussians. Napoleon directed Marshal Grouchy to move on Wavre, and his failure at Waterloo he attributed to a disobedience of orders on the part of Grouchy, not joining him. The Prussians were more than our strength, therefore to dispose of them, and keep their Army in check, it could not be considered a large detachment in employing one Corps of 30,000 Men and in weakening his force to that amount, he must be considered fortunate if by so doing he disposed of the Prussians. I have little doubt but that Napoleon considered them so beat on the 16th that the corps he sent would prove sufficient to keep them in play, whilst he acted with the remainder of his force against us – If ever the real orders to Grouchy are known, I much question if it will not be seen, that his directions were, to act against the Prussians without any reference to the British and that had the Prussians retired before him he was to have continued his advance on Brussels, turning our left or rather obliging us, either to fall back and cover Brussels or abandon it. Likewise effecting by his movement a more important object, that of to *entrecoupe* us and the Prussians. When the Prussians made their appearance on the right of the French, Officers from Napoleon's staff were sent to tell their Troops that Grouchy was in sight and up to the last moment Napoleon persisted they were not the Prussians. He was well aware that his only chance was carrying our position. He determined to persevere to the last and in this resolution he knew that a report of fresh Troops acting on his flank at the close of such a day would so damp the spirit of his Men that any attack would prove nearly hopeless – He did right to conceal this truth and has nothing left him but supposing his real instructions to Grouchy – It appears since Waterloo (which about the time of the Action we were not aware of) that Grouchy attacked the Prussians at Wavre. This rather proves his orders were to act against them without reference to the Main Army under Napoleon, as we can hardly suppose he would do so without Orders and unsupported – I fancy he had the 2nd & 3rd Corps with him –

Luard Journal:

June 18th I slept with my feet near a fire, & with my cloak kept the upper part of my body dry, but the rain was so heavy that the water run down underneath me & soak'd my clothes. – at 9 o'clock I went to Colonel Hay & he order'd me to mount the Regiment which I did – my horse was so cold & shiver'd so much that he could scarcely stand up for one to mount. – the Regiment was placed on the left of the position – & we dismounted under a rising ground, waiting for orders – at 11 o'clock – a cannonade was commenced by the French – & a furious attack made on the centre of our position – the conflict became general & bloody, a hill on the left of our position was attack'd by Infantry & Cavalry – Lord Ed[w] Somersets Brigade of Heavy Cavalry & General Ponsonbys charged brilliantly & repulsed them with great loss. – on reforming they were pursued by Lancers, when our Brigade, Sir John Vandeleurs, charged & drove them back – Colonel Hay fell here shot thro the body, but he lived many years afterwards – & died a General Officer – after our Regiments had charged here – the Brigade was moved to the right – & form'd on the right of & close to the Hussar Brigade – I saw my brother George – the 18th Hussars being close to us. – while in this position I was talking to Lieut. Philips of the 11th Lt Dragoons, when his head was shot off by a cannon shot – poor fellow he was much loved in his Regiment – The Belgians began to give way, the enemies fire being too hot for them – we closed our squadrons and would not let them go to the rear – Sir John Vandeleur & I moved to the front & encouraged them – the fire rather slacken'd & they held their ground. – The Battle became general & very sanguinary – the enemy succeeded in gaining the heights & some of our guns were at one time in their possession – the limbers retired behind our squares of infantry who advanced, & repulsed with the Bayonette the assailants – the Artillery then opened grape & canister shot on them – our Brigade & Gen[l] Vivians Brigade of Cavalry, moved rapidly down the hill, charged squares of Infantry, Cavalry &

Artillery – going through every obstacle as if they were made of pasteboard – taking a quantity of Artillery & provisions. – we pursued until the moon got up & were very nearly charged by the 1st German Hussars, who mistook us for French, as we return'd from a considerable distance in front – The Prussians were engaged with about 10,000 men on the extreme right of the French at about 4 o'clock & being fresh & not having lost many men, pursued the French after dark. – we bivouac'd close to a wood. – Our Regiments loss was not very severe – Captn Buchanan, Cornet Hay – two Serg^{ts} – six rank & file & thirty five horses kill'd – Lieu$^{t.}$ Co^{l} James Hay, Captn Ric'd Weyland Lieu$^{t.}$ Osten Lieu$^{t.}$ Crichton – two Serg^{ts} 16 rank & file & 20 horses wounded my horse was shot in the head & kill'd – I rode a Trooper afterwards

Luard Diary:

18th – it rained all night dreadfully – at 9 we mounted & moved up on the left of the position called Mount St Jean, having the Hussars only on our left.

At 11 a cannonade was commenced by the French & a furious attack made upon our Centre – The conflict became general & bloody – a Hill on the left of our position was attacked by Infantry & Cavalry – Genl : L^{d}: Ed^{d}: Somerset's Brigade & Genl: Ponsonby's Brigade of Cavalry charged & repulsed them with great loss – our Brigade supported them – The conflict became more sanguinary on the right – Buoneparte who Commanded in Person – repeated his attacks on the same point at about 5 p.m. – our Brigade, Genl Vandeleur's & Hussars were moved to the right – The Enemy's attacks were repeated at the same point & the last supposed to have been headed by Napoleon Buoneparte [*sic*], was very vigorous – They succeeded in gaining in the height & some of our Guns were in their possession 2 or 3 times for a few minutes, the Limbers retired behind our squares of Infantry – who advanced & repulsed the Bayonet the assailants – the Artillery then opened Grape and Canister upon them – & Genl: Vivian's & Genl: Vandeleur's Brigade advanced rapidly charged their squares of Infantry that had formed a long way in the rear – their Artillery & their *Curassier* & took an amazing quantity of Artillery – & prisoners – thus ended the day which cost the French – about 25,000 men killed & wounded & 15,000 prisoners – with 210 pieces of Cannon & the Materiel of the Army – The French force Estimated at 130,000 men ours at 70,000 – At the close of the day the Prussians under Marschal Blucher were engaged with about 10,000 men & turned the Enemies' right flank – they pursued during the night – we encamped near a wood . We had killed Cap^{n}: Buchanan L^{t}: Hay – wounded Col: Hay, Cap^{n}: Weyland, L^{t}: Osten, L^{t}: Crighton.

Tomkinson:

19th June – I rode this morning over the Field – The loss on both sides has been immense and the face of the Hill near La Haye Sainte and from there to

Hougoumont has more the appearance of a breach carried by assault, than an extended Field of Battle –

There were three Men of the 32nd lying wounded together from Grape. They begged a little water from me with such earnestness that I got off and gave them a taste of some Brandy I had in a flask. The two first I gave it to were wounded in the leg, and on my putting it to the mouth of the third, who was wounded in the body, one of the others requested me to give him his share, for his comrade was wounded in the belly, and the Brandy would only do him harm – I was aware it was not good for any, yet having been out all night and probably had nothing on the 18th I thought a taste could not injure them – They begged me to send their Doctor and were afraid they would remain out a second night.

A Man of one of the Highland Regiments was employing himself in carrying water to the wounded on both sides and had been doing so from day Light. Many were looking after plunder and excellent French Watches were sold at a low rate.

A French Colonel wounded near La Belle Alliance was on the shoulders of four peasants in a Blanket going to the rear – On seeing I was an Officer, he spoke much of his unfortunate situation , on being wounded and not better attended to – He requested me to go to the Duke of Wellington and tell him how little attention a French colonel had received, when he assured himself, the Duke would provide for him in future – Compared to many of our own Officers he was well off and none of his Army had met with his good fortune in finding hands to carry him off the Field –

On going over the ground where we supported the charge of Gen[l] Ponsonby's Brigade & drove back the enemy's Lancers which were pursuing them I saw the Muskets of two Lines of Infantry lying on the side of the Hill. The second Line was about 200 yards behind the first – The Muskets showed the exact position where the two Lines had been & no doubt they were so placed on our heavy Brigade coming down upon them. The Infantry here taken were all young Men (very young) & had run away from our Cavalry grounding their Arms.

The Wounded have remained all night on the spot they were hit and from their numbers and want of means of immediately carrying them away. I fear some will have to remain out a second night. The Weather is now fine and if they are dressed and supplied with a little water and bread they will not take any injury – Many of the enemy must remain out a second night and some a third. In Hougoumont our Troops had suffered greatly and from the *Chateau* being on fire I almost fear some wounded were burnt to death. The Trees in advance of the building were cut to pieces by musketry and will I hope be allowed to stand in confirmation of the heavy fire out Troops were exposed to and the resistance they must have made to hold it through the day against such an attack – The road from Waterloo to Brussels was completely blocked up with Commissariat Waggons either broken down or deserted and by other carriages belonging to the Army – From the many carriages and Horses which had passed along it the road was one puddle, and independent of the obstructions on it, had a retreat been attempted to Brussels it would have been found nearly impracticable. There was some very disgraceful conduct in Brussels, from Soldiers, and in some few instances I fear Officers, riding into the Town and saying all was lost and that the enemy would enter immediately.

An Officer of Cavalry galloped to Malines and on his arrival there, he stated, that as he left the upper Town in Brussels he saw the enemy's Troops in the lower part of the Town – Some person with the Baggage advised his informing the *commandant* of Antwerp, and possibly thro' his report the gates of Antwerp were shut. They were closed for a short time.

A Corporal of the Guards stationed in Hougoumont having left his Regiment passd through the 95th on his way to the rear. He was not wounded and assigned no reason for leaving his corps. He told the 95th that the enemy had possession of the *Chateau* and that all there were lost. From the point the 95th occupied in the line, they saw our fire proceeding out of Hougoumont against the enemy and therefore knowing his report to be false, they caught him, gave the Corporal a good booting, telling him in future to beware how he spread such incorrect dispiriting reports –

The loss and confusion from these reports spreading through those in charge of the Baggage, occasioned such an alarm that in one instance a Bat Man was seen throwing his Masters Baggage into the Canal going to Antwerp. Many English Families had remained in Brussels and had not conveyance to take them away – They ran a great risk – The Duchess of Richmond and her Family were there and had they been obliged to move must have gone with the line of Baggage or Troops without the power of getting out of it – The wounded from being so numerous were some time before they met with proper attention. They were in the first instance placed under what little cover there was, some Farm Houses and Cottages near the Field, and then removed to Brussels when transport could be provided for them. The people in Brussels behaved well to them, taking into their Houses the Officers as they arrived and assisting in providing Convents or large Buildings as Hospitals for the Men. The day after the Action they gave Beer away to the Soldiers going and returning to Waterloo. In many instances procuring old Linen for the Hospitals. To judge of this assistance we should attend a large Hospital after a General Action, where from want of Linen the same is used Week after Week, and the very bandages put round Wounds to cover them are doing more injury than good – Many Surgeons came out from England for the practice and on things being arranged no wounded could be better attended to – The wounded generally of a British army receive more attention than those of other Nations. The French system is to run great risk with a Man's Life, in hopes of saving a Limb from knowing that a Soldier without a Leg or Arm is incapable of Service and probably a burthen to the state – With us the practice is possibly too much in favour of hasty amputation. There have been instances of Officers saving their Limbs from not allowing the Surgeon to operate, choosing rather to run the risk of losing their life, than being cut out of their Profession –

There is one circumstance greatly in favour of all Men wounded. An Army is commonly on short allowance and particularly when before an enemy, neither Men nor Officers are in the habit or have the power of eating more than is requisite to support them. Very early rising, little rest and frequently none at all, all tend to keep down the system and prevent inflammation. The Surgeons attribute the rapid and extraordinary recoveries to this cause.

The inflammation to contend with in a gun shot Wound on such a habit of body as a London Alderman, or indeed of any Englishman in his own country would endanger his life or at all events retard his recovery –

The scanty fare of an Army is possibly more applicable to Troops in the Peninsula than the *Pays Bas* – and to officers doing Regimental duty than to those in Staff employ – Some of the generals think considerably of their Table.

[At this point there is a table of casualties for 16, 17, and 18 June. This is omitted.]

The Army marched this day to the neighbourhood of Nivelles. Genl Vandeleur's Brigade Bivouaced at Arquennes, about two Miles from Nivelles – head Quarters this night at Nivelles.

Luard Journal:

The next morning an officer of the 18th Hussars came to where we were bivouac'd to enquire after his friends in the 16th – I did not dare to ask after my dear brother George, but overheard him say that Luard was safe altho his horse was shot – it is a curious fact that throughout the Peninsula War, altho we were between us in every general action from Talavera, to Toulouse & in several cavalry affairs we were neither of us wounded: at Waterloo we both had our horses shot. – it was reported that the French lost 25,000 men kill'd & wounded & 15,000 prisoners – with 210 pieces of canon & the whole materiel of their army – June 19th – we march'd at 10 am thro Nivelles & encamp'd at a small village.

Luard Diary:

June 19th: – marched at 10 am thro' Nivelles & encamped at a small village.

Luard:[38]

Camp near Waterloo ye 19th

My dear Father

Every reason have we to be thankful to God for George's and my preservation during the battle of the most sanguinary description. He has just left me to ride on the ground we yesterday charged over – I, acting as adjutant, would not attend

38 Cohen, 'Brothers in war', pp.72–73. The original letter has been lost and reconstructed from copies by Clive Cohen. Another version can be found in Gareth Glover (ed.), *The Waterloo Archive, Volume 1: British Sources* (Barnsley: Frontline, 2010), p.82.

him – I have not now time to describe the battle. I can only say that is the bloodiest ever fought by the British and the returns will show they [?] sustained the brunt. The French were commanded by Bonaparte who fought in the most furious stile, making repeated attacks with their nest troops well filled with liquor on our position which had he ultimately carried would have opened the road to Brussels. They did carry our position several times & which was as often retaken from them, and the French repulsed with dreadful carnage on both sides. Our Brigade indeed and most of the British Cavalry were on the left in the morning. General Ponsonby's Brigade consisting of the 1st and 2nd or Scotch Greys and 6th Enniskillans [*sic*] charged their cavalry which were attacking out principal height: we then charged successfully – Col. Hay of out Reg^{t} is seriously wounded – he is not dead yet but as the ball passed through his body his death is hourly expected. At the close of the day the enemy made a last furious attack upon our right wing and carried it, but were again repulsed. We then [went] into play and with the Hussars charged everything – Infantry, Cavalry, and Artillery, took about 30 pieces of cannon and about 3000 prisoners – in that the day finished in the entire defeat of Bonaparte's army and the loss of about 150 guns and 50,000 men. The household brigade and Ponsonby's Brigade are completely annihilated as a brigade – Fenton is safe and well. I had my horse shot, but he is not yet dead – the greatest confusion prevailed in the rear amongst the baggage. I lost mine and the horses. I have therefore nothing but what I stand in – I am in good health and spirits, our loss is horrid to think of, for we have lost the greater part of the British Army. We are to march immediately for the Frontiers.

Cornet William Beckwith, 16th Light Dragoons:[39]

In bivouac near Waterloo June 19th

My dear father

I merely write to let you know I am safe, after the Battle of yesterday. When we think of it today our only surprise is to find ourselves alive. No one who was in ever saw such a fight before. You will see by the Gazette the particulars in general. I think Buonaparte is ruined. We charged four times. It was impossible for any Regiment to behave better. We were at first on the left, afterwards on the right. After they retreated we charged their Guns, and the solid squares of Infantry. Co^{l} Hay is I am afraid mortally wounded. I was at Antwerp when the Battle with Blucher near Charleroi was fought. I however joined them the following Morning near Nivelles. We were without rations for three days. They are just now issuing them for the first time. I am not touched, my mare is wounded but not badly. We march on Nivelles

39 The Queen's Royal Lancers and Nottinghamshire Yeomanry Museum, letter of Cornet William Beckwith, 19 June 1815.

in ten minutes. My baggage mare died at Ninove. I however took a French one yesterday which I expect they will let me keep.

Yours affectionately
W Beckwith

Lieutenant William Harris, 16th Light Dragoons:[40]

Bivouac } Near Waterlieu
Camp }
And Wood }June 19th 1815

My Dearest Father –

Thank God, I have escaped this bloody scene unhurt. My feelings will not at present allow me to express to you any particulars – As I know it will afford great consolation I have with great difficulty procured this bit of paper I am most concerned to say that I was within a yard of Co[l] Hay when I fear he received a mortal wound charging with us at the head of a body of Lanciers – I may say that those of us that have escaped aught to be thankful to God Almighty, our brigade suffered seriously, but our triumph was complete – Besides Co[l] Hay, 5 or 6 others were sufferers, but again I say the gazette will give you an account of officers, which really my feelings will not allow me now to mention –

We have been engaged 3 times, the 16th of this month we marched from Denderwindeke to beyond Nivelles, a distance of I am sure 40 miles, and our brigade arrived on our the lines in the evening about 1/2 past seven, having made a brisk trot for 12 miles, [deleted words] as more Cavalry were particularly wanted for the [deleted misspelt *Cuirassiers*] *Cuirassiers* who were so destructive upon our infantry – The 17th Lord Wellington retreated to Wais le Hutte a mile and a half beyond which he took up his position, the Cavalry covering the retreat – This bit of paper will not allow me to write at greater length, poor Lord Uxbridge is wounded in the thigh, scarcely any of our officers escaped without their horses, or some of their accoutrements being shot thro – God help you all.

Affectionate respectful
son
W Harris
The advance the Prussians make [?]

40 Private collection, Geneva, Lieutenant William Harris to his father, 19 June 1815.

Swetenham:[41]

Camp on the field of battle near Waterloo
16 miles south of Brussels

June 19th 1815

My dearest Mother

To relieve your anxious mind I take advantage of two or three minutes –

Thank God I am able to write my present safety after three days hard fighting, nothing that ever I experienced equalling yesterday, the action commenced at 12 midday and did not cease before 11 at night, most tremendous and bloody was the fight, our loss consequently is most severe – Unhappily it falls upon me to impart the melancholy tidings of my good and ever to be lamented friend poor Buchanan, I shall write to his poor Mother the very instant I have time but really the present state of my mind does not admit of it, this gallant fellow fell last night in a charge about 9 o clock last night, he was shot through the breast. I have had his remains decently interred, I cannot dwell on the subject, it quite overcomes me, never was a man more lamented, fine gallant fellow, I feel for him as I should have done for my own brother, I have got his horse which I shall keep, the remainder of his goods and chattels will be disposed of – Poor Col. Hay mortally wounded as I fear also Lt Crichton and Cornet Hay in short never was there so bloody a day but thanks to Providence after a long and dubious contest, a corps of Prussians under Bulow coming up on our left attacking the right flank of the Enemy decided the day in the complete route of the French Army, it was in this pursuit where we sustained our principal loss – I had my Horse shot under me from the splinters of a shell, the horse Kynnersley gave me –

My orderly was killed by which means I lost my Cloke which at this moment is a serious loss – The chances and near escapes I shall not enter into thank God I am able to tell the story –

I leave it to you to write as you think proper to Mrs Buchanan poor Buchanans friends, I will write the instant I am able – The Prussians are now gone in advance to follow up our success – we march immediately

Your affectionate Son
Clement

I am writing on the ground covered with dirt have not seen our Baggage for 4 days

41 Private collection, letter of Captain Clement Swetenham to his mother, 19 June 1815.

5

After Waterloo

Order Book:

RO 20th June 1815 Boussoit [sur Haine]

For the Day tomorrow Lieu$^{t.}$ Swinfen

Lt Osten will take the Command of the late Capt. Buchanans Troop –

Lt Monkton is appointed to Cap$^{t.}$ Weylands Troop, Corn^{t} Polhill to Captn Swetenhams

Watering order to morrow morn^{g} at 10 o'clock with Blankets –

Tomkinson:

20th Boussoit sur Haine, a March of 18 Miles to near Roeulx. The Prussians are gone in pursuit of the flying Troops of the enemy and it is probable we shall not meet with any resistance for some distance.

Order Book:

RO Bellignies 21st June 1815

For the Day tomorrow Lt Baker

Com^{g} Officers of troops are requested to see that the men carry nothing with them but what is strictly Regimental and that nothing is carried in their Corn Sacks but Corn – A muster roll is to be cald every evening at 7 o'clock and report made of all absent men

Com^{g} Oficers of troops are requested to have troop states ready whenever the Regt may be ever order'd on Parade

St Stewart of Maj. Bellis troop is reduced to the Ranks for misconduct on the 18th Ins^{t} for being absent without leave – St Payn [Payne] to be Acting St Maj^{r} of the Reg^{t} *vice* Baxter killed in action Corp^{l} Ashworth to be Serj^{t} in Maj^{r} Bellis troop *vice*

Stewart Corp^{l} Hayes of Maj^{r} Bellis troop to be Serj^{t} in Capt^{s} Weylands troop *vice* Rey killed in action the above appt^{s} to take place from the 19th Ins^{t} Serg^{t} Prout to be troop Sr Maj^{r} *vice* Baxter[1]

Tomkinson:

21st Wednesday. Marched to Bellegely [Bellignies?] near Malplaquet. Whilst waiting for orders to know where we must halt for the night The Duke of Wellington passed us. It was our first time seeing him since the Action and being two or three Brigades of Cavalry together we all cheered him. He held his Hat off for a short time and appeared gratified with the reception – I got this night into a cottage and a short time after dark a Dragoon of the Belgian Cavalry rode into my quarter. He came into the House on Horse back intending to frighten the occupiers in order to extort money or some other bribe to induce him to leave their House. He was not aware it was occupied by any of the Army – We got hold of him, pulled him off his Horse and gave him in charge to the Guard of the 16th for the night. He was reported the following morning by Major Murray who commanded the 16th to the Duke and a reference took place respecting it – Severe orders had been issued to prevent the Troops plundering on entering France, and this being a flagrant attempt and committed almost immediately on the first Village we have occupied in France, the Duke was desirous of making an early example – I was asked if I could swear to the Man and on saying I could not he was given over to be punished by his Regiment. Had I been quite clear about it, or indeed had stated that which was really the fact I believe he would have been tied up on the first Tree. The Man came into my quarter with his Pistol loaded in his hand, was pulled off his Horse and taken by us to the Guard of the 16th. They kept him secure all night and had no other foreigner under there charge.

Order Book:

Camp Mem^{m} 22nd June 1815

In order to insure certain communications from Cavalry Head Quarters with different Brigades in Bivoac or Quarters an Intelligent Non CO must be selected who have been instructed in the Duty he is to perform and be particularly directed to make himself acquainted with the Roads, so that he may be able to return back to the Brigade by night to Insure this written Instructions must be given to such NCO signed by the Major of Brigade or Off^{r} appt^{d} to do that duty – these NCO will report themselves to Major Childers A.A.G. at Cavalry Head Qr^{s} One S^{t} of the 4th Brigade

1 The reorganisation of the NCOs of the regiment presents some difficulties. Troop Sergeant Major Baxter, killed at Waterloo, appears to have been replaced by two different sergeants, one of whom (Prout) does not appear on the Waterloo Roll.

& one private from each of the others are to be sent to Cavalry Head Quarters to form a Guard –

One Serjt from the 6th Brigade and 2 privates from each of the other Lt Brigades will be stationed at Head Quarters of the Army – these men will parade at the quarters of the A.A. General at 7 o'clock this evening when the Brigade marches into camp or new quarters an offr of each Regt must attend at Major Childers quarters now head Quarters Cavalry

Camp 22nd June 1815

For the Day tomorrow Lt Lloyd

The Troops to be out in watering order tomorrow morning at 9 o'clock

Officers commanding Troops will give in the names of two men for Corpls of each Troop

Tomkinson:

22nd Marched to Cateau Cambresis – We were ordered to Pommereuil about three Miles from Cateau. Blucher is advancing with all haste in pursuit of the enemy – He wished the Duke to proceed without a halt pushing on to Paris with the least possible delay or rather without a single halt. From the extent of our loss on the 18th our Army is much more disorganised than the Prussians and a day or two to collect those left to carry away the wounded and allow the Cavalry to shoe their Horses, is requisite, in order that our advance may be made with a little order. The Men are all in great spirits and have not much idea of stopping before we obtain possession of Paris – Looking at our present march up to Paris with a view to dethrone the great Napoleon and our commencement on a strip of land in the lines of Torres Vedras. Then the only Army he had not subdued and that Army but a handful in comparison to his hordes on every part of Europe, it appears so great a conclusion to such a poor commencement that we can scarcely revert to the up hill campaigns we have fought and believe ourselves the same Army now on our advance to the gates of Paris. Napoleon has left his Army and gone to Paris – After the defeat he has encountered his cause may be so weakened as to render his presence necessary to keep down any political which maybe hostile to his Government and under cover of his defeat, now presume to show itself.

Lille is said to have a Garrison of 1,500 Men with a small force in Valenciennes – It is probable the Garrisons in any of the Towns around this are not large, as every Man would be collected for the advance against us, previous to the Battle –

Order Book:

BMO 23rd June 1815

Return of sick men and sore-backed horses of the Brigade to be sent in this afternoon by 3 o'clock

Sign^{d} Jn Sicker
11th Lt Drs

RO Camp 23rd June 1815

The Troops will parade this Evening in watering order at 7 o'clock officers to attend

The Mail starts for England tomorrow morning at 8 o'clock

Each Troop to give in or return the number of rounds good and bad in possession immediately –

RO Pommerueil June 23 1815

The following men & horses are at Brussels the latter wounded

Men	Horses
A Troop McGrath	} A Troop N°16 McGraths Horse
D Troop Williams & Herbert	} G N°39 Heaps Horse
	} C N°45
H Troop Corp^{l} Gwyllym	} D N°24 & 36
	} H N°36 not wounded

Cavalry horses had their troop number burnt into one fore hoof and one back hoof.

Serj^{t} Whitaker of Cap$^{t.}$ Swetenhams Troop exchanges with Serj^{t} Pain of Cap$^{t.}$ Kings Troop from this Troop

Corp^{l} Coward of Cap$^{t.}$ Buchanans Troop is reduced to the Ranks Jno Leakin [Laken] of Capt. Tomkinsons Troop & Jas. Green of Cap$^{t.}$ Kings Troop are appointed Corp^{ls} in Major Bellis Troop Wm Castens [Caston] of Cap$^{t.}$ Swetenhams Troop & Robt Needham of Major Bellis are appointed Corp^{ls} to the late Cap$^{t.}$ Buchanans Troop – & to date Date for the 19 ins^{t}

Camp 24th June 1815

The Troop to parade this evening at 7 o'clock under arms in full Dress

Memberandum

The Brigade will saddle and Reddy to turn out at 1/2 past 5 o'clock tomorrow morning

Mem^{m} Faust [?] 24th June 1815

The Brigade major of the 4 Brigade will cause all officers which are absent from their several Regts which are wounded are to be struck of the strengths in there daily states stating in the colum of Remarks when the are so struck of – he will likewise be so good as to transmit them forthwith

M. Childers Maj.
A.A.A. Genl

Memm Foust [?] 24th June 1815

Officers Com^{g} Regts are requested to Recommend without delay two steady serjts for the duties of Ass^{t} Provost Martial and also Baggage master to the Cavalry which recommendations must be transmitted forthwith to Cavalry H^{d} Quarters

M. Childers Maj
A.A.A. Genl

BO Fontaine [Uterte] 25th June 1815

Captn Ch King of the 16th Lt Dragoons is appointed Maj^{r} of Brigade to the Forth Brigade of Cavalry – the Brigade will saddle and be Redy to turn out tomorrow morning at 1/2 past 5 o'clock

Signd G. Jackson [?] M.B.

Mem^{m}

A Court of Inquiry having been demanded by Serj^{t} Hay in consequence of Acquasation made against him by Private McCaid the Court assembled accordingly when Serj^{t} Hay was most honourably acquitted and the acquasation of Private McCord found malicious and without foundation

Tomkinson:

25th Marched to Fontaine Uterte –

Order Book:

RO Camp [?] June 26th 1815

For the Day tomorrow Lt Buchamp
The Regiment to saddle & be Redy to turn out at Day Break tomorrow morning

Tomkinson:

26th Marched to Fluquières, a small Village on the High road between St Quentin & Ham

Order Book:

RO 27th June 1815

For the Day tomorrow Lt Hay
The same orders for tomorrow as ordered for this day

Tomkinson:

27th To near Royes [Villers-les-Roye]

Order Book:

RO Camp 28th June 1815

For the Day tomorrow Lt Napean
The Regiment to saddle & be redy to turn out tomorrow morning at Day break

Tomkinson:

28th Ricquebourg

The enemy on the 28th attacked the advanced guard of the Prussians at Villers Cotterêts. The main body of the Prussians coming up they retired across the Marne being driven by General Bulow on the road near Meaux. He took from them 500 prisoners. On the 28th in the attack at Villers Cotterêts they lost 6 pieces of Cannon and 1,000 prisoners

29th Bivouaced on the other side the Oise which we passed at the Pont St Maxence. The Bridge was destroyed on the advance of the Prussians in 1814 by blowing up the centre Arch – It is repaired in a temporary manner – Deputies are daily coming out of Paris to treat with the Duke and attempt to prevent the further advance of the Army. No terms whilst Napoleon remains at the head of affairs will be listened to. Blucher with the Prussians is in our advance and attempts have been made by them to treat with him. I believe he will not see them, saying in Paris alone will he listen to any terms – The Duke will not of course make a separate treaty, therefore they must wait for an interview in Paris –

Marshal Grouchy with his Corps from Wavre has arrived at Paris – he has made a rapid march and brought all his materiel complete – The enemy have near 50,000 Troops of the Line, beside the National Guard and a new Levy called the *Tirailleurs de la Garde* – In all near 70,000. Grouchy's retreat was very rapid and well conducted.

30th June. Marched to Goussainville near Louvres within four leagues of Paris – It is on the high road from Senlis the St Denis. We made a detour from the high road to avoid interfering with the other columns. This took us through the Wood of Chantilly. Previous to passing the Pont St Maxence nothing could be more uninteresting than the country – It is flat and extensive chiefly covered with corn without Timber and not affording the least variety. For the last three days we have followed the route of the Prussians, they plunder every village. There are not many inhabitants remaining at their houses.

There were long Avenues of Cherry Trees in the neighbourhood of Goussainville. More Cherries around this village than I ever saw collected in one spot.

Order Book:

[The following section of the order book is a record of General Orders and Brigade Orders. It is possible there is a page missing here, as the section appears to start in mid-order.]

NCO as there may be occasion they will always accompany the Baggage of their respective Brigades –

2. Officers Com^{g} Reg^{ts} will be pleased to send in a return tomorrow to the A.A.A. Genl of the number of Carts or Waggons employed to transport –

3. On a march where the head of the column is turned onto a new direction every part of it must be made to follow out of the old direction to the exact point where the Head of the Column left it

The Baggage must also do likewise [or] as was the case the other day the Baggage will be straggling all over the country –

M. Childers
A.A.A.G.

GO Joncourt 25th June 1815

N°6 The Comm^{r} of the forces has observed the greatest irregularity among the Baggage and women & private Baggage are put upon the Carts destined to carry Tents & Hospital Stores & the consequence is that they cannot get on and delay everything else – If the Comd^{r} of the forces should observe such practices again he will order the private Baggage to be burnt & will bring the Officers to whom it belongs to a Court Martial for disobedience of orders –

N°7 The women must not be allowed to get upon the public Carts –

N°8 The Comr of the forces begs that the divisions will start from their ground at the hour ordered – particularly the cavalry & that they will march in the order fixed in the Rout. The Baggage must be kept well up in the rear of each Division or Corps according to the order given upon the subjects through the Quarter Mr Genl

GO Nesle 27 June 1815

N°1 the Officers comg companies are responsible that the soldiers do not fall out on the march it is scandalous to see the number that straggle from many of the Regts of the Army solely for the sake of plunder –

GO Nivelle 20th June 1815

N°2 the Field Marshall takes this opportunity of returning to the Army his thanks for their Conduct in the glorious action fought on the 18th Inst and will not fail to report his sense of their Conduct in the terms which it deserves to the several Sovereigns –

N°3 The Field Marshall has observed that several soldiers and even Officers have quitted the Ranks without leave and have gone to Brussels and some even to Antwerp where and in the country through which they have passed they have spread a false alarm in a manner highly unmilitary and degrading to the character of soldiers –

N°4 The Field Marshall requests the General Offrs Commg Divisions in the British Army and the Genl Officers Commg the Corps of each Nation of which the Army is composed to report to him in writing what officers & men the former by name are now & have been absent without leave since the 16th Inst –

N°5 The Field Marshall desires that the 14 Article of the 14 section of the Articles of War may be inserted in every orderly book of the British Army in order to remind officers & soldiers of the punishment affixed by Law to the Crime of creating false alarms –

N°6 As the Army is about to enter the French Territory the field Marshall desires it may [be] understood by the troops of the several nations composing the Army which he has the Honor to Command that their Sovereigns are in alliance with the King of France therefore must be considered as a friendly Country –

N° 7 No article is to be taken from any individual by any officer or soldier without paying for the same. Commissary of the Army will supply the troops for all they require in the usual manner and no requisitions to be made direct on the country or its Magistrates by any officer or soldier –

N° 8 The Commissary will receive directions either from the Field Marshall or from the Generals comg the troops of the several Nations (if these troops should not be supplied with provisions by the British Commissary) to make such requisitions as may be necessary for the supply of the troops for which they will give the usual vouchers & receipts and they will understand that they will be responsible to these and account for what they will thus receive from the Country in France in the same manner as they would if they purchased supplies for the troops in their own Country respectively –

N° 9 In order to preserve order and provide for attendance on the Hospitals of Brussels Commr of the Forces desires that one Off^{r} one NCO & three private men for one hundred men sent to the Hospital wounded in the late action of the 16th & 18th Ins^{t} may be sent from the sev^{l} Reg^{ts} to Brussels tomorrow and place themselves under the order of the *Commandant* there –

N° 12 As soon as the Off^{rs} Non CO and private men should arrive at Brussels they will send to the Comm^{t} a nominal list of the Offr^{s} and men of their Several Reg^{ts} who were then in Hospitals or on the duty of attending Hospitals –

13 the Comm^{t} at Brussels does hereby positively forbid to allow a billet or the issue of rations to any Off^{r} or soldier who will be at Brussels whose name is not in the list above ment^{d} or who does not proceed thither by Rout from the Quarter Master Genl or order from the field Marshall

Signed
J. Wates L.C.[2]
A.A.G.

Malplaquet 21st June 1815

N°1 With a view to preserve order in the Army is Essentially necessary that a Corps of *Gendarmerie* should be formed who will be employed under the direction of the Field Marshall –

2 This Corps shall be formed of those men from each Reg^{t} of Cavalry in the Army and the Generals Com^{g} troops of the sev^{l} Nations are requested to select the best and steadiest men for this service and if Possible those who can talk French –

3 When selected they are to be sent to Head Quarters with their Horses where they will receive rations for themselves & their Horses & additional pay of one *Franc per diem* while so employed which will be paid to them by the Field Marshall –

4 He requests the Com^{g} Offr^{s} of Reg^{ts} of the British Army & of the German Legion to select such men for this service as may have served before in the staff Corps –

5. Lt Col Schofield is appointed to Comm^{d} the Corps of *Gendarmerie* – Lt Rook late of the Staff Corps is appointed L^{t} of the Corps of *Gendarmerie* –

2 Lieutenant Colonel J. Waters, unattached.

6 The Offrs of the *Gendarmerie* are to be paid and are to perform the same duties as the officers of the late Staff Corps –

7 Field Marshall begs that all Horses belonging to the British Cavalry or to Cavalry of any other Nation which may have been detained by any individual may be returned to the Regts to which they belong –

10 Major Childers of the 11th Light Dragoons is appointd to act as A.A.G. and is appointd to do duty with the Cavalry till Col Elly shall have recovered from his wounds –

Signed
J. Waters Lt Col
A.A.Gl

GO Le Cateau 23 June 1815

1. Mr Deputy A Commy Gl Spencer is removed from the Commissariat for quitting the third Division to which he was attached without leave during the important operations recently carried on –

2. The Comr of the Forces gives notice that he will dismiss from the service forthwith any commissary or any Offr of the Civil Departt of the Army who quits his station witht leave

Croix [?] 25 June 1815

Serjt Matthews of the 11 Light Dns is appointed to act as an asst pro [?] Baggage Master until further orders he will proceed to mounted to Cavalry Head Quarters this day and report himself to the A.A.A.G. –

No2. Generals & Officers in Command of Brigade are referred to the General Orders Dated the 30th of April 1815 No 2 and General Cavalry Orders Dated 10th May 1815 No 1 & 11 June 1815.

No1 and are requested to order immediately all Dragoons that are absent except those furnished by General Cavalry Orders –

Signed
M. Childers
Ma. A.A.G. –

General Cavalry Orders
Eshelles 26 June 1815

1 Officers on out posts duty will be pleased to make regular reports to the Cavalry Head Quarters daily of the information obtained by their patrols and the state of the Roads and features of the Country in the front –

2 Officers Comg Regts & Brigades are requested to make every Exertion to occupy the place assigned them in the Column of the March but in case that object

cannot be obtained without obstructing or inconveniencing Corps already in their place they will remain behind them till a favourable opportunity occurs –

3. As arrangements are made by the Quarter Master Generals of the Allied Armies to prevent the clashing of Columns & Cantonments assigned in consequence –

Officers Com^{g} Brigades are requested not to occupy any other villages than those pointed out by the A.Q.M.G. as such deviations are productive of great inconvenience –

Should they find troops of other allies in these villages they may be sure that they are only passing through or there by mistake and will be moved by a proper application –

Officers so situated will therefore report to Cavalry Head Quarters before they quit the grounds assigned them in the General arrangements –

Officers in Command at out posts will be pleased to forward any reports they may have to make to Cavalry Head Quarters as early as possible after having ascertained them –

M. Childers
M.A.A.A.G.

Roye [Villers-les-Roye] 27 June 1815

In order to prevent as much as possible harassing the troops Off^{rs} Com^{g} Brigades which march in the rear of the Infantry are requested to form up in column & Dismount & let the Horses feed whenever it can be done without inconvenience to other Corps –

3. Whenever a Brigade or Reg^{t} being out of its place is permitted to pass through a Column it & its Baggage must be previously formed in Close Column of Squadrons or half-Squadrons & pass the Road so as to retard the troops in March as little as possible the circumstances must also be reported to the Off^{r} Com^{g} the troops that are to be passed through & sanctioned by his permission

M. Childers M.A.A.A.G.

RO 1st July 1815

Lt Osten is to proceed to Chantilly to take charge of [the] cavalry depo he will receive his instruction from Colonel Sligh[3] previous to marching –

Lt Baker will take the Command of the late Captain Buchanans Troop Filton of Captn Tomkinsons Troop is appointed Farrier Maj^{r} from this date Gibson of C Troop is appointed assistant Farrier in G Troop & Farrier Coates[4] to H

3 Lieutenant Colonel J.W. Sleigh, commanding the 11th Light Dragoons.
4 There is no Coates listed as being at Waterloo; this might be John Courts, listed as being in G Troop.

The Officer Com^{g} having heard of several instances of most outrageous attacks made on the houses and property of the inhabitants in the course of this march in which he as great reason to suspect some of the 16th and particularly the Women of the Reg^{t} are implicated he calls upon the Officers to support him in maintaining the most strict discipline and desires the Officers upon no acc^{t} to overlook the crime of a soldier caught plundering Dragoons are particularly forbid entering the Houses or Premises the People they are not Quartered on and Officers will never detach men on foraging duties without an Officer or NC Officer who must be responsible for the conduct of is Party

Any woman belonging to the Reg^{t} seen with articles about her which she cannot satisfactory acc^{t} for must be delivered up to the Provo Martial Genl of the Cavalry and provided the Conduct of the Women attached to the Reg^{t} is not in every Respect Regular and Creditable to it he desires Officers comm^{g} troops to dismiss them

The English soldier should be reminded he as no Excuse for Retaliating on the Peaceable Inhabitants like the facing troops and that the are not to follow there example in Pillaging the have the advantage of Commissaries to supply them with Regular Rations which is not the case with facing troops

Watering Order tomorrow morning at 9 o'clock

GCO Rocssa [?] July 1st 1815

N°1 The Cavalry depo will be formed at Chantilly for sick men and lame horses a Genl Hosp^{l} will also be established there –

N°2 A Subaltern from each Brigade and a Serj^{t} Maj^{r} or steddy Serj^{t} from each Regt will accompany the sick men and sick and lame horses the number of men sent with the horses must not be in disproportion than one man to two horses the will take there arms and appointments with them the sick sent into hospital will take a list of there necessaries including Arms and Ammunition Signed by Officer Comm^{g} the troops

N°3 Officers Comm^{g} Brigades will be so good as to send proportionate numbers of NC Officers and Farriers from there respective Brigades

N°4 the Second Brigade will furnish a Cap$^{t.}$ who will take charge of the depo until further orders he will attend this evening as early as possible to the Cavalry H^{d} Quarters to receive is instructions

N°5 Spare app^{ts} of the Reg^{ts} to be sent at same time the will be collected by the Reg^{ts} and deposited in the proper store under the charges of Serj^{t} maj^{r} of the Reg^{ts}

N° 6 Mr Deputy Commissary Genl Harris will be pleased to take charge of the depo

N°7 the first Brigade will furnish a Vitanry [*sic*, veterinary] Surgeon for the Depo

N°8 The Commissariat Officers attached to Reg^{ts} will provaid the Necessary means of transport for the sick men and spare app^{ts}

N°9 Sick men & Horses and Stores will march to morrow morning at 6 o'clock under charge of a subaltern Officer of Brigades direct to Chantilly when the will Report themselves to the Capt. in charge of the whole

N°10 A Return of the number of sick men and horses of each Regt to be sent into morrow morning to the Asst Adjt Genl

N°11 A Medical officer of each Brigade will attend the sick to Chantilly to morning when the will remain until the medical department of the Hospt is established

Signed
M. Childers
A.A. Genl

An orderly Dragoon of each Regt will attend the Serjts ~~of~~ that attends for orders

Letters for Hd Quarters to be sent by the Serjt only that attends for orders

BO 1st July 1815

The Brigade to be saddled and ready to turn out at day break

Officers Commg Regt are requested to pay particular attention to the Genl Cavalry Orders of this day, and be carefull the men they send are sober –

Detail Regts	Sublts	Serjts	
16th Lt Ds	1	1	
11 Lt Ds	Asst surgeon 1	1	
12 Lt Ds	-//-	1	1 Farrier

One Private to two Horses from each Regt the whole to march to morrow morning at 6 o'clock Returns of their Necessaries and Appointments the men take to be given in to the subaltern who Commds the detachments and the cause of the Horses being sent to the rear.

C. King
Mr B.

GCO Brussels 21 June 1815

Lieut. Genl the Earl of Uxbridge as the honor to announce to the Cavalry and R.H. Artillery that he is about to proceed to England –

He cannot leave here without feelings of regret at the separation, but he at the same time enjoys those of admiration and gratitude for there Conduct whilst under is Command –

The Brilint [*sic*] conduct of many of the Brigades in the face of a Cavalry so greatly out numbering them justifies all praise that [...] attempt to offer he requests the Genl Officers, and all other Officers will accept is warmest thanks for there readiness and zeal with wich they executed every duty and that the NC Officers & Privates may feel assured that there gen^{l} good conduct and there Bravery in Battle have made an indelible Impression on him

Signed
M. Childers
M.A.A.A. Genl

GCO Chateau de Roissy 13 June 1815

N°1 Maj^{r} Genl Sir John Vandeleur having observed in the Column of Baggage this day Waggons and Carts conveying the Private Baggage of Officers who are not entitled to them begs to refer officers Comm^{g} Brigades & Reg^{ts} to the repeated Genl Orders on the subject

N°2 comm^{g} Officers of Reg^{ts} are held responsible that no wheel carriges accompany there Reg^{ts} except those that are allowed by the Genl Orders of the Army and that have been impressed by the authority of a Commissariat Officer –

N°3 Should the Ma^{j}r Genl observe this disobedience of Orders he will report the Regt to the Comm^{r} of the forces

Signed
M. Childers
A.A.A. Genl

Tomkinson:

July 1st Marched to Argenteuil and bivouacked in the Garden of the Minister of Marine – The Prussians have passed before us and done all the damage in their power to the House – The Looking Glasses are all broken, many of which were large & handsome. A Bust of Napoleon is split from top to bottom and the Iron railings around the House have been pulled up. I am sorry the Prussians act in such spite, though it is exactly the conduct of the French when in their Country. The French deserve it, yet it would have been nobler conduct not to avail themselves of such petty advantages altho' the enemy acted to them the same, or possibly in a more oppressive manner – It is difficult to say what is right. The French should not allow their Army to act as they have & come off themselves with impunity.

Blucher on the 2nd was strongly opposed in taking possession of the heights of St Cloud. He however affected his object and pushed his advance close to the gates of Paris – They occupied the village of Issy – They were attacked at this point on the morning of the 3rd at day light – the enemy advanced on the Prussians in considerable force and the affair became severe. They were driven back into Paris and knowing Blucher would bombard the Town, they sent to desire the firing might cease and that terms being arranged for the withdrawing of the Army they would evacuate Paris – Blucher had applied for our Rocket Brigade and would probably have employed them the instant they could have got up against the Town –

The Duke having thrown a Bridge over the Seine at Argenteuil and by an advance on Neuilly the Bois de Boulogne would have been occupied and the two Armies in possession of the ground up to the Gates of the Town. It is a fortunate the affair ended here for had we advanced up to the Town, had a successful affair, and in the hurry of the Troops have followed the enemy into the Town, it is impossible to say what would have been [the] result. Had the Men left their ranks and attempted plundering a Town of such an extent as Paris with a population half Soldiers, I fear we should have lost half the Army – It is fortunate the business has closed and the Troops in bivouac a short distance from the Town.

July 3rd A Pontoon Bridge was thrown over the Seine yesterday at Argenteuil. We crossed this morning and with the second Division moved on Courbevoie situated on the Seine close to the Pont Neuilly. The second Division of Infantry crossed at the same time and moved on Courbevoie. A convention has been agreed upon and signed this day at St Cloud –

On the 4th July St Denis, St Ouen, Clichy & Neuilly are to be given up.

5th Montmartre is to be surrendered.

6th All the Barriers around Paris are to be given up. The French Army to retire over the Loire within eight Days –

The enemy are to retire over the Seine and give up Courbevoie, they pretended ignorance of the terms agreed on and fired on our advance. We had a skirmish with them in driving in their Piquet, they knew of the Convention being signed, in which we lost a Man & Horse with three or four Wounded. After they had retired into Courbevoie we had the greater difficulty in persuading them to suffer our Piquet to be stationed (as specified) close to the Bridge. Lt Gen[l] Clinton talked with them for some time and then allowed them ten minutes to determine. He moved the second Division to attack if they did not retire, when they evacuated the post allowing our piquet to be stationed on the Bridge – When they saw us determined they became very civil and came forward to converse with us – They were dreadfully enraged at the Bourbons, saying how they supposed now, that they must receive a King from the English, but that they preferred the Duke of York or the Duke of Wellington to a Bourbon – An Officer of Hussars put himself in a dreadful passion, pulled the Cloke he had before him in a manner to pull it off his saddle – saying he had seen the Duke du Berri strip an Officer's epaulettes from his shoulders on parade – We bivouacked in the Garden belonging to a *Chateau* [de Becon?] close to Courbevoi.

Order Book:

RO Camp near Argentuil 3 July 1815

The Reg^t this date will be formed as follows

Right Squadron
Brevet Major Belli C Cap^n Swetenhams D

Centre Squadron
Cap^n Tomkinson A Cap^n King F

Left Squadron
Cap^n Whealan [Weyland] H Cap^n Buchanan [dead] G

Lt Swinfen to take Command of Cap^n Swetenhams Troop[5]

Lieut. Lloyd to do duty in Major Bellis *vice* Swinfen removed

Mem^m Chateau de Roissy 1st July

Off^rs Com^g Reg^ts will report tomorrow to the Deputy Inspector of Hospitals Cavalry Head Quarters the names of the medical officers absent from their respective Reg^ts specifying authority –

M. Childers
M.A.A.A.G.

G O Louvres [?] 30th June 1815

N°1 Major Marly 14th Foot is appointed in the an assistant in the Adjutant Generals Departm^t till the pleasure of his Royal Highness the Prince Regent is known and is attached to the 2d Division of Infantry Date of appoint^t 25 Ins^t

2. Cap^n Shaw 4th Foot is appointed Brevet Major till the pleasure of his Royal highness is known and is attached to 10th Brigade of Infantry

3 Ensign the Honble J.S. Bathurst 1st Guards is appoint^d aide de Camp to Major Genl Marslan [?] date of appoint 25 Ins^t

Signed J. Waters Lt Col
A.A.G.

5 There is no reason given for Captain Swetenham's apparent absence from the regiment.

G.O. H^{d} Q^{rs}

Genappe 2nd July 1815

N° 1 the Field Marshall has great pleasure in publishing in GO the following letter from the Comm^{r} in Chief and the Secretary of State expressing the approbation of His royal Highness the Prince Regen of the conduct of the Army in the late action with the Enemy –

Horse Guards 21st June 1815

My Lord Duke

I have to acknowledge the receipt of your graces dispatch of the 19th Inst Conveying a report of the Military operations up to that Date –

Marked and Distinguished as these operations have been by the glorious and Important victory gained over the French Army on the 18th Inst I have infinite pleasure in Communicating the high feeling and approbat^{n} which the Prince Regent has viewed the Conduct of the troops upon this memorable occasion no language can do justice to the sense His Royal Highness Entertains of that Distinguished merit which has even surpassed all former Instances of their Characteristic firmness and Discipline allow me to desire that your grace will also accept yourself and convey in my name to the Off^{rs} NCOs and troops under your Comm^{d} the thanks of his Royal Highness for the great and important Services which they have rendered their grateful Country –

From my partiality and well known opinion of the Prussian nation and their troops your Grace will readily believe that I also concur in those expressions and thanks which have emanated from the Prince Regent for those important services rendered to the common cause by Prince Blucher and the Brave Army under his Com^{d} the triumph of success cannot lessen the regret felt by all for the loss of the many valuable Lives which has as considerably attended the accomplishment of their great achievement and par[ticu]larly [?] deplore the fates of Sir Thos Pickton & Major G. Sir Wm Ponsonby

I am my Lord Duke
Yours Sincerely
Frederick Comm^{d} in Chief

War Department, London June 24th 1815

Copy
My Lord

Your Grace will be pleased to convey to General His Royal Highness the Prince of Orange the Satisfaction the Prince Regent has expressed in observing that in the actions of the 16th & 18th Inst His Royal Highness has given an early promise of the Military Talents of which his ancestors have been so renowned and that by freely shedding his Blood in the defence of the Motherland he has summented [?] a Union of the People with the House of Orange which is to be hoped will thereby become Indisolvable [*sic*] –

The Prince Regent is fully sensible of the Meritorious services performed by the Earl of Uxbridge who had the Command of the Cavalry and Commands me to desire you will Communicate to his Lordship His Royal Highness most gracious acceptance of them –

The Judicious conduct & Determined Courage displayed by General Lord Hill and by the other General Officers in Command of His Majesty's Forces upon this Glorious occasion have obtained the High approbation of the Prince Regent Your Grace will be pleased to communicate to the General Officers the graceful approval of their exertions and your Grace will also be pleased to make known to the Army at large the High approbation with which the Prince Regent has viewed the Excellent Conduct and Invincible Valour Manifested by all ranks under your Graces Command –

His royal highness commands me on no account to omit expressing his deep regret on receiving so large a list of officers & men who have either fallen or being seriously wounded in the action of the 16th & 18th Ins^{t} and the Prince Regent particularly Laments the loss of such Highly Distinguished Officers as Lt Genl Sir Thomas Pickton and Major General Sir Wm Ponsonby –

It cannot be expected that such Desperate conflicts should be conducted and so Transcendent a Victory be obtained without considerable loss. The chance of war must at times expose Armies and the ablest Commanders to great Casualties without any adequate advantages to be derived in return and whoever contemplates the immediate effects and the probable results of the Battles fought on the 16th & 18th Inst cannot but think that although on the list of killed and wounded several of his Majesties most approved officers unfortunately Inscribed many endered [endeared] to your Grace and whose Names have become familiar to the Country by their Distinguished Service in the Peninsula the loss however severe and however to be Lamented bears but a small proportion to the Magnitude of the victory which has been achieved the military glory of the Country has protected from Invasion and spoiled the territories of his Majestys allies the King of the Netherlands and has opened the finest prospect on a lasting foundation the peace and liberties of Europe –

I have the Honor to be ye
Signed – Bathurst

His Royal Highness has been pleased to appoint the following General Officers on the Staff of the Army –

Lieut. Genl	Lord Combermere GCB
Major General	Sir Kennett Howard KCB
" "	Sir Thomas Bradford KCB
" "	Honble Sir R WA Callaghan KCB
	Sir John Keane KCB

N°2 His Royal Highness the Commander in Chief has been pleased to approve of Doctor Grant Inspector of Hospitals being appointed Inspector General of the medical Dept of the Army serving under the order of his Grace the Duke of Wellington Date of appointment 21st June last –

3 All Regimental Surgeons and assistants except those doing duty with the Hospitals by order of the Inspector General are to join their Regiments forthwith –

N° 5 Officers Commanding Divisions of Cavalry & Infantry and the Comg Offr of Artillery are requested to send in the names of those officers for the obtaining of Brevet P[ro]motion to his Grace the Duke of Wellington addressed to the Military Secretarys Office –

Signed J. Waters Lt Col
A.A.G.

Head Quarters
Gonesse 4 July 1815

N°1 The Field Marshall has great Satisfaction in announcing to the troops under his Command that he has in Concert with Field Marshall Blucher Concluded a Military Convention with the Commander in Chief of the French Army in Paris by which the Enemy are to evacuate St Denys St Hosaw [?] Clishly [?] and Louily [?] this day at Noon the Heights of Montmartre tomorrow at Noon and Paris next Day –

2. The Field Marshall congratulates the Army upon this result of their Glorious Victory. He desires that the Troops may Employ themselves this Day & tomorrow to Clean their Arms Clothes and appointments as it is his intention that they should pass him in review –

3. Major General Sir Manley Power KGB is appointed to the Staff of this Army

Copy, Signed J. Waters Lt Col
A.A.G.

BO 4th July 1815

The Brigade to saddle and ready to turn out at Day Break –

Officers Com^{g} Reg^{ts} are requested to Inspect the mens kitts tomorrow and throw away all Superfluous Articles

Mem^{m} Roissy 3d July 1815

Reg^{tl} Quarter Masters will wait on Major Campbell A.Q.G. Cavalry H^{d} Quarters tomorrow with the monthly returns of Camp Equipage the Quarter Masters of Reg^{ts} that have already sent in their returns will also attend

CO Chateau de Roissy 2d July 1815

N°1 All Regimts when they are posted will send back a man to their Brigade in order to insure a communication, an extra Dragoon might be sent with the Piquet for that purpose –

M. Childers
A.A.G.

GCO Chateau de Roissy 4 July 1815

N°1 Officers Com^{g} Brigades of Cavalry and troops of Horse Artillery are requested to send in immediately the names of such officers as they may wish to recommend for Brevet Promotion in consequence of the Glorious action of the 18th *Ultimo* –

M. Childers
A.A.G.

GCO Chateau de Roissy 4 July 1815

N°2 Reg^{ts} that have not sent Camp Kettles with their Detachm^{ts} to Chantilly will forthwith send a sufficient number according to the description of Kettle

The Seignor Company of the Brigades will furnish the necessary means of transport for the whole Brigade –

M. Childers
A.A.A.G.

Found by a Dragoon of the 13 a Grey Mare with a mark of a broken knee the letters B.D. on the Cloathing also a Black Baggage mare –

They will her Deliver to the owners when applied for C. King

Tomkinson:

> 4th July. The Convention being signed we moved a short distance down the Seine occupying the village of Asnières – We were well put up and within two Miles of Paris.

Order Book:

> RO July 5th 1815
> Asnières
>
> Offr Comg Squadrons are call'd upon to see that the offrs & NCO exert themselves in turning out their respect troops tomorrow in the most creditable manner for the Review of the Field Marshall the Duke of Wellington on the march of the Army into Paris –
>
> The appoints of men & horses to be inspected this evening at 5 o'clock when it is hoped that all the Overalls will be mended & that every man has a pair of overall straps –
>
> The officers to wear Jackets & Pouch Bech [?] Belts the Facings of officers & men to be turned out Cap Lines & feathers to be worn –
>
> Officers to appear in Velices & without Cloaks –
>
> The parade as ordered at 4 o'clock this evening will not take place –
>
> BO 5th July 1815
>
> Regiments will be ready to turn out at any hour required tomorrow morning as clean as possible
>
> Memberandum) Not to saddle

Luard:[6]

> Asnières, July 5th, 1815
> 3 miles from Paris
>
> I should like much to have dated this my Dear Mother from Paris but however it is at present the same thing & for fear of losing the post I will not defer it. – This morning I received a very kind letter from my Dear Father of the 25th Inst – in which he seemed to think it would reach me in France, but no suspicion was supposed of my receiving it at the Gates of Paris – but so it is: & thus gloriously has terminated the war – we have beaten the French Army near the Capital of Flanders – pursued them to their own & there dictated our own terms – An Armistice has been concluded by which treaty the Army of Buonaparte is to retire behind the

6 Luard Family Archive, Letter 406.

Loire with the whole of their material – yesterday it evacuated St Denis – today Montmartre becomes garrisoned by the Allies – & tomorrow the Capital is put in our possession – the Army of Napoleon is of course discontented with these terms & is in a perfect state of insubordination – but however necessity compels them to comply with our terms & we have it all our own way – Napoleon with some of his steady adherents has vanished for some days passed & no certain information is gained of him but report has him at Cherbourg about to be embarked for America. –

I wrote to my Father from Ricquebourg on the 28th ult^{o} – on the 29th we marched & crossed the L'Oise at Pont St Maxence 30th through Vermeuil & Louvres to Goussainville – 1st we halted when George[7] dined with me – 2d to Argentuil 3d crossed the Seine by a bridge of boats & encamped near Courbevoie – yesterday we came here. – The Prussians upon whose line of march we have now & then entered have destroyed & pillaged every thing – the villages they passed thro have been deserted by the inhabitants – & plundered by the Prussians – I confess I am not sorry for it but am happy it is not the English that have done it. –

Since writing the above Major Murray has been with me & given me an order for the Reg^{t} to brush up as smart as possible – for the Duke of W reviews the whole British Army as it passes thro Paris tomorrow. – what a humiliating sight this will be for the Parisians, whilst a glorious one for our History. – So short, brilliant & decisive a campaign has never taken place – I regret much that Charles[8] was not with us – tell him with my kindest regards my Capt^{ns} brother, Tomkinson, with whom he was at Rugby & Cambridge was with us, of course he did not interfere in the Battle he saw it & rode over the field after & will enter Paris with us tomorrow in Triumph, I should like much our Brother Bourragau[9] have done the same – I should like to remain in France for a couple of years – but we shall only I fear for as many months – our Village here is very delightfully situated on the Seine – a bridge of Pontoons is thrown across by which we shall cross tomorrow – The inhabitants have not deserted. Some have not vanished their houses – George was in excellent health & spirits on the 1st – I shall most probably see him tomorrow: We have an order to send an escort for the Emp^{r} of Russia

I fear I shall be obliged to avail myself of my Father's kind offer with respect to money – could I it should be avoided & if I get an allow^{ce} for my losses I hope I shall be able to refund it – Thank dear Loui[10] for her few kind lines, as well as Tomasina[11] Gordon wich most probably not reach us for I should think they would

7 Brother George, 18th Hussars at Waterloo (1788–1847).
8 Eldest brother Charles Bourragau (1785–1855).
9 Bourragau was the maiden name of John's grandmother, Jane. Whether John is here referring to his brother Charles (whose second name it was) or to some other member of the extended family is unknown.
10 John's sister, Louisa Susannah (1798–1885).
11 Tom Fenton had a sister named Thomasina, but it is not known if she married a Mr Gordon.

be halted before they got far from Ostend – I thank you for the shirts – they are always useful but I have not immediate occasion for them I believe George has – To the Armytages[,][12] Fentons[13] & all your kind neighbours who have interested themselves about me pray remember me to kindly – Now is Jennys opportunity to come to this country Tom has nothing to do but obtain leave of absence & search for a place where she could reside comfortably – we have now beautiful weather I am quite elated by our intended Entre to the Capital de L'[…]

God bless you my Dear Mother my best wishes attend all the family – I will write again when we are settled

Believe me to be
Your Affect Son
John Luard

It is true we suffered greatly on the 18th but we cannot fight without killing nor conquer Nations without bloodshed – & this Nation has been conquered with much less loss of blood than Spain was saved –

Order Book:

RO Asnières 6th July 1815

Squadrons to be out this evening in Watering Order at the most convenient hour for the Inspection of the Com^g Off^rs of Squadrons – Corp^l Hodgson of A Troop is reduced to the ranks for repeated neglect of duty from this day inclusive –

RO Asnières 7th July 1815

The Troops to parade this afternoon in full Dress with the whole of their arms at 4 o'clock

Officers Commanding Troops are Riquested to send in for the information of the Commanding officer a Lang Roll of ther Troop to the acting adj^t accounting for ever a man thay are also desired to see that every officer has a Lang Roll and every Serj^t a Squad Roll and that thay may allways have then with them –

Lt Swinfen will proced immediately to Malmaison to ascertain what number of Capt. Swetenhams Troop is there that he may be able to account for them

12 John's brother Charles married Henrietta Armitage (d. 1783).
13 Captain Thomas Fenton (1790–1841) was a close friend; he charged with the Scots Greys at Waterloo, and survived.

RO Asnières 7th July 1815

The […] & drunkenness of the men in of certain troops of the Reg^t has been carried to such an excess of late that the officer commanding requests Com^g office^rs of Squadrons to continue as much in the quarters as possible till a better discipline is observed.

At no time is a troop to be without the presence of one officer and moor & every stables must be dismissed agreeable to the SO of the reg^t by an officer – the quarters must also be inspected once a day by an officer of Troop –

A piquet consisting of – subaltern officer 1 serj^t 1 corp^l & 9 men to mount daily. The subaltern officer on no account whichever to be absent from his command. He will aid is cmding officer superintend the Drills with the acting adjutant and see that […] order is maintained in the cantonments of the Reg^t –

RO Asnières 7 July 1815

The troops to be out to morrow morning at 7 o'clock in riding School Order for foraging

Foot Parade at 4 o'clock in full Dress with the whole of the Arms –

Clearks of troops to bring in the Pay List to morrow morning at 9 o'clock to the Pay Master for the 24th June with the Accts of Non Effective Men to 24th June 1815 –

Detail

	[…]	Serjts	Corpls	Privates	Horses
A				2	2
C				2	2
D	1		1	1	2
F				2	2
G		1		1	2
H				1	1
	1	1	1	9	11

Lieut. Harries for the above duty

All awkward men or men that has misbehav'd or been confined with the exception of men that have been try'd by a Court Martial since the march from Denderwindeke at 3 o'clock this afternoon

GCO Roissy 5th July 1815

N°1 Officers comm^g Brigades & Regiments are requested to direct a proportion of the officers always to encamp with their Regiments.

A Field Officer per Brigade, a Captn per Reg^{t} & a Subal^{n} per Squadron will always be on Duty & will be responsible for the regularity of the Troops –

N°2 Such patroles will be ordered as may appear necessary in order to take up stragglers & prevent marauding – Officers Comm^{g} Brigades will be pleased to order a Guard either by Brigades or Reg^{ts} to furnish these patroles & receive prisoners

N°3 Officers in Commnd are requested to put a stop to the unmilitary practice of discharging fire arms in camp, any person found guilty of this offense will be punished severely

N°4 Officers in commnd of Reg^{ts} are requested to recommend without delay 2 NC Officers calculated to fill the situations of Adjutant & Serjt Major

Signed
M. Childers
A.A.G.

Tomkinson:

7th July. Rode this day into Paris. The Barriers having been only surrendered yesterday not many Officers have entered. They rather looked at us as we rode along the Streets. The greater part of the Infantry are in bivouac in the Bois de Boulogne – We find a Regiment of Cavalry daily for duty which occupies the Champs Élysées close to the Place Louis Quinze – On the 16th marching from Asnières, the first day they took this duty, we did not go the direct way but marched through a part of Paris, across the Place Louis Quinze to our station – It was singular to find a British Regiment of Cavalry marching peaceably through the Streets of Paris – Paris in three days after signing the Convention was full of Officers from both Armies and the Parisians enjoying the concourse equally with us, at least to all appearance –

Louis the 18th entered Paris on the 8th. He was tolerably well received – Many I think went to see his entrance from the mere pleasure of witnessing such sights, and not from any respect or liking to him. This was I think the motive which induced the people in whose House I was Quartered at Asnières. They spoke for a couple of Days of going to see him yet had not any particular dislike to Napoleon.

The Lady of the House and her Sister feel the situation their Nation has sunk to. They were speaking of their Troops before the Russian Campaign, stating that had they been properly managed 'they could have given Laws to all the World.'

The Emperors of Russia and Austria with the King of Prussia are arrived.

A detachment from one of our heavy Regiments of Cavalry was sent to escort the Emperor of Russia into Paris – He paid them the compliment to say 'he was flattered by being escorted by such brave Men.'

Napoleon left Paris on the 20th or 21st for Malmaison where he remained until obliged to leave from the advance of the Armies – He has embarked at Rochefort and given himself up to a British Man of War. She has sailed with him for England. Cap^{n}. Maitland of the Bellerophon.

The Prussians carry the thing with a high hand, and in every house they occupy the owners keep a table for the Officers billeted on them – We generally attend any duty required early in the morning and then pass the day in Paris –

The Prussians were reviewed by the Emperors of Russia, Austria & King of Prussia. They assembled on the *Boulevard* with their right on the Place Louis Quinze, where the Sovereigns stood to see them pass in review order. Each Regiment as it moved played the downfall of Paris. The Men are fine young looking fellows, yet I think rather disfigured by the stuffing they use in their jackets to pad them out and swell out their chests –

The Prussians having played the downfall of Paris at their review an order was issued for the British Regiments wither to play God Save the King or the national air of their Country, applying the latter distinction to the Scotch. It is right to avoid these petty annoyances, the more so as nothing enrages the French more than the good conduct of our Army, thereby removing all plea for abuse from them to us –

The British Army was reviewed in about a fortnight. We formed along the road to Neuilly with our right on the Place Louis Quinze. The Artillery on the right, then the Cavalry in Line and the Infantry in close columns of Regiments. The Troops looked well. The foreigners particularly admired the Artillery – and also the Cavalry – The Infantry not being selected for any particular Corps (as in all their services) there was no Regiment distinguished above the rest and did not call for any particular comment. There is however a steady determined look in the clean shaved face of an English Soldier which we do not find in the Whisker'd Mustachio'd countenance of a Foreigner –

The Landwehr of Prussia (Militia) are very fine Troops – nearly equal to their Regts of the Line – It is said they kept up a considerable force under the name of Landwehr during Napoleons power, being restricted in treaties with him from having above a certain number of Troops in the pay of Government – Their Militia appear to be nearly equal to their Troops of the Line –

Order Book:

Regimental Morning Orders 8th July 1815

A Court Martiall to assemble at the Presidents Quarters at 11 o'clock

President Capt. Weyland

Lt Swinfen} { Lt Baker

Lt Beauchamp} Members { Lt Harris

All evidence to attend

Not with standing the above orders the Court Martial will sit at the Picquet Room

Hd Quarters Neuilly, 5th July 1815

GO The Comm^{r} of the forced has the greatest satisfaction in Communicating to the Army the thanks of the Houses of Lords & Commons for their conduct in the Battle fought on the 18th June –

Resolved *Nuncio Dissetante* by the Lords Spiritual & Temporal in parliament assembled that the thanks of the House be given to Genl his Royal Highness the Prince of Orange, Knight Grand Cross of the most honourable Military Order of the Bath Lieu$^{t.}$ Genl the Earl of Uxbridge Knight of the Grand Cross of the most honourable Military Order of the Bath Lord Hill Knight Grand Cross of the most Military Order of the Bath Sir Vincent [?] Clinton Knight Grand Cross of the most honourable Military Order of the Bath Chas Baron Altan Knight Comm^{r} of the most Military Order of the Bath Maj^{r} Genl Sir Jno Ormesby Vandeleur Knight Comm^{r} of the most honourable Military Order of the Bath Geo Coote James [...] Knights Comm^{r} of the Military Order of the Bath Sir [...] Danbury Knight Comm^{r} of the most Military Order of the Bath Sir Edward Baines Knight Comm^{r} of the most honourable Military Order of the Bath Sir Jno Byng Knight Comm^{r} of the most honourable Military Order of the Bath Sir Dennis Pack Knight Comm^{r} of the most honourable Order of the Bath Lord Edward Somerset Knight Comm^{r} of the most honourable Order of the Bath Sir Jno Lambert Knight Comm^{r} of the most honourable Military Order of the Bath Sir Colquhoun Grant Knight Comm^{r} of the most honourable Military Order of the Bath Peregrin Maitland Sir Colin Halkett Knight Comm^{r} of the most honourable Military Order of the Bath Frederick Adam Sir R.H. Vivian Knights Comm^{r} of the most honourable Military Order of the Bath and to the Several Officers under their Command of their indefatigable Zeal and Exertions upon the 18th June when the French Army commanded by Bonaparte received a signal & complete defeat. –

Die Lunae 25th *Junius* 1815

Ordered by the Lord Spiritual & Temporal in Parliament Assembled that his Grace the Duke of Wellington be requested to signify the said Resolution to them
Signed
George Rosen
Cler. Parlementum

Die Veneris 23rd *Junius* 1815

Resolved *Nuncio Dissetante* by the Lord Spiritual & Temporal in Parliament assembled that this house doth acknowledge and highly approve the distinguished valour and discipline displayed by the NC Officers & Private soldiers of his Majestys forces Serving under the Comm^{d} of Field Marshall the duke of Wellington in the Glorious Victory obtained on the 18th June.

Die Lunae 25th *Junius* 1815

Ordered by the Lord Spiritual & Temporal in Parliament assembled that the same be signified to them by the Commg Officers of the Several Coars [Corps] who are desired to thank them for their Gallant and exemplary Behaviour
Signed
G. Rosen
Cler. Parlementum

House Commons 25 June 1815

My Lord

I am commanded to transmit the unanimous thanks of this house to the Several Gen[l] Officers named in the inclosed resolution and the Officers serving under their Command for their indefatigable Zeal and Exertions upon that Memorable day Requesting your Grace to signify the same to all the officers therein named except Lieut. Gen[l] Sir H Clinton KGCB & Majr Gen[l] Lord Edw[d] Summersett KCB they being members of this house and at the same time I have to communicate to your Grace the unanimous Voate of this house acknowledging abd highly approving the distinguished Valour and discipline displayed by the NC Officers and Private Soldiers of his Majestys Forces Serving under your Graces Comm[d] in that Glorious Victory –

I am further commanded to transmit to your Grace the unanimous Resolution of thanks to the Gen[l] Officers, Officers and Men of the allied forces serving under your Graces immediate command for their distinguished Valour and intrepidity displayed by them in that hard-fought Battle –

I have the honor to Remain ever with the Sincerest Respect and devotion
My Lord your Gracious Majesties servant
Signed Chas Abbot

Veneris 23d Junius 1815

Resolved *nemine contradicente* that the thanks of this house be given to Gen[l] his Royal Highness the Prince of Orange Knight Grand Cross of the most honourable Military Order of the Bath Lieut. Gen[l] the Earl of Uxbridge KGCB Lord Hill KGCB Sir Henry Clinton KGCB Chas Baron Alten Knight comm[r] of the most honourable order of the Bath Maj[r] Gen[l] Sir J. Ormesby Vandeleur KCB Geo Cook Sir James Cook KCB Sir Wm Danbury KCB Sir Ed[w] Barnes KCB Sir Jn[o] Bing KCB Sir Dennis Pack KCB Lord Ed[w] Summersett KCB Sir Jn[o] Lambert KCB Sir Colquhoun Grant KCB Sir Colin Halkett KCB Frederick Adam Sir R.H. Vivian KCB and to the several officers under their command for their indefatigable Zeal and Exertions upon the 18th June when the French Army comm[d] by Bonaparte received a signal and complete defeat and that the Grace the Duke of Wellington be requested by Mr Speaker to signify the same except Lieut. Gen[l] Sir H Clinton KGCB and Maj[r] Gen[l] Lord Edwd Summersett KGCB being members of this house –

Resolved *Nemine Contradicente* that this house does acknowledge and highly approve the distinguished Valour & discipline displayed by his Majesties forces serving under the comm^{d} of Field Marshall the Duke of Wellington in the Glorious Victory obtained on the 18th June and that the same be signified to them by the Comm^{g} Offciers of the Several Coars who are desired to thank them for their exemplary behaviours –

Ordered that Mr Speaker do communicate the said resolution to Field Martiall the duke of Wellingtom

Signed
J. Dysan

A Tru Copey, A.D. [...] [...]

Signed
J. Waters Lieu$^{t.}$ Coln^{l}
A.A.G.

G O H^{d} Quarters Neuilly 6 July 1815

N°1 Lieu$^{t.}$ Genl the honourable Sir G Lowry Cole his appointed to the staff of this Army from the 24th May last and his to Command the 6th division of Infantry –

N°2 Maj^{r} Genl Sir Manley Power is app^{td} to the Comm^{d} of the II British Brigade

N°3 Captn Maud of the 4th Foot his app^{td} Maj^{r} Brigade till the Pleasure of his R. Highness the Prince Regent his known and is attached to the II Brigade of British Infantry –

N°4 Lieu$^{t.}$ Christie 5th Dragoon Guards is app^{td} Aid de Camp to Maj^{r} Genl Sir Dennis Pack

N°5 Ensigne Algernon Greville 1st Foot Guards his app^{td} to act as extra A D Camp to Maj^{r} Genl Sir Jno Lambert

N°6 Brevet Maj^{r} Johnson 71 Regt is app^{td} *Commandant* of Chautilly

N°7 Serg^{t} Matthew Bellingery 11th L^{t} D^{s} is app^{td} as Baggage Master to the Cavalry

N°8 Serg^{t} Wm White 40th Reg^{t} is app^{td} an Ass^{t} Provost Martial and attached to the 6th Division –

N°9 Serg^{t} Robt Arthur 4th Reg^{t} is app^{td} Baggage Master to the 6th Division

N°10 Serg^{t} Smith R Welch fusiliers is app^{td} ass Baggage Master to the 4th Division *vice* St Majr [...] killed in action

N°11 Officers on their arrival at a Military Station will invariably report themselves to the *Commandant*

Signed
J. Waters
Lt Col^{nl}
A.A.G.

A.G.O.
Neuilly 6 July 1815

Mem[m]
The sick of the several divisions are not to be sent to Gen[l] Hosp[l] until further orders

Signed
J. Waters
Lieu[t.] Col[nl] &
A.A. Gen[l]
A.A.G.

True Copey
M. Childers

Mem[m], Malmaison 8th July 1815

The Reg[ts] which is at Paris and which is directed to Relieve daily will always send a man to the Reg[t] which is to Relieve to Conduct it to the post it as to occupy

M. Childers
A.A.G.

BO
Courbevoie 8th July 1815

The 16th/or Queens/Light Dragoons will march to morrow morning at 6 o'clock to place Louis 15th to Relieve the 12th L[t] D[s] – it is Requested that the mens dinners may be cooked this day for to morrow
The daily state to be sent in before the march of the Reg[t] –

Signed
C. King
A.B.M

NB The Baggage not to move –

RO, Asnières 8 July 1815

For the day to morrow Lieut. Monkton
The Regt to march agreeable to BO of this day
Baggage Lead Horses & dismounted men to remain at this place

Paris 7th July 1815

General Orders
N[o]1 Major Genl Baron Muffling of ye Prussian Service has been appointed Governor of Paris by ye common accord of y[e] field Marshall & Field Marshall Prince Blucher

No2 The Allied Army under ye Command of ye Field Marshall are to occupy ye Posts and Barriers in 6 of the *mairies* on ye right of ye Seine; that is to say No 1, 2, 3, 4, 5, 76

No3 Col Barnard of ye 95th Regt is appointed to Command in those *mairies* under ye General Discretion of Major General Baron Muffling –

No4 Col Barnard is appointed to act as colonel on ye Staff till further Orders –

No5 Brevet Lieut. Col Auchmuty, 7th Royal Fusileers, is appointed an Assistant Adjut Genl till ye Pleasure of H.R.H. ye Prince Regent is known, and is attach'd to ye 6th Division of British Infantry –

A True Copy

Sign'd
J. Waters, Lt Colonel
A.A.G.

Genl Cavalry Orders, Malmaison 9th July 1815

In consequence of a following Extract of a Letter from Lt Col Scovell, Officers commanding Brigades and Regiments will be good enough to give him any assistance he may request, as to ye subject contain'd in ye Extract –

Paris 8th July 1815

Extract/– I am directed by ye Commander of ye Forces to request of ye Officers commandg Brigades of Cavalry in ye Vicinity of Places when ye Troops of that description may be Quartered, to relieve with sufficiently good men such parties of ye English *Gendarmerie* as I may require to be so relieved, and also to furnish such safe Guards or Patrols for ye preservation or Order and Discipline as may from time to time be required

Signed G. Scovell
Lt Col
True Copy
For ye actg A.G. Cavalry

Memm Regiments that have sent in requisitions for ammunition, will send a NC Offr and as many men as may be necessary to ye Offr Commdg ye reserve Artillery to receive it –

BO, Courbevoie 10th July 1815

In future ye Brigade Majors Orderly will be relieved every day at 3 o'clock and will bring with them ye daily state for ye following day –

RO Asnières 10th July 1815

For ye day tomorrow Cornet Polhill

The Reg^mt^ to be out in watering order tomorrow morning at 9 o'clock – Foot parade in Stable Dress with Side Arms at 4 in ye afternoon –

GO H^d^ Quarters Paris 8th July 1815

N°1 The pay masters of Reg^ts^ are to wait upon the pay master Genl to receive their Balances due upon there several estimates to the 24th June 1815

N°2 These Balances are to be paid to the troops in the mode pointed out by the Genl Orders of the 3d of June last

A True Copy Signed
J. Waters Lt Col^nl^
A.A.G.

BO Courbevoie 11th July 1815

Notwithstanding the Orders of this Morning the 16th Lt Drag^s^ will not Relieve the 12th Lt Drag^s^ to morrow Morning – but a Reg^t^ of Hussars on the following day

Signed
C. King
A.B. Maj^r^

Mem^m^
Malmaison 10th July 1815

The Majors of Brigades will transmit Daily to Cavalry Head Quarters all the letters returning them by the serg^t^ who comes to relieve the one waiting for Orders – who will arrive by 10 o'clock a.m. every day if the Reg^t^ or Brigade are not moving

Signed M. Childers
A.A.A. Genl

BO 11th July 1815

The Serg^t^ and Orderly Man for H^d^ Quarters will parade at the Brigade Maj^rs^ every morning at 7 oclcok – the 16th Lt Drag^s^ will march in sufficient time to relieve the 12th Lt Drag^s^ at 7 o'clock to morrow morning

Signed
C. King
A.B. Maj^r^

RO Asnières 11th July 1815

For the day to morrow Lt Wheeler

The Officer comm^{g} was extremely concerned to be under the necessity of resorting to the measure of ordering the Officer of the Guard of last night under arrest – in deffience of the Orders of the 7th Ins^{t} that Officer absented himself from his Quarters alledging as an excuse is having obtained another officer to perform is duties

Major Murray had no Idea that any Officer coming on Service would entertain the notion of such a practice being allowed in the Reg^{t} and requests that Officers and Cap^{ts} will take the trouble to instruct them in Military and Reg^{t} duties –

The following Certificate to be made by the Orderly Officer on the back of his Guard Report –

I certify to have made frequent visits throughout the Cantonments of the Regt where every thing was found regular (far as the case may be) that no wine as been allowed to be sold in the Village and that I have visited the wacking [waking?] men

The Reg^{t} to be out in Watering Order to morrow at 9 o'clock – Foot Parade in stable dress with side arms at 4 in the afternoon

Confidential, Adjut^{nt} Genl Office
Circular, Paris 11 July 1815

I am desired by his Grace the Duke of Wellington to inform you that as the Emperor and the King of Prussia have expressed a wish to see the British Troops it is his Graces Desire that you should take such measures as you may think most conducive to enable the Troops to appear in the best possible state of equipment

True Copy
Signed A.Childers
A.A.A. Genl

I have the Honor to be
Sir, y^{r} ob^{t} serv^{t}
Signed Jno Waters

Mem^{m} A return of Forge Carts in possession upto the 10th Ins^{t} to be sent in forthwith to Lord Grenock Ass^{t} Quart^{r} Master Genl

The Reg^{ts} undermentioned are to send an Non Commiss^{d} Officer forthwith to St Dennis for the portable Forges sent from England

11th Lt Dragoons
12 do do

Signed M. Childers
A.A.A. Genl

BO 12th July 1815

Officers Command^{g} Regiments will take the necessary Orders for the good appearance of their respective Corps

The 16th Lt Dragoons will march to morrow morn^{g} in sufficient time to relieve the Hussar Regiment of the 6 Brigade at 7 o'clock at there old Post

Signed C. King
A.B. Major

R Ord^{s}, Asnières

For the Day tomorrow Lt Swinfen

The Regt to parade in march^{g} order tomorrow morn^{g} at 1/2 past 5 o'clock for the purpose of relieving a Hussar Regiment on duty at Paris –

The sore-backed and lame horses to be out in watering order –

Head Quarters Paris
Genl Orders, 11th July 1815

N°1 Lt Genl Lord Combermere is to command the cavalry of the Army date of appointm^{t} 25th June

N°2 Captain Shakespear 10th Hussars is appointed Aid de Camp to Lt Genl Lord Combermere from the date of the Lt Gen^{ls} appointment

N°3 Brevet Major Wade of 42 Reg^{t} and Lieut. Stewart of the 11th Lt Dragoons are appointed Aids des Camps and Cap^{tn} Hutchardson 78 Regt extra Aid de Camp to Lt Genl Sir G Lowry Cole from the 24th May last –

N°4 Lt Macpherson 21st Reg^{t} Foot is appointed Major of Brigade until the pleasure of His Royal Highness the Prince Regent is known and is attached to the 9 British Brigade of Infantry date of appointment the 17 June –

N°5 Serj^{t} Myer of the 1st Regt of Light Drag^{ns} K. German Legion to be appointed an Ass^{t} Provost Martial to the Cavalry date of appointment 29th June

Signed
Jno Waters Lt Coll^{l}
A.A.G.

GC Ord Malmaison 13th July 1815

N°1 Captain Frazer 7th Hussars is appointed to act as Major of Brigade to the 6 Brigade until further orders

Captn Shakespear is app^{td} Aid de Camp to Lt Genl Ld Combermere

N°2 Captn Fenton North British Dragoons is app^{td} to act as *Commandant* at the Cavalry Depot Chantilly he will proceed there and take Command forthwith

N°3 Officers Command^{g} Brigades will be pleased to send in as soon as possible to the Acting Ass^{t} Adj^{t} Genl the names of Officers who Commanded Reg^{ts} and of those who succeeded to the Command in the Battle of Waterloo

Signed
M. Childers
A.A.A. Genl.

BO 13th July 1815

The serj^{t} and orderly for Head Quarters of the 16th Lt Drgs will parade at the Brigade Majors at 7 o'clock to morrow morn^{g}

Signed
C. King
A.B.M.

Head Quarters Paris
13th July 1815

Extract
Memorandum

The emperor of Austria will receive the Genl Officers of the allied Army, Officers Command^{g} Brigades and Genl Staff to morrow at Twelve the Field Martial requests they will assemble at his Quarters at half past eleven –

Signed
J. Waters
A.A.A. Genl

Asnières 14th July 1815

Mem^{dm} The Horses Manes Tails &c to be trimmed and squar'd this afternoon and the whole of the Foot and Horse Appointments to be put in the best order possible previous to the Inspection

RO Asnières 14th July 1815

For the Day tomorrow Lt Lloyd

Officers Commanding Squadrons will inspect there squadrons in watering order tomorrow morning at 9 o'clock –

Foot parade in stable dress with side arms at 4 in the afternoon –

Circular 284, War Office 6th July 1815

Sir,

The naturel anxiety entertained by the Relatives of Officers and Soldiers on foreign service regarding their fate, having been much increased by the losses incurred by the recent Battle in Flanders, I am to desire that you will cause me immediately to be furnished with returns of the men of the Regm^{t} under your command who became non effective during the month terminated on the 24th *Ultimo* and to aquaint you that the same may be forwarded agreeably to the form enclosed, without reference being made to the state of effects and credits; it is however to be clearly understood that the usual casualty returns are to be prepared and transmitted with as little delay as possible –
I have the Honor to be

Sir
Your most Obed^{t}
Humble Servt
Palmaston [*sic*]

Officer Commanding
16th Reg^{t} Lt Drag^{s}
France

RO Asnières 15th July 1815

For the Day tomorrow} Lieu$^{t.}$ Nepean

The Troops to be out in watering order tomorrow morning at 5 o'clock –

Foot Parade in Full Dress with side arms pouch belts & haver sacks at 10 o'clock –

Mem^{o} one man p^{r} troop to be recommended for L^{c} Corp^{l} –

The Commanding officer felt very much for the credit of the Regiem^{nt} in the Complaint preferred by Monsr de Prone [?] of this village against the officer quartered in his house his conduct was so very reprehensible that the Commanding Officer would be deficient in his duty if he did not reprobate such an example offered to the Dragoons in the strongest terms –

He desires the adj^{t} will see that this officer removes from Monsr de Proney's [?] House immediately

General Cavalry Orders Malmaison 14th July 1815

N°1 Lt Genl Lord Combermere feels very proud of the Honour which his Grace the duke of Wellington has conferred upon him by appointing him to the command of the Cavalry –

N°2 the Lt General has heard with the greatest satisfaction the unqualified praise & admiration which the British Cavalry merited by their gallant conduct on the Glorious 18th of June under their late distinguished Commd^{r} the cause of whose temporary loss to the service has [...] with the whole Army must regret –

3 Lt G^{l} Combermere has to lament the loss of many brave officers & soldiers who fell upon the 18th of June many of whom he has had the Honour to Command and to whose Zeal & Gallantry he has upon many occasions felt so much indebted –

4 The Orderly Hour will be at 12 o'clock

Me^{d} –

The effects & Horses of the Maj^{r} Beane of the R. H. A. will be sold at Columba at 1 o'clock on monday next

Signed M. Childers
A.A.A. G^{nl}

A. G^{l} Office, H. Guards 5 July 1815

List of promotions & appointments –

11 Lt Dragoons

Cornet Barton P Brown to be Lt without purchase *vice* Binney promoted 22d June 1815 –

16th Lt Dragoons

Ensign George G Tuite from the 97th Foot to be Cornet by purchase *vice* Harris promoted –

Hospital Ass^{t} Denis Murry to be Ass^{t} Surgeon *vice* Evans resigned

Sigd H. Jarvis

True Copy
Signd J. Waters Lt Colonel A.A.G^{l}

Asnières 16th July 1815

RO For the Day tomorrow – Lt Harris

Private J^{no} Hall of A Troop is appointed Corp^{l} in the same *vice* Hodgson reduced for repeated neglect of duty. Private Chambers of H Troop is appointed Corp^{l} in the same *vice* Pat Riding by the sentence of a regimental Cort Martial

Private Thos Rytes of F Troop is appointed Corp^{l} in the same *vice* Lewis reduced for drunkenness & unsoldierlike [conduct]

The above appointments are until further orders and to take date from the 6th Ins^{t} Inclusive

Officers Commanding Squadrons will inspect their squadrons in watering order tomorrow morning at 9 o'clock – Foot Parade in stable dress with side arms at 4 o'clock in the afternoon

RO Asnières 17th July 1815

For the Day tomorrow Lt J. Luard

Officers Commanding Squadrons will inspect their squadrons in watering order tomorrow morning at 9 o'clock

Foot Parade with side arms at 4 in stable dress at 4 in the afternoon

All Watch Setting reports to be collected by the St Maj^{r} and given to the Orderly Officer every evening who will state the same in his report to the Commanding Officer

RO Asnières 18th July 1815

For y^{e} day tomorrow Lieu$^{t.}$ Monckton

Off^{rs} Command^{g} Squadrons will inspect their respective squadrons in watering order tomorrow morning at 9 o'clock –

Foot parade with side arms in stable dress at 4 in y^{e} afternoon

RO Asnières 19th July 1815

For the Day tomorrow –

The Detachments to be out in Watering Order tomorrow morning at 9 o'clock –

Genl Orders

N°1 Lieu$^{t.}$ y^{e} Honble Augustus Stanhope, 12th L^{t} D^{gns} and Lieu$^{t.}$ Robert Webb, 3rd Dragoons, are appointed Aides de Camp to Lieu$^{t.}$ Genl Lord Combermere untill y^{e} pleasure of His Royal the Prince Regent in known -; date of appointment 25th June last –

N°2 Lieu$^{t.}$ Chas Wyndam, half-pay, is appointed extra Aide de Camp to Major Genl Sir Denis Pack –

N°3 Cap^{tn} King 16th Lt Dragoons is appointed Major of Brigade, untill y^{e} pleasure of H.R.H. The Prince Regent is known, and is attached to y^{e} 3rd Brigade of Cavalry; date of appointment 19th June past –

N°4 Lieu$^{t.}$ Boldero 14th Foot, as appointed a deputy Assistant in y^{e} Adju^{t} Generals Department until y^{e} pleasure of H.R.H. the Prince Regent is known

Sign'd J. Waters Lt col
A.A.G.

N^{o} General Orders on 17th Ins^{t}, Head Quarters

General Orders, Paris 18th July 1815

N°1 (Birch Mayor) A common Council holden in ye Chamber of ye Guildhall of ye City of London, on Friday ye 7th day of July 1815

Resolved unanimously that ye thanks of this Court be given to General H.R.H. ye Prince of Orange Knight Grand Cross of ye most Honble Military Order of ye Bath: Lieut. Generals ye Marquis of Anglesey KGCB Lord Hill KGCB Sir Henry Clinton KGCB Charles Baron Alten, Knight Commander of ye most honourable Order of ye Bath, Major Generals Sir John Ormsby Vandeleur KCB George Cook, Sir James Kemp KCB, Sir Wm Dornberg KCB Sir Edwd Barnes KCB Sir John Byng KCB Sir Denis Pack KCB Lord Edwd Somerset KCB Sir John Lambert KCB Sir Colquhoun Grant KCB Peregrine Maitland, Sir John Halkett KCB Frederick Adam, Sir R.H. Vivian KCB and to ye several Officers under their Command for their Indefatigable Zeal and exertions upon ye 18th June when the ye French Army commanded by Bonaparte received a signal and complete Defeat and that His Grace the Duke of Wellington be requested to signify ye same to ye Officers above named –

Signed
Woodthorpe

(Birch Mayor)
A common Council holden in ye chamber of ye Guildhall in ye City of London on Friday ye 7th day of July 1815

Resolved unanimously that this Court do most warmly admire & thank ye NC Officers & Private Soldiers under ye command of F M ye Duke of Wellington, for ye distinguished Valour & discipline displayed by them in ye glorious Battle of ye 18th June & that His Grace be requested to cause this vote to be signified to them by ye Commanding Officers of ye several corps

Signed
Woodthorpe

Circular No 224 War Office 25 April 1815

Sir

I have the honor to signify to you His Royal Highness Pleasure in the name & on ye behalf of His Majesty, that in future whenever an Officer shall prefer a claim in this Country, on account of a loss which he may have sustain'd on foreign Service, he shall (unless he shall have been taken Prisoner, & shall come hence instead of returning to ye Station where he was taken) produce to ye Board of Claims a Certificate from ye General Officer Commanding on the Station where ye loss shall have taken place that no indemnification has been, or will be granted under his orders for ye loss in Question; and, that he is not aware of any objection to ye Officer receiving such allowance for his loss, as may upon investigation appear to be fair & reasonable –

I am to add to these H.R. Highness Orders are to take effect from ye day on which they shall be given out in General Orders, by ye General Officer Commanding ye Forces under whom you are serving –

To Officers
Commandg Regts

I have ye honor to be Sir,
Your most obedt humble Servant
Synd [*sic*]
Palmerston

N°3. The 23rd Regt are to be in Major General Sir M Powers Brigade, in ye 6th Division

N°4. The 30th Regiment are to be in ye 4th British Brigade in ye 4th Division –

N°5. Col. Sir C Belson, and Sir Chas Greville are appointed to act as Colonels on ye Staff till ye pleasure of H.R.H. ye Prince Regent in known –

N°6 – Col. Sir C Belson is appointed to Command Major Genl Sir C Halketts Brigade in ye 3rd division till further orders –

N°7. The 12th, 36th & 64th Regiments are to be ye 12th British Brigade & to be under ye Command of Colonel Sir C. Greville

Sign'd C. Barnes
A.G.

BO Courbevoie 20th July 1815

Major Genl Sir John Vandeleur will see ye 16th Lt Dragoons in Marching Order tomorrow morning at 8 o'clock on ye same ground on which he saw ye 11th & ye 12th this morning.

RO Asnières 20th July 1815

For ye day tomorrow} Cornet Nugent

The Regimt to be out in Marching Order without forage or corn tomorrow morning at 1/4 past 7 o'clock agreeable to ye above BO

The men to appear in Cap Lines, Feathers, & ye red facings outwards – The horses unfit to be rode to be out in watering order, & ye men leading them in Full Dress with Side Arms – Every man & horse must be on ye Parade –

Corp. Mowbury[14] of G Troop is reduced to ye ranks for drunkenness & unsoldierlike conduct from this day inclusive –

14 Corporal Mowbury does not appear on the Waterloo Medal Roll.

RO Asnières 21st July 1815

For the day tomorrow Cornet Ball

Cornet Ball is attached to Major Bellis Troop until further orders[15] –

Watering order tomorrow morn^{g} at 9 o'clock. Foot parade in stable dress with Arms at 4 in ye afternoon

GC Orders

N°1 Regimental returns are required to be sent in to Cavalry Head Quarters as soon as they can be accurately made out of ye number of dismounted men which will be required to join their respective Regiments so that each horse may be mounted –

N°2 The horses now at Brussels belonging to Regiments – as in No 5 of this Order are altogether without saddles, & ye return call'd for in No 1 must specify whether saddles can be furnished. Provided such horses should be order'd to join

N°3 The men at Brussels are nearly all without appointments or necessaries, and it is intended to send such men and horses of that Depot to England which cannot be appointed, or may not be required with their respective Regiments.

N°4 The return call'd for in No 1 must include ye remounts now on ye march to join, & likewise have in view ye men, horses, & appointments at ye depot at Chantilly –

N°5. State of Cavalry Detachments at Anderlecht near Brussels –

[Omitted table: 'State of ye Cavalry detachments at Anderlecht, near Brussels']

[Omitted table: 'Return of ye Horses considered unfit for H.M. Service']

N°7 Lieut. Col. Ellis of ye 6th Dragoons/Inniskillings/will be pleased to take charge of ye 2nd Brigade till further orders –

8 – Cap^{tn} Wallace 23rd Lt Dragoons is to act as Major of Brigade with ye 2nd Brigade untill further orders –

9 – All Official Letters for Cavalry Head Quarters must be addressed either to Co^{l} Sir John Elly or to Lt Co^{l} Lord Grenock according to ye nature of ye Communication

10 The Majors of Brigade are desired to establish more punctuality in ye arrival of ye orderly men with ye morning reports & communications of ye day, as several do not arrive untill eleven o'clock – instead of ye ordered hour which is ten –

Memorandum

Found on ye 2nd July near Roissy a foreign Grey Horse whoever will give ye proper description of him may recover him by proper application to ye General Office of ye Cavalry

A Troop horse of ye 2nd Hussars KGL was lost while foraging on ye 10th Inst – Description

15 William Hawkins Ball had joined the regiment as a cornet on 27 October 1814. He was not present at Waterloo. Tomkinson (ed.), *Diary of a Cavalry Officer*, Appendix 1.

Bay mare 6 years old 14½ Hands, small star mark'd on ye off fore hoof 2 & on ye near fore foot & ye No 23 is cut on ye near shoulder & has a sore back on ye off side –

No letters for England will be received at Cavalry Head Quarters unless they are made up in a packet by each Regiment & transmitted by y^{e} Orderly of y^{e} Day on Mondays & Thursdays –

Majors of Brigade will take care that y^{e} directions contained in this paragraph are attended to

Sign'd J. Elly
Co^{l} – D.A.G.

RO Asnières 22nd July 1815

For the day tomorrow – Lieu$^{t.}$ Wheeler

Cornet Nugent will proceed tomorrow morning to Chantilly & relieve Lieu$^{t.}$ Osten on duty at that place –

The troops to parade for Divine Service tomorrow morning at 10 o'clock with side arms –

BO Courbevoie 22nd July 1815

Off^{rs} Command^{g} Regim^{ts} will be pleased to prevent irregular foraging – No party is to be sent out to collect forage or provision without an officer – The Commissaries will always point out ground on which forage or vegetable are to be taken – Individuals found disobeying this order will be punish'd as marauders

This order to be read to every Individual in ye Brigade & particularly to Off^{rs} Servants, Sutlers & Followers –

Letters for England will be received at ye Brigade Majors Office on Sunday & Wednesday by ye relieving orderlies

In future y^{e} attendance of an orderly only is required at Cavalry Head Quarters

All letters for England to be put up in a packet & docketed – Letters for England

Letters for Head Quarters or y^{e} Army may come separate

Sign'd
M. Childers
M.B.

RO Asnières 23rd July 1815

For the day tomorrow Lieu$^{t.}$ Swinfen

The Regt to assemble in complete Marching Order without forage or corn for the inspection of His Imperial Majesty the Emperor of Russia tomorrow morning at 1/2 past 5 o'clock

The men and horses left in will be in readiness to turn out on the return of the Reg^{t} in its present quarters in marching order for muster

RO Asnières 24th July 1815

For the day tomorrow Lieut. Baker

The Honourable Capt. Brown[16] will take the Command of Capt. Kings Troop and Lt Barra the Command of the late Capt. Buchanans Troop Lieut. Osten will do duty in Major Bellis and Lieut. Crichton in Capt. Tomkinsons Troop untill further orders –

The Troops to turn out to Water tomorrow morning at 7 o'clock

Foot Parade with side arms at 4 in the afternoon –

GO Paris Hd Quarters 22d July 1815

N°1 His Imperial Majesty the Emperor of Russia will see the allied Army under the Command of the Field Martial on Monday at 10 o'clock and it must be found for the purpose in the following order –

N°2 The British Cavalry with the Artillery attached with their right to the Champs Elyse [*sic*] and their left to the Bariere [?] Letaire [?] –

N°3 The Infantry with the Artillery attached with their right to the Triumphal Arch the left to the Bridge Neuilly Reserve Artillery will be on the left of the Infantry

N°4 The Cavalry attached to the Corps of Infantry to be formed in line behind the Infantry. That is Colnl Estaffs[17] Brigade behind the 2d Corps a Cavalry of the Netherlands behind the 1st Corps and the Brunswick Cavalry behind the 5th & 6th Divisions

N°5 British Cavalry will be formed in two lines and the Artillery attached to the Cavalry on the right of each Brigade the Guns will be formed as close to each other as possible and the Ammunition Waggons immediately in their rear and close –

N°6 The Infantry will be formed in close column of Battalion with their right in front –

with the Artillery attached to each division formed in Close Order on its right the Ammunition Carriages including those for Muskett Ammunition must be formed likewise in Close Order immediately in rear of those of Artillery

The bands and drums of each Battn are to be formed at close Order on the right of each Battn

N°7 The Second Corps must be on the right then the First Corps and then the 5th Division the 6th division Colnl Grevilles Brigade and Infantry of Brunswick Corps

N°8 The Reserve Artillery will likewise be formed at Close Order

16 Joined the regiment from half-pay on 30 March 1815. Not present at Waterloo. Tomkinson (ed.), *Diary of a Cavalry Officer*, Appendix 1.

17 Colonel Baron Estorff.

N°9 On the arrival of the emperor in front of the Cavalry Swords will be drawn and the Genl Salute will be given in the usual manner and Arms are to be carried when his Imperial Majesty will pass down the lines the bands &c playing God Save the King or the National tune of the Nation troops belong to –

N°10 those Battns that are of the number of 350 men and under that number are to be formed for this occasion 6 divisions those Battns of the strength from 550 men to 350 are to form for this occasion 8 divisions those of above 550 will form 10 divisions –

Those Battns of above 900 men will form 20 divisions

N°11 The British Cavalry are to march to their ground by the Bridge of Neuilly & will keep the pavement on their right till the come to the triumphal Arch where the will proceed to take up their ground –

N°12 The 5th & 6th Divisions and Brunswick Infantry and reserve Artillery will be ready to cross the road and take up their ground as soon as the British Cavalry will have passed Neuilly –

N°13 The Neatherland [*sic*] Infantry will Camp tomorrow evening in the Bast[ion?] at Bologne –

N°14 The Second corps will move out of the Bast of Bologne by the gate of Passey and thence to its ground –

N°15 The 1st Corps will move out of the Bast of Bologne by the port Maulatt [Maillot?] –

N°16 All Guards will be relieved tomorrow and all Safe guards are forthwith to be called in –

N°17 The Field Martial begs that the Officers may be dressed uniformly and if possible according to the Kings orders

N°18 Lieut. Colnl Belli[18] half-pay is appointed Asst in the department of the Qr M Genl from the 16 June 1815

True Copy — Signed
E. Barnes
A.G.

Malmaison 23d July 1815

GCO

N°1 A board of which Majr Genl Sir J.O. Vandeleur is President will assemble on Tuesday next at 10 o'clock a.m. at Carberry [Courbevoie?]

N°2 Detail of the Members

18 Not to be confused with Major Belli of the 16th.

1st Brigade	Capt. 1
2 do.	1 Field Officer
3 do.	1 Field Officer
6 do.	1 Captain

N°3 The duty of this Board is to Inquire into and Report upon the claims made by Farriers for an increased allowance and each member will ascertain the Prices which as been generally paid by the Farriers for coal and iron in this Country – by which the Board will be inabled to form an opinion what additional allowance shall be made

N°4 In Pursuance of the Gen[l] Orders of yesterday the different Brigades will move from their respective Cantonments at such hour as will enable them to pass the Bridge of Neuilly before 7 o'clock

Should the heads of any two Brigades arrive at the Bridge at the same time the senior Brigade will take precedence the other forming in column under the Avenue by the Road side and halting till the first as passed –

The horse Artillery unattached will pass the Bridge before any Brigade except the 1st & 2nd Should the happen to arrive at the same time otherways the will follow in the rear of any Brigade that may happen to be in their front to the ground upon which the line is to be formed-

N°5 The Cavalry and Royal Horse Artillery will be formed in two lines as directed by the Gen[l] Orders with the exception of the latter which will form in the manner hereof specified –

The different Brigades will be posted as follows –

1st Line on the Center of the paved road	
	In [?] Col[nl] Gardiner R.H. Artillery
Right upon the Place of	}1st Brigade
Louis the 15th left extending	}2 – do –
Towards L'Étoille de Champs Élysées	}
On the left of the 2d Brigade and	}Maj[r] Bulls troop R.H. Artillery
Extending across L'Étoille de Champs Élysées	}Captn May [?] – do –
As close Order as possible	}Captn McDonalds – do –
	}The Rocket Troop
On the left of the guns of the Centre	}3d Brigade
And Extending to the Barrière L'Étoille	}7 – do –
	}Lieu[t.] Col[nl] H. Smith troop R.H.A.

N°6 Second line in rear of the first in the Avenue

4 Brigade 5th & 6th Brigades should there not be sufficient space for the whole troops named and the horse Artillery in the 1st Line the 7th Brigade will form on the left of the 6th Brigade in the 2d Line –

N°7 All the Brigades with the exception of the 3d will move to the ground right in front – the 3d Brigade left in front after passing the Barrier de L'Étoille –

Brigade open columns of divisions will be formed in the order specified under the trees on the left of the road in readiness to move into alignment when taken –

N°8 The Officer Comm^g the 5th Brigade will Communicate immediately with the Officers in charge of Pontoon Bridges at Chatou & Argenteuil and endeavour to get one of them established in time for the Brigade to pass the river in the morning –

Should there however be the least doubt on this subject and either of their Bridges not be passable by this evening the 5th Brigade must move today by the Bridge of St Germain and barrier [...] in the Common of Marliu [?]

At all Events Comm^g Officers of Brigades must take the greatest care that every thing must be across the bridge of Neuilly before 7 o'clock a.m. –

N°9 The 3d Brigade must march so as to arrive on the ground when the lines are formed by 8 o'clock in the morning

N°10 Reg^ts will be in ranks closed in line and in passing by half-squadrons

N°11 The R.H. Artillery will be accompanied by all their ammunition waggons and spare carriages

Signed
J. Elly Col^nl
D.A. Genl

BO Courbevoie – 23rd July 1815

The Brigade will assemble on the ground below Courbevoie near the river at 6 o'clock a.m. and form in Reg^t column of 1/2 squadrons at 1/4 distance in marching order baggage & forge carts left in –

Signed
M. Childers Lt Coln^l
M.B.

RO Asnières 25th July

For the day tomorrow Lieu^t. Beauchamp

Each man to be charged 5/ in the accts to the 24th June 1815 towards payment for a pair of overalls agreeable to his Majesties Regulations after which the accts to be closed tomorrow for the above period and the balance paid to them agreeable to GO 3d June 1815

The undermentioned men to be trooped as follows *viz* Philip Schooby & Wm Late to Captⁿ Weylands troop & Izack [?] Davis in Captⁿ Kings troops and take date for this day of July inclusive

Memᵐ The horses of the late Captⁿ Sandys and Lieuᵗ· Barton [Bertie] of the 12th Lt Drags to be sold by auction at Courbevoie tomorrow morning at 10 o'clock –

Watering order at 7 o'clock foot Parade under arms at 4 in the afternoon

BO Courbevoie 26th July 1815

The 16th Light Dragoons will relieve the Regt of the 6 Brigade on Paris duty tomorrow morning at the usual hour

A party of the 16th Lᵗ Dragˢ consisting of one Officer two Sergts two Corplls & sixteen men will march tomorrow morning to Lagny on the road to Coulommiers by Vincennes and through St Denis sur Marne to relieve the Officer of the 12th and the party of the Brigade that is there stationed this party will take rations with them for three days and will be supplied by the Mayor of Lagny for the remaining three days of the week as this party is relieved weekly the Officer will receive his instructions from the Officer of the 12th and will report by him to the Major of Brigade weather there is any difficulty in procuring provisions

Signed M. Childers
M.B.

RO Asnières 26 July 1815

For the day tomorrow Lieut. Lloyd

The troops will turn out in marching order tomorrow morning at 1/2 past 5 o'clock with one days provisions & forage to relieve a Regt on duty at Paris – the horses unfit to be road will be out in watering order –

A detail from the following troops will be in Rediness to march to Lagny at the shortest notice

	Officers	Sergts	Corpls	Privates	Horses
A			1	2	3
C		1		3	4
D	1	1		3	4
F				4	4
G				2	2
H			1	2	3
Total	1	2	2	16	20

Officer for the above duty Lieut. Swinfen this detach will be selected on the parade tomorrow morning

Circular, Horse Guards 8th July 1815

I have the honor to enclose for your information & guidance a copy of a proclamation which his R. Highness the Prince Regent in the name and on behalf of his Majesty has been pleased to issue requiring that all soldiers serving in the Army for limited period shall in consequence of the recommencement of hostilities may remain for the further turn of 3 years after the expiration of such limited periods respectively and I have the Comm^r Chiefs Commands to desire you will be pleased to explain to the men under your orders that it is only in consequence of the unexpected renewal of hostilities that the Prince Regent as considered it expedient to have recourse to this measure in conformity to the provisions of the Act of Parliament –

It is the same time to be understood that the enclosed proclamation does not apply in the case of soldiers whose engagement expired previous to the 2d June (The date of the Parliamentarian) and whom from having been [...] or from peculiar circumstances of the service may have been prevented receiving their discharges

I have the honor –
&c &c &c
Signed
H. Calvert
A.G.

To the Officer
Comm^g the 16th L^t D^s

Copy

By his R. Highness the Prince of Wales George P.R. – Regent of the United Kingdom of Great Britain and Ireland in the name of and on behalf of his Majesty

A proclamation

Whereas [?] soldiers now serving in his Majestys Army under the provisions of the Muting Act passed in the 46th year of His Majestys Reign Chapt^r 66th and of another Act passed in the 47th year of His Majestys Reign Chapter 32d & in another Act passed in the 48th year of His Majestys Reign Chapter 15th and of another Act passed in the 49th year of His Majestys Reign chapter the 12th and of another Act passed in the 50th year of His Majestys Reign Chapter 7th and in another Act passed in the 51st year of His Majestys Reign Chapter 8th & in another Act passed in the 52d year of His Majestys Reign Chapter 22d and in another Act passed in the 53d year of His Majestys Reign Chapter 17th and which said several Acts as severally and respectively intitled, an Act for Punishing Mutiny and desertion and for the better pay for the Army and their Quarters, Dated same time as the respective indictments engaged to serve His majesty for the Limited Periods –

Therein respectively expressed provided his Majesty should so long require the same and for such further time not exceeding 3 years (as should be directed by any Proclamation of his Majesty) provided always that the case of such direction the said additional period should termined [?] when ever 6 months of continual peace to be reckoned from the ratification of any definite treaty should have elapsed. Subsequent to the expiration of such limited periods and whereas the recommencement of hostilities renders it expedient to exercise the power vested in is Majesty of prolonging such period limited of services we have therefore thought fit the name and behalf of his Majesty & by & with the advice of his Majestys Privy Counsel to publish this proclamation and we do hereby direct that all soldiers now serving his M Army the [...] Battl^{ns} excepted who have been inlisted for such limited periods aforesaid shall continue the same therein for the period of 3 years after the expiration of such limited periods respectively provided always that the said additional periods that shall determine whenever 6 months of continual peace to be reckoned from the ratification of any definite treaty shall have relapsed subsequent to the expiration of such limited periods respectively

Given at the Court of Carlton House –

The 2d day June 1815 in the 55th year of his M. Reign

God Save the King

RO Asnières 28th July 1815

For the day tomorrow Lieu$^{t.}$ Luard

A Regt Court Martial to assemble tomorrow morning at 11 o'clock for the trial of all prisoners as may be brought before it

	President Captn Brown	
Lt Harris }		{ Lieu$^{t.}$ Leyton [?]
Cornet Baillie }	Members	{ Lieu$^{t.}$ McDougall
	All evidence to attend	

Comm^{g} Officers of Squadrons will inspect their squadrons in watering order tomorrow morning at 9 o'clock

Foot parade with arms at 4 in the afternoon

RO Asnières 29th July 1815

For the day tomorrow – Lt Harris –

The troops to parade for Divine Service tomorrow morning at 11 o'clock – all working men to attend –

Corp^{l} Thos Shooter of Major Bellis Troop is reduced to the ranks for unsoldierlike conduct from this day inclusive –

RMO – Asnières 30th July 1815

The billeting parties to parade at 1/2 past four o'clock a.m. and the Reg[t] to be in readiness to march off at 1/2 past 8 –

RO Asnières 30th July 1815

For the day tomorrow Lt Mockton

The Troops to march tomorrow morning from their present quarters precisely at 1/4 before 8 o'clock & assemble at Inauces [?]

The Baggage & led horses to march off at the same time –

The billeting party to assemble at Marein [?] at 1/2 past 5 o'clock tomorrow morning

RO Chaumount [en Vexin] 31st July 1815

The Troops to assemble tomorrow morning on the main road leading to Gournay [en Bray] at 7 o'clock

Baggage & led horses to parade at the same time

L[t] Swinfen will proceed tomorrow morning to Chantilly agreeable to BO of this day

Tomkinson:

July 31st. Forage becoming scarce the greater part of the Cavalry was ordered away from Paris to the neighbourhood of Neuchatel – 5 Days march – The 16th occupied Aumale – The inhabitants expected the same treatment from the British thay had heard of the Prussians exercising in many Towns they had occupied, and were rather alarmed on hearing any Troops were moving to their neighbourhood – I found in the House I was billeted, a dinner prepared and every attention – We soon established a Mess at our own quarters and were on the best of terms with the Inhabitants –

Whilst at Aumale Lord Harcourt came out from England and reviewed his Regiment on his way to Paris. He was much delighted and could only observe that he never expected to have reviewed his Regiment in France.

Order Book:

RO Aumale 3d Aug[st] 1815

The Troops to be out in watering order tomorrow afternoon at 3 o'clock every horse to be present

RO Aumale 4th Augt 1815

For the day tomorrow {L[t] Monckton

The Troops at this place *viz* F G & H will be out in marching order tomorrow morning at 7 o'clock

Capt. Tomkinsons Troop will march tomorrow morning at the most convenient hour & occupy the villages of Barques & Marques untill further orders Major Bellis Troop to occupy the villages of Villers & Haudricourt Capt[n] Swetenhams Troop the villages of Ellecourt & adjacents

Copy, Circular no 287

69823, War Office 31st July 1815

Sir,

The Prince Regent having taken into consideration y[e] distinguished Gallantry manifested upon all occasions by y[e] Officers of y[e] British Army, and having more particularly accounts to the conspicuous valour displayed by them in the late glorious victory gained near Waterloo, by the Army under the Command of Field Marshall, the Duke of Wellington, & His Royal Highness being desirous of testifying the strong sense entertained by him of their devotion to His Majesty's Service I have the honor to acquaint you that his Royal Highness has been pleased to order

1st that the regulations under which pensions are granted to wounded officers shall be [...] & that the pensions which has been or may be granted to officers for the loss of an eye or limb or for wounds certified equally injurious with the loss of a limb shall not be confined to the assessment [?] attached, by the scale to the Rank which the officer held at the time when he was wounded, but shall progressively increase according to the rank to which such officers may from time to time be promoted – The augmentation with regard to the pensions of such officers now upon the list beginning to take date from the 18 June 1815 inclusive.

2nd that every subaltern officer of infantry of the line who served in the Battle of Waterloo or in any of the actions which immediately preceded it shall be allowed to count 2 years service in virtue of that victory in reckoning his service for increase of pay given to Lieutenants of 7 years standing and every such subaltern will there fore be entitled to the additional shilling a day whenever he should have served 5 years of Lieu[t].

3rd That this regulation shall be extended to every Subaltern of cavalry and to every Ensign of Foot Guards who served in the above mentioned actions and every such Subaltern and Ensign will therefore be entitled to an additional shilling a day after 5 years service as a Lieu[t.] in the Cavalry or as an Ensign in the Guards.

His Royal Highness being also desirous of thanking his sense of the distinguished Bravery displayed by the NC Officers & Soldiers of the British Army in the victory of Waterloo as been most graciously pleased to order that henceforward every NC Officer, Trumpeter, Drummer & Private Man who served in the Battle of Waterloo or in any of the actions which immediately preceded it shall be bourne upon the Muster Rolls and Pay Lists of their respective Corps as Waterloo Men and that every Waterloo Man shall be allow'd to count 2 years service in virtue of that victory in reckoning his services for increase of pay or for pension when discharged.

It is however to be distinctly understood that this indulgence is not intended in any other manner to effect the conditions of their original inlistment or to give them any right to their discharge before the expiration of the period for which they have engaged to serve.

The Duke of Wellington has been requested to transmit the Returns of Subaltern Officers to whom these orders may be considered by His Grace to apply together with the accurate Muster Rolls containing the names of the 'Waterloo Men' in each Corps, such Muster rolls being to be preserved in this office as a record honourable to the individuals themselves, and as documents by which they will at any future time be enabled to establish their claim to the benefits of this regulation.

I have great pleasure in communicating these instances of the Prince Regents gracious consideration of the Army & request that you will be pleased to take the earliest opportunity of announcing the same to the Officers and men of the corps under your Command.

I have the Honor to be
[? ? ?]
Signed
Palmerston

Officer Comm^{g}
16 LD

Luard:[19]

Marques – 1/2 a league
From Aumale
August 5th 1815

I shall address this to you my Dear Louisa: for I find a letter of yours bearing date May 4th & I do not remember writing to you since the receipt of it – the latest I have from Northampton was penned by me Dear Mother on the 16th of July, & received by me a few days before we marched from Asnières – we left that place with regret on the 30th & marched to Pontoise 31st Chaumont [en Vexin] 1st August Gournay [en Bray] 2d Forges [les Eaux] 3d thro Neufchatel [en Bray] to Aumale where 3 troops remain, & 3 are in small villages in the vicinity – Tomkinsons Troop in which I am,

19 Luard Family Archive, Letter 407, John Luard to his sister, 5 August 1815.

arrived here this morn^{g} & we are comfortably fixed up considering the secluded situation of the village & the hardship of the Country – The 11th occupy Neufchatel & our Cavalry so cantoned all around Rouen I do not know yet where George is, but shall soon learn, I fear not near enough to meet often – I am only 10 leagues – about 25 English miles from Dieppe which place I intend to see one of these days – don't be surprised if I take a trip to Brighton & back for it is but 14 or 15 hours passage – it is possible you may see me at Northampton, but not probable –

Of course we were sorry to leave the Gaieties of Paris we were delightfully situated for them we mounted our horses after dinner & rode to see some spectacle or saw the lions in the morning & returned to dinner by which we avoided being cheated at a rascaly restauranteurs George & myself met there often. –

The Great Emperor Tyger has at last arrived at Plymouth, I certainly think his political life is finished for I believe that St Helena will be perfectly secure – Thus My Dear Loui has fallen our great Military Friend, the [...] enemy of England. –

I am sorry you have lost the 5th D^{gn} G^{ds} – there are some excellent fellows in the Reg^{t} – I have not the happiness of hearing that sweet little man Mr Watson – but it appears he has made dreadful havoc at Northampton amongst the fair sex –

I hope Jenny is again stout – it grieved me much to lose her mameduke[20] she was the sweetest little Animal I ever had I had refused £40 for her frequently – Our claims are not yet gone in & it is yet doubtful if we shall be allowed our losses for our Noble Duke is not [page torn] out of the field I confess I think he [page torn] sufficiently regret that Army which has gained him every thing – the Battle of the 18th was gained as much by British perseverance as Albuera – I am convinced had the Duke commanded any other Troops they would not have held their ground.

The Prussians have stripped the Louvre of some of their own paintings – I have not heard that the Prince of Orange intends taking his – I think he ought – if so he would take the better part of the paintings from the gallery – as much as from the Luxembourg – he has taken from the Hospital des Invalides the models of all the Frontier Towns –

In spite of all reports respecting Col^{l} Hay many of which appear to have been well founded, particularly that relating to his death, I am extremely happy to say that he is now allowed by the medical men to be out of danger – Tomkinson has written to England for his Dogs & Gun & I wish my Gun to come by the same conveyance – I will thank Charles to open the case (my mother has the key) & See that it is properly cleaned & has every thing complete – that there are plenty of Flints & powder & shot sent with it to Lt Luard – 16th D^{gs} Hughes's Livery Stables, Bruton Mews, Bruton Street London – to be left till Captn Tomkinsons Servant calls for it –

Give my love to H[21] & do tell her I fear I cannot fulfil my promise of dancing with her at the Race Ball but hope to do so in the Winter – I think it most probable

20 This may be Luard's horse, killed at Waterloo.
21 *H* may be Aunt Harriet Spooner, née Luard (d. 1833).

we shall remain here for 3 or 4 months – There is some Game here & Tomkinson & myself intend to frighten them extremely – there are also Trout in a neighbouring stream, but the season is past – This is not a good part of the Country & the people are ill disposed we therefore treat them more as conquerors than we used – Indeed it appears the intention to humble them a little, for we draw our rations without paying for them & they are very much astonished to find they are not treated as they were last year when we marched thro – We thrash a Mare now and then which makes a whole department civil. – My detestation of the national character is not lessen'd – You must have been very gay lately in Abington Street I do not recollect Miss Booth[22] but should like to be acquainted & to see her [...] productions

I wrote to Charles last a few before we left Asnières & invited him there to come to us, but said he would have no amusement – I shall get into the *Diligence* one of these days to go to Rouen a Town I believe worth seeing – as well as Amiens & Dieppe – If Charles has a mind to see how we live – he has nothing to do but put himself onto the Packet Boat at Brighton – it will cost him a Guinea & it will take him to Dieppe & from there to Aumale a dist[ce] of 25 miles he will go in the *Diligence*[23] for a few *Francs* – George would perhaps give him better quarters than I could – but however he could sometimes be with me & sometimes with the other & I need not say how happy we would be to see him. – I should think he could put up with one Trunk of Cloaths & I could carry that for him when we marched – but however there is nothing alluring in the offer for we lead a very stupid life –

I must now ride into Aumale to learn the news – My most affect wishes always attend you all, my dear Loue that every happiness may be your lot is the prayer of your affec[te] Brother

John Luard

Order Book:

RO Aumale 8th Aug[t] 1815

Private Caleb James of G Troop is appointed Corpl in the same untill further orders, Nick Mowbury reduced for drunkenness & unsoldierlike conduct from the 25 July 1815 inclusive.

Head Quarters Paris 3rd Aug[t] 1815

General Orders

N°1 At a General Court Martial assembled at Ath on y[e] 17th May 1815 by virtue of a warrant from Field Marshall His Grace y[e] Duke of Wellington KG & GCB Commander of y[e] forces &c &c &c, and continued by adjournments untill 14th

22 *Miss Booth* is probably Miss Sarah Booth (1793–1867), dancer and actress.
23 A French coach.

July 1815, & of which Col Du Plat 4th line Batt^{n} KGL was President & Cap^{tn} R. Glassing 95 Reg^{t} acting deputy Judge Advocate – Private John Can 95 Reg^{t} was arraigned upon ye undermentioned charge – *viz* –

For highly mutinous conduct in loading his rifle & declaring an intention of shooting ye first person who should attempt to put him in confinem^{t} at Luzee [?] on or about ye 20th day of May 1815

Opinion & Sentence

The Court having maturely considered ye Evidence against ye prisoner Private John Can together with what he has stated in his defence is of opinion that he is guilty of ye crime laid to his charge, & ye same being in breach of ye Articles of War doth sentence him ye Prisoner to receive a Punishment of One Thousand Lashes at such time & place as ye Commander of ye Forces may direct. Which opinion & sentence His Grace ye Commander of ye Forces has been pleased to approve & confirm

N°2 The Sentence of ye Court Martial on Private John Can, 95th Reg^{t} will be carried into execution on ye 6th Inst under ye Direction of ye Assistant Provost Martial attached to ye 2nd Division Infantry and in presence of such troops as can be conveniently assembled for that purpose.

N°3 The Commander of ye Forces begs ye Officers of ye Army will not go out shooting without leave of ye proprietor of ye Estate on which they may shoot and particularly on ye Royal Estate – ye Soldiers must not be suffer'd to go out shooting on any account.

N°4 The 3 Companies of ye 95th Reg^{t} under ye Command of Lt Col Guilmer [?], & ye 62nd Reg^{t} are placed in ye 12th Brigade of Infantry untill further orders.

Erratum of y^{e} Genl Orders of y^{e} 2nd Ins^{t} of N° 2 for Major Shaw 95th Regt read Major Shaw 43rd Regiment.

Sign'd
E. Barnes
A. Genl

Adju^{t} Genl Office

Paris 3rd Augt 1815
Horse Guards 26th July 1815
List of Promotions and Appointments
To be Lieu$^{t.}$ Colonel in y^{e} Army
Major G.H. Murray 16th Lt Dragoons

Date 18th June 1815

Sign'd
E. Barnes
A.G.

Mem^{m} Head Quarters, Paris 3rd Augt 1815

N°1 Soldiers who are entitled to be discharged under y^{e} authority of y^{e} A Gen^{ls} Circular Letter dated Horse Guards 8th July 1815 & addressed to Officers Command^{g} Regiments are to be sent to Ostend in conformity with ye following GO

N°2 Soldiers who have given themselves up as deserters and are entitled to a free pardon under ye Prince Regents Proclamation & do not belong to Reg^{ts} serving with ye Army & in like manner to be sent to Ostend – their accounts being settled up to 24th this month & their provisional discharges &c being sent to Lt Col Burton

Sign'd E. Barnes
A.G.

Head Quarters, Brussels 25th July 1815

All soldiers with ye British Regiments whose period of Service may from time to time expire are to be sent to Ostend without any further Orders – their provisional discharges & all other papers being at ye same time sent to Lt Col Gregory (now Lt Col Burton)

RO Aumale 9th Augt 1815

The Regiment to assemble in marching order on Friday next at 9 o'clock – A Subaltern of each of the out Troops will parade at the Adjutants quarters tomorrow morning at 11 o'clock to ascertain the ground on which the Troops are to be assembled.

Those Officers who are desirous of becoming Members of the Royal Military Club – the particulars of which are in the Orderly room, will leave their names at the Adjutants Office in the course of tomorrow morning.

RO Aumale 10th Augt 1815

The whole of the horse fit for duty to be mounted if possible – sick, sore-back'd & led horses to be left in.

The Troops at this place to march off at 1/4 past 8

RO

The Troops to be out tomorrow morn^{g} in watering order at Head Quarters at the following hours *viz*

F G & H Troops: at 1/2 past 9 o'clock
A C & D: at 10 o'clock

Head Quarters

General Orders, Paris 10th Augt 1815

N°1 H.R. Highness the Prince Regent in the name and on behalf of His Majesty, having been Graciously pleased by a warrant under His Sign Manual dated 17th *ultimo*, to grant to Field Marshal His Grace the Duke of Wellington, in trust for the British Army, which served under His Graces immediate Comm^{d} in Portugal, Spain, & France from ye Year 1809 to 1814 the sum of Eight Hundred Thousand Pounds for ye Ordnance, Army Stores, Magazines, Shipping, & other Booty captured by it from the Enemy during that period, & appropriated to the Publick Service, to be distributed according to the Provisions of the aforesaid warrant & the Agents appointed by His Grace on the part of the Army, to conduct & arrange the Business, having prepared & submitted to him the forms of prize lists necessary to be fill'd up by the different Departments & Corps, entitled to share in the said prize money, together with instructions for filling them up. It is hereby order'd that the said lists and instructions be forthwith circulated, fill'd up, & return'd with every possible dispatch, so as to enable the Prize Agents to pay over the money to the different persons entitl'd to receive it, with as little delay as possible.

N°2 Such of the Corps entitled to share, as now compose part of this Army, will return the lists for each of their respective payments as soon as completed, under cover to the Adju^{t} General of this Army, marking on the cover thereof the Corps to which they belong, & the numbers on the lists contain'd therein;

N°3 The paymasters or adjutants of the Regiments in or about Paris, will call on Mr Cambell at No 18 rue de Madelaine for the forms of the prize lists and any information they may require upon the subject.

Mr Cambell will be at home between the hours of eleven & three daily.

N°4 The 39th Regm^{t} is placed in the 12th British Brigade

True Copy — Sign'd E. Barnes
A.G.

GCO Malmaison Augt 11th 1815

N°2 The undermentioned sums having been charged by the Vitanry Surgeon Ship 23d L Ds and witnessed by Vitanry Surgeon Vincent of the 6th Lt Drags [Vincent was VS to 6th Dragoons]

Comm^{g} officers of Reg^{ts} are requested to take the necessary measures for reimbursing Vitanry Surgn Ship in the several sums expended in the cure of troop horses belonging to these Reg^{ts} – Viz –

1 Life Guards	2	4	9½
2 " Do	1	5	10½
R.H. Guards	1	10	5½
1 Dragn Do	1	2	3½
Royal Drags	3	6	3½
2 RNB Drags	4	18	6½
7 Hussars	2	3	"
10 Do	"	7	1½
15 Do	1	13	3
11 Light Ds	"	10	11
12 Do	"	14	7
13 Do	2	11	10½
16 Do	1	5	1
1 Hussars KGL	"	8	11½
	£21	5	2½

N°2 A representation having been made by the Officer Comm[g] the Royal Waggon Train of the extreme misapplication & abuse of the spring waggons attached to the Regts – Comm[g] officers of Regts are desired to refer to the Gen[l] Orders of the 13th [...] which particularly expresses that the waggons so attached are for the purpose of conveying 12 sets of hosp[l] bedding and the sick of the Reg[s]

N°3 Whenever damages may arise hereafter to the spring waggons so attached by a disobedience of the Gen[l] Orders describing the service the are to [...] the expense will fall upon the Reg[t] such Baggage so required may be attached to

Signed
J. Elley Coln[l]
D.A. Gen[l]

Tomkinson:

16th August. The procuring of Forage in the Town being rather troublesome my Troop moved to the Village of Marques, occupying some Farm houses around the Village. The Village only consisted of a Farm house, a poor old *Chateau* and a few Cottages –

Order Book:

RO Aumale 18th Aug[t] 1815

The troops to assemble tomorrow morning at 9 o'clock in marching order on the same ground as Friday last all horses fit for duty to [be] mounted Sick & Lame horses to be left in

Officers to appear in Pelices to march off at 20 minutes past 8 o'clock

RO Aumale 19 Augt 1815

The troops to parade for divine service tomorrow morning at 11 o'clock

The mens balance due on the 24 June last will be paid to them after parade tomorrow after which the accts to be closed to 24 July 1815 – and the balance paid to the NCO & Privates daily agreeable to the Genl Orders of the Army 5 shillings to be charged to each drag^{n} in the accts of 24 July in part of payment for pair of overalls

Officers Comm^{g} troops will be responsible for such sums stopped from each dragoon in part of payment for overalls.

Private Joseph Hobbs of Major Bellis Troop is appointed Corp^{l} in the same untill further orders *vice* Shouter reduced for unsoldierlike conduct the above apt to date from the 30th July 1815 inclusive.

G. Cavalry Orders Malmaison 20th Augt 1815

N°1 Lieut. Genl Lord Combermere desires the Instructions contained in the Adj^{t} Genl Office of which the follow is a coppy may be particularly attended to by the Staff Off^{rs} of each Brigade & the G^{l} Off^{r} Commanding are requested to observe whether the Staff Officer attached to their respective Brigades are acquainted with the principal on which all alignments should be determined.

Copy, H^{d} Quarters

Paris 15th Augs 1815

Sir I am desired by Field Martial Commanding the Army to desire that the staff off^{rs} and the Adj^{t} of the divisions under your command must be practiced in taking up alignments and distances for the formation of troops & also in prolonging of alignments for troop movements in column manoeuvres –

N°2The several brigades of cavalry may expect to be seen by Lord Combermere about the latter end of this month or early in Sept^{r}

Sigd J. Elley
Collonel A.A.G^{l}

RO Aumale 24 Augt 1815

The Regt to assemble in marching order tomorrow morning at 9 o'clock on the exercising ground near the H^{d} Qu^{t} – sick and lead horses to be left in – Off^{rs} not having Pelice [*sic*] will wear jackets without epaletes – the troops claims for kitts lost in action to be made out in duplicates by each troop and sent in to the adj^{t} office on the 26th ins^{t} by 10 o'clock –

RO Aumale 27th Augt 1815

A regimental Court Martial to assemble tomorrow at 12 o'clock at Head Quarters – for ye trial of all prisoners that may be brought before it

President Major Belli

Lieut. Lloyd }		{ Lieut. Luard
Monckton }	Members	{ Cornet Nugent
	All evidence to attend	

Memm

Major General Sir John O. Vandeleur will see ye Regiment in marching order on Sunday next ye 29th Inst – the place of assembly & hour will be made known to ye troops tomorrow –

Correct marching states will be sent in tomorrow afternoon at 2 o'clock – all horses fit to march to ye field will be out – Forge Carts to be left in.

RO Aumale 29th Augt 1815

The troops at Head Quarters and ye troops at Marque will assemble in watering order tomorrow afternoon at 3 o'clock – half way between head quarters and Marque –

RO Aumale 30th Augt 1815

The Commanding Officer forbids Private James Picket of Captain Tomkinsons troop being employ'd by any person otherwise than as a Dragoon.

RO Aumale 1st Septr 1815

The Regiment to assemble in marching order tomorrow morning at 9 o'clock on ye old exercising ground near this place – led horses to be left in – blue facings outwards –

Corpl Fitzpatrick of Captain Swetenhams troop is reduced to ye ranks for drunkenness & unsoldierlike conduct – from this day inclusive

GO Head Quarters Paris 14th Augt 1815

No1 The following letters are publish'd for general information

No2 Horse Guards 8th Augt 1815

My Lord Duke

As I perceive by ye return of ye 2nd Battn 81st Regt dated 21st *ultimo* that Captain Taylor is still reported 'Prisoner, at Ostend' I have deem'd it necessary to transmit to your Grace a duplicate of ye letter I have ye honor of addressing to your Grace on ye 19th June last

H. Calvert
A.G.

Field Marshall
Duke Wellington

Horse Guards 19th June 1815

Duplicate, My Lord Duke,

The Judge Advocate having submitted to ye Commander in chief ye procedure of a Genl Court Martial held for ye trial of Cap^{tn} P.G. Taylor of ye 81st Regim^{t} together with his report thereon (a copy of which is enclosed) and likewise a letter from your Grace dated 1st Ins^{t} H.R. Highness requests me to express to your Grace his regret that ye award of ye Court was not framed in terms more decisively declaratory of ye perfect acquittal of Captain Taylor, grounded on ye circumstances which demanded his interference, which unfortunately occasioned ye infliction of ye wound on Private James Rain 52 Regt. In wading [sic] over ye proceedings, ye Commander in Chief observes that certain men belonging to ye detachment under Captain Taylors command presumed to declare that they would not obey him, or any other officer, except those of ye Regim^{t} to which they immediately belong; H.R.H. cannot but consider that as a very great aggravation of ye crime for which they should be brought to trial, nor can he suppose that any soldier can be so ignorant of his duty as to imagine it is not equally incumbent on him to obey ye order of any officer under whose Command he may be placed to whatever Regiment ye Off^{r} may belong; If however your Grace may be of the opinion that such an idea is entertained by any part of ye troops under your command H.R. Highness recommends ye issue of a Genl Order explicitly and decidedly condemning so erroneous & so dangerous a principle.

Sign'd H. Calvert
A.G.

Cap^{tn} Taylor is to be released from his arrest and is to return to his duty –

The Field Marshall observes that it is contrary to Orders for ye Q^{r} Master of ye 12th Regim^{t} to carry his baggage on a waggon, & he desires ye Commanding Off^{r} of ye 12th Regiment to take care that this does happen in future –

GO N°1 Head Quarters Paris 14th Augt 1815

H.R.H. ye Prince Regent has been pleased to appoint Major Genl Lord Beresford to ye Staff of ye Army from ye 22nd June last –

N°2 Major Gabriel of ye 2nd or Queens Dragoons is appointed A D C to Major Gen Lord George Beresford –

3 – Brigade Major Humberg is appointed to do duty with ye 1st Brigade Infantry KGL –

4 –The prices to be charg'd against ye Troops for ye undermentioned articles of Equipment are fix'd as follows –

Camp Kettles with Bags for 6 men each	---------	3/
Do Do Do 4 do do	---------	2/
Shoes per Pair	---------	6/2

Sign'd E. Barnes
Gen.

GO N°1 Head Quarters Paris 21st Augt 1815

The 2nd & 3rd Dragoon Guards, & 3rd Dragoons, are to form ye 8th Brigade of Cavalry & to be under ye Command of Major General Lord Beresford –

N°2 Major Dunbar 66th Regim^{t} is appointed a Brigade Major upon ye Staff of ye Army from 25th June last –

N°3 Brigade Major Dunbar is attached to ye 8th Brigade of Cavalry –

4. The 3rd Batt^{n} 27th Regim^{t} is to attached to ye 12th Brigade of Infantry untill further orders –

Ensign Hanley 40th Regiment is appointed to act as Town Adjutant of Brussells – *vice* Shraeder resign'd

Signd E. Barnes
– A.G. –

GO Head Quarters Paris 24th Augt 1815

N°1 The 1st & 2nd Brigade of KGL are hereafter to form one Brigade & to be in ye 3rd Division –

N°2 The 5th British Brigade is hereafter to consist of ye 3rd, or Buffs – the 12th Reg^{t} – 1st Batt^{n} 33rd 2nd Batt^{n} 30th and to be in the [blank] Division

N°3 The 4th British Brigade is hereafter to consist of ye 1st Batt^{n} 5th 14, 51, & 69th Reg^{t} –

Clarks of Troops will keep a book & enter daily the supplies the may Receive from the Commissary which book will be Coaled for by the Regimental Quarter Master when he thinks necessary –

An account of Provisions & Forrage received by a troop from the 16th June 1815
Form

[Column Headings]

Dates – No of Men – No of Horses – Pounds of Bread or Biscuit – Pounds of Meat – Pounds of Corn – Pounds of Long Forrage – Pints of Spirits or Wine – Remarks

[Dates listed are 16th June to 30th June inclusive. There are no entries.]

A Return to be given in tomorrow Evening Ac. Qr. Mr. Harrason of what the have rec'd since the 16th June 1815

[The following entries in the order book follow on from the above, but are clearly out of date order.]

Memm Courbevoie 21st July 1815

The Horses & effects of y[e] late Cap[tn] Sandys and Lieu[t.] Bertie 12th L. Dragoons to be disposed of on Saturday 22nd July at 2 o'clock at y[e] Bridge at Courbevoie

[Continues from GO N[o]3, Head Quarters Paris 24th Aug[t] 1815, with page turned upside down.]

N[o]4 The 12th British Brigade is to consist of y[e] 38th, 73rd, 41st & 36th & to be in y[e] 2nd Division

N[o]5 The 4th Batt[n] Royal Scotts is to be in y[e] 9th British Brigade

The Q[r] M[r] General will give orders for y[e] movement of y[e] Troops to join their several Divisions & Brigades

GO Head Quarters Paris 25th Aug[t] 1815

N[o]3 The Paymasters of Regiments will wait upon y[e] Pay Master General – to receive y[e] balances due upon their several estimates to y[e] 24th Ins[t] –

N[o] 4 The Staff to be paid up to same period

Major Cambell [*sic*] 45th Regiment is appointed to act as a Brigade Major from y[e] 25th Ins[t], & attached to y[e] 14th British Brigade –

A General Court Martial will assemble at Paissy on Monday 28th Ins[t] –
Major Gen[l] Sir Tho[s] Beresford President
8 Field Officers}
6 Captains } Members

Sign'd E. Barnes
A.G.

Mem^{m}

Whenever the Reg^{t} marches the clerk of each troop will parade dismounted & sore-backed horses and give over [?] with a list of the names to the NCO in charge of the Baggage who will call the roll of the dismounted men each of the troops when they join the Baggage and also prior to entering the Quarters or Bivouac when a Serj^{t} of each troop will receive them from the NCO in charge of the Baggage –

When the troops arrive in camp or quarters & the order is given to unsaddle every dragoon will clean his appoint^{s} & place then in a compact & regular order so as to be ready to turn out at the shortest notice.

By order of the A.A.

J. Blood
[...] Major

Whenever the Orderly Serj^{t} should go on duty and leave the line on any occasion he must invariably apprize the next Serj^{t} of it that no delay may take place whenever the trumpet sounds upon immediate attendance.

Memd

No wallets to be worn or bags of any description, Corn Sacks the exception, Water Buckets to be carried on the off side tins & nose bags on the near side –

7th July 1815

All awkward men or men that has misbehav'd or been confined with the exception of men that have been try'd by a Court Martial since the march from Denderwindeke at 3 o'clock this afternoon

[This list of names is written across the bottom of the page; most appear on the Waterloo Roll for Tomkinson's troop.]

Duffield – 1
[?]raddle – 1
Hardman – 1
Richards – 1
McGinn – 1
C. Smith – 1
Siddle – 1
~~DeLancey [?] – 1~~
Worthington – 1
Hall – 1
Skinner – 1

Hudgson – 1
Janes – 1
Parsons [?] – 1
Taylor – 1
Granty – 2
Urnu [?] – 2
Rortharm [?] – 1
Smith – 1
Reynolds – 1
Hooley – 1
St Jodesh [?] – 5
St Moon – 5
Dunbar – 1
Ogden – 1
C. Packer – 1
Malsom – 1
Wedin – 1
Collins – 1
Simister [?] – 1
Hammond – 1
Ogden Sgt – 1
Price – 1

1 Stable Jacket
1 Flannel trousers
1 Pair Slings
1 Flannel waistcoat
1 pr Trousers
1 Forage cap
1 Sash
Corn bag & log
Three shirts
Stock & clasp
2 prs worsted Stockings
1 pr Shoes
2 Shoe Brushes
Cloath Brush Worm & Picker
Main Comb & Spung
Water Spung
Turn Screw
Horse Picker
Lock cover
Valice

Denderwindeke 7th June 1815
Mem

The Clerks of Troops to Pay into the hands of the Hospital Serjeant 3d *Per Diem* for each man in Hospital Commencing on the 8th *Ultimo*

By Order of
Surgeon Robinson

It is requested to pay a week }
In advance previous to a }
Man going into Hospital }

RMO Camp 23rd June 1815

A Return of Sick

Memorandum for the officers of the 16th D.

The English Horses Baggage Horses and effects of the late Cornet Hay will be sold by publick auction in the Camp at 7 o'clock this evening

Bivouac near Pommerueil 24th June 1815

Denderwindeke

The whole of the orderly serjeants quartered out of the village will sleep at the Serj[t] Majors untill further orders.

Whenever a man is ordered for duty the orderly Serj[t] is to parade him and see him to the Serj[t] Majors

When an order is sent to a troop the first Serj[t] the Dragoon delivers it to whether orderly Serj[t] or not he is to see the order put in execution

Each Dragoon previous to his being sent as an orderly to Head Quarters or any other place is to have the name of the Head Quarters of the Brigade Regiemnt and Troop given to him in writing and also to know where the officers of his troop are quartered

Wm Harris Lieut. 14th May 1815

Camp Kettle Horses to be on the parade tomorrow morning –

Mem[o] Clarks of Troops to be over at Cap[t.] Waylands Quarters tomorrow morning at 4 o'clock and to take a man with them

[A draft form]

A State from each Troop agreeable to the following form as they will appear on Monday next to be sent in to y[e] Adjutant tomorrow morng by 8 o'clock________

State of Captn Troop

[Column Headings]

Captain – Subaltern – Serjts – Trumpts – R. & File – Horses

[Categories for each column]

Present in the Field

Men sick	{In Regimt Hospital {In Quarters {Absent

On letter parties

Offrs batmen & dismounted men left in
Confined

Horses	{ sore-backed { sick or lame {forge cart Effectives

[This is the end of the Order Book.]

Tomkinson:

October 12th. We this day moved to Ville d'Eu, 20 miles nearer the Coast than Aumale – The people at Ville d'Eu having heard we were not inclined to give any trouble at Aumale presumed on this, and were very impertinent on our arrival. They would scarcely allow us to come into their Houses – We were as much at variance with the Inhabitants of Ville d'Eu as we had been otherwise with those at Aumale.

It is arranged that a certain proportion of the Army is to remain as a Corps of occupation for three years, and that Russia, Austria and Prussia are to furnish their contingent – I fear it is our turn for Ireland and that we must leave France for that country – The whole of the Army of occupation is to be under the command of the Duke of Wellington –

A sketch of Eu in 1815 by John Luard. (Luard Family Archive)

Luard:[24]

Eu Novr 4th 1815

A joint Epistle my Dear Loui of Oct 4th written in the kindest way by my Dear Mother Tomasina F[25] & yourself reached me yesterday!

I cannot give you an exact History of the […] it has […] as I would, for it would prove interesting I know it has been to Rouen & Bris [?] & I believe to Marques & Aumale as it has however arrived at this destination […] in a pitiful state, the old address scratched out newly directed & that again defaced with a third address – torn dirtied & hardly legible, however its internal fully compensated for its external appearance for I found it replete with kind expressions & information of all your welfares

I received my Fathers letter of the 3d Oct & answered it last week –

Our correspondence of late has certainly ceased to be so brilliant as formerly – it is to be accounted for on my part because we have no longer long marches to make, no wet bivouacs to endure, nor Bloody Battles to fight the relation of which afford ample & interesting subjects for a letter and told without much trouble or consideration – At present stationary in a quiet Country Town in France amusing ourselves precisely as we should in England, Hunting shooting fishing breakfasting

24 Luard Family Archive, Letter 408, John Luard to his sister, 4 November 1815.
25 Tom Fenton's sister.

at 9 dining at 6 & then when I sit down to write to the [?] friends, imagining I must fill a long sheet of Foolscap Paper, I am at a loss for subjects so I have recourse to the same means that I am now adopting, that of composing this letter with the relation of something, such as follows but which I am confident will please you as they all tend to this composition [?]; that I am well, happy, & amusing myself all of which I owe to constant employment. –

We have a splendid Pack of Hounds, I do not know if I am right in saying pack for I am not certain that 5 dogs constitutes a pack, but however we hunt with these, sometimes we collect as many as 12 of them we always stalk a Hare. this in that way we have passed two days a week since we have been here – Then we shoot but without destroying much game, for our Country is so open here, that the Partridges pack (that is several coveys join company) & when in this state they are so wild it requires the greatest cunning to approach sufficiently near to shoot them.

Five days have elapsed my Dear Loui since I wrote the above – I was going to relate what I had done fishing, for altho Novr it is such wether these few days that I have given up that amusement – I intended to have gone over to have spent a week with George on the 5th but Major Whale[26] having joined from Paris, brings information that there is a probability of our going to Ireland – therefore I shall defer my vist until it is ascertained whether we do so or remain here during the Winter I think the latter most probable – & rather hope it will be the case – George is about 10 leagues from here not far from Abbeville I believe amusing himself well –

The absence of Tomasina & Jane Fenton from Northampton must be much felt by you – & I fear they have left a quiet home for a very disturbed one, their family is in a shocking state & I see no prospect of their improving. – I expect to hear from Charles ere long. – I was delighted to hear so good an account of Dear little Bessy she certainly is a great pet of mine. – Your Lincolnshire trip appears to have afforded you much pleasure; your expression of Aweful Aunt [?] is very applicable, it precisely conveys an Idea of that Venerable Piece of Antiquity. – Altho Gerard Bouverie has obtained leave of absence, you must not expect to see me; for there is a wide diff^ce^ between us, in as much as he has plenty of money, & a power of interest – In both of which I fail, or I would long since have had my Troop for it grieves me to consider I am still a Lieutenant. –

Your account & Tomasinas respecting H.A. does not agree – she says she is very very thin, you that she is improved, I hope the latter is the case; tell her with my kind love that I fear some happy partner will be in my place at the Winter Ball – I however thank her for her consideration – How does M.A. and the little man get on – The officers of the 3d D^g^ G^ds^ were as long as I remember them a very mixed set – you will find a poor substitute for Gordon or Watson in Watts or Skinner which excepting Gra[n]t are the only men I know – the latter is a vulgar man that rose

26 John Whale joined the 16th from the 1st Life Guards: Tomkinson (ed.) *Diary of a Cavalry Officer*, Appendix 1.

from the ranks – Watts is a gentlemanly quiet unhappy melancholy man – Skinner I hardly knew – There were two or three only in the regiment with whom I was intimate & I believe they are killed or left the Reg[t] – The Comd[g] Off[r] Sir Granby Calcraft a great Brute, said he never wished to have a gentleman in his Reg[t] – I am glad Octavius has taken to school life I am in hopes he will be a man after all I despaired it at one time

When you write to Tomasina pray give my love & thank her for her few lines in your letter – I shall always be most happy to hear from her, or any of her dear sisters What is become of Bell? – Having given over Old Armytage is a bad subject – Madame I suppose proceed as usual. I must now write to my old friend Light – Give my warmest affection to my Dear Father Mother Brother & Aunt Look [?] – & Believe me my Dear Loui

Your affec[t] Brother & sincere Friend
John Luard

I never hear from Peter

Tomkinson:

We moved from Ville d'Eu on our route for Calais on the 15th December – There were a certain number of our Horses transferred to the Regiments remaining in France. These we gave up at Abbeville and then proceeded on our Route –

The weather on the march from Ville d'Eu to Calais was the most severe I ever experienced. It was so cold for a couple of days the Men could not ride their Horses, they were occasionally obliged to dismount and walk to prevent their being frozen or rather cut through by the coldest Easterly wind I ever experienced – The frost was severe.

On arriving at Calais the weather was very stormy, it was some time before we could embark. The *Commandant* of Calais threw every obstacle in the way of our embarkation. He would not allow us inside the Walls of the Town causing us to make the detour of the Walls to the point of embarkation.

We arrived at Romford near London on Christmas day 1815 – We left England for Lisbon April 1809 – Returned from France in June 1814. Embarked for Waterloo in April 1815 and returned from France December 1815 making a period of service of nearly six years –

We were the only Cavalry Regiment in the service that went through the whole of the Peninsula, (excluding sir John Moore's Campaign and no Reg[t] served in both – Those with Sir John Moore were not with Sir Arthur Wellesley) – and had the good fortune to be present at Waterloo. The 14th L Dragoons served the same length of time in Spain, but were not at Waterloo having left the Spanish Army at Bordeaux for America – where they were in 1815 –

Epilogue

Compared to many other cavalry regiments, the 16th escaped Waterloo with relatively few casualties. However, this was not a matter of pure luck. As Tomkinson pointed out, the severe losses in the Ponsonby's Union Brigade were due in no small part to inexperience. As he wrote, 'had they halted after completely routing the enemy's troops … their loss would have been trifling.'[1] In comparison, the charges made by the 12th and 16th were controlled, limited and effective. This was the difference between regiments with years of campaigning experience in the Peninsula and those with none, such as the 2nd and 6th Dragoons.

It is notable that while much is made of the havoc wrought on the retreating Union Brigade by French lancers, the 16th do not appear to have experienced any difficulty with them worth mentioning. Here again, their experience in the Peninsula must have come into play. It has to be wondered what they thought when informed they were to be converted to lancers.

In 1816 the 16th were sent to Ireland, based initially at Clonmel and then moving to Dublin. It was in Ireland that they became lancers, Lieutenants Luard and Crichton being sent to London to learn the new lance drill and then train the regiment. The regiment returned to England in 1819, and a period of home service followed until 1822, when the regiment was ordered to India. The 'Queen' in the title of the regiment was George IV's estranged wife, Queen Caroline. The decision to send the 16th to India was said to have been a consequence of them continuing to drink to her health.[2]

In December 1825 and January 1826 the regiment was involved in the campaign and siege of Bhurtpore.[3] In 1830 the regiment's colonel, Field Marshal Earl Harcourt, who had been the colonel since 1779, died and was replaced by Lieutenant General Sir John Ormsby Vandeleur, under whose command they had been at Waterloo.[4] After 1834 the last of the officers who had served at Waterloo, Murray and Osten, disappeared from the regimental list.[5]

1 See Chapter 5.
2 Graham, *History of the 16th*, p.69.
3 Graham, *History of the 16th*, pp.72–77.
4 N.B. Leslie, *The Succession of Colonels of the British Army* (London: Society for Army Historical Research, 1974), p.30.
5 Graham, *History of the 16th*, p.290.

Appendix I

The Uniform of the Officers of the 16th at Waterloo

In the National Army Museum, Chelsea, is a uniform of Cornet Polhill of the 16th Light Dragoons.[1] Polhill joined the 16th in July 1813 and served with the regiment at Waterloo. The uniform is of the style worn by Light Dragoon officers before the new uniform of the 1812 Warrant was adopted. Because of this it has often been stated that at Waterloo the officers of the 16th were wearing the old style uniform.[2] This is not the case. Indeed, the inspection return for the regiment in February 1815 states 'The clothing of the officers, noncommissioned officers and privates is according to regulation.'[3]

The dress regulations for Light Dragoon officers post 1812 states: 'On Ordinary Duties, or on the March, they are to wear Overalls of a Colour similar to the private Soldiers, and a short Surtout or Great Coat made according to Pattern, which is calculated to be worn likewise, as a Pelisse on Service.'[4]

One officer of the 16th at Waterloo was Lieutenant John Luard. Later in life, having reached the rank of lieutenant colonel, he published *A History of the Dress of the British Soldier*. In this he wrote:

> On the change of the Lt. Dragoons dress in 1812, the officers were also instructed to wear a jacket, called a pelisse, as undress. It was very plain, double-breasted without ornament of any kind, with a rough shaggy lining; the collar and cuffs of the same and of the colour of the facings of the Regt. Certainly it was not brilliant in appearance, & there was nothing about it to denote the officer, but it was very comfortable, put on and off in a moment and in the dreadful weather of the night before Waterloo it was very useful.[5]

1 Both the uniform and the portrait of Polhill wearing the uniform are in this book. Images of the uniform can also be found on the National Army Museum website.
2 Godfrey Brennan, 'Uniform, 16th Light Dragoons, Waterloo', *Journal of the Society for Army Historical Research*, 18:72 (1939), p.242.
3 The National Archives, Inspection Returns 1815, WO 27/134.
4 Horse Guards General Order, 24 December 1811, 'Regulations relative to the Dress of Officers'.
5 John Luard, *A History of the Dress of the British Soldier* (London: W. Clowes, 1852).

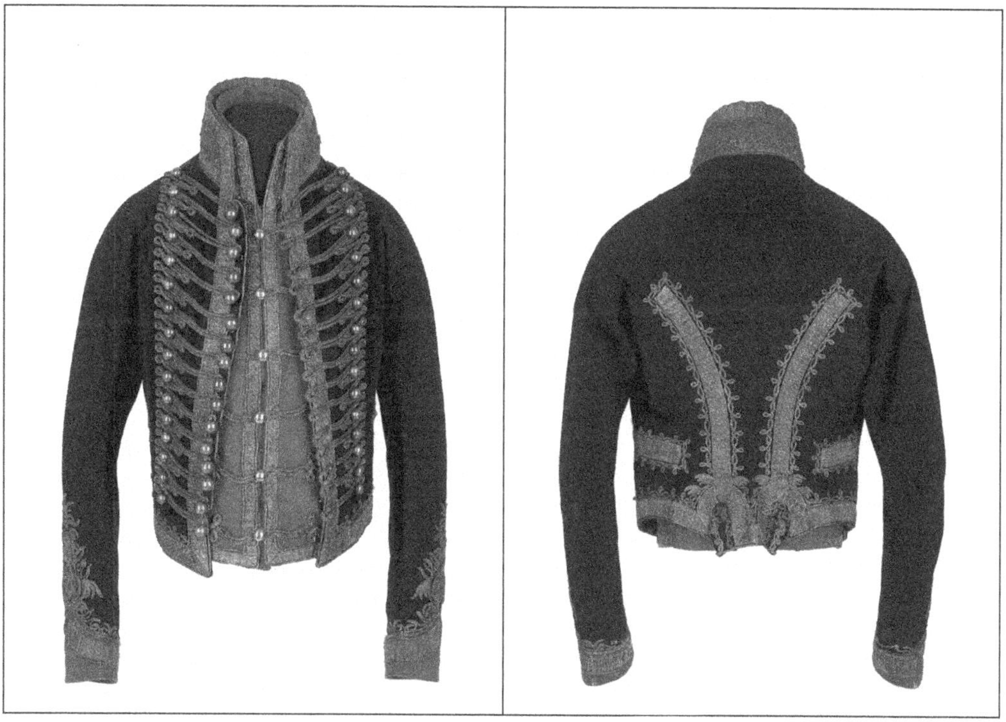

William Polhill's dress uniform in the National Army Museum. (Accession Number 1963-9-215. Reproduced courtesy of the Council of the National Army Museum)

The Stothard Pattern Book in the Anne S.K. Brown Collection, Providence, Rhode Island, contains a drawing of the pattern for this pelisse. It is, in general form, the same as the short coatee adopted for Light Dragoons in 1812. In addition to this, there is a pencil sketch in the Royal Collection by Lieutenant Luard, dated 1815, of Major Lygon of the 16th wearing such a pelisse.[6]

The order book for the 16th for 1815 includes the following instructions for 24th August: 'Offrs not having Pelice [*sic*] will wear jackets without epaletes [*sic*].' The pelisse, unlike the dress jacket, did not have epaulettes, and thus, at a distance, a jacket without epaulettes would appear the same. There is no doubt that the undress pelisse was the workaday jacket of Light Dragoon officers following the introduction of the new uniform in 1812 and was worn at Waterloo by the 16th.

6 Royal Collection Trust, 'Henry Beauchamp Lygon, 4th Earl of Beauchamp; Lieutenant General, Colonel of 10th Hussars, After John Luard (1790–1875)', RCIN 658287, https://www.royalcollection.org.uk/collection/search#/3/collection/658287/henry-beauchamp-lygon-4th-earl-of-beauchamp-lieutenant-general-colonel-of-tenth (accessed 12 February 2019).

William Polhill in his dress uniform, curiously there is no sabretache shown. The shako is obscured by later damage. (Polhill Collection)

That the earlier style uniform continued in use after 1812 is not in question. As already mentioned, Polhill joined the Army and the 16th in 1813. In October 1813, Lieutenant John Vandeleur of the 12th Light Dragoons wrote home asking to be sent 'epaulettes, cloth, and buttons to make a jacket of the new pattern; lace cloth, and buttons to make up a jacket of the old pattern.'[7] Vandeleur also wrote home in August 1813 that he had 'worn out most completely my pelisse and jacket.'[8] It would seem that the early style uniform remained popular with officers and continued in wear as a form of unofficial dress uniform. Further, family tradition has it that Cornet Polhill attended the Duchess of Richmond's Ball in the very uniform now in the National Army Museum; the family have his ticket or invitation to the ball, and not having had time to change he was still wearing the uniform in the battle. So it is possible that one officer of the 16th was in the old style uniform on the 18th of June.

7 Andrew Bamford, *With Wellington's Outposts* (Barnsley: Frontline Books, 2015), p.16.
8 Bamford, *With Wellington's Outposts*, p.110.

Appendix II

Biographies

Unless otherwise stated the information given is from Dalton.[1]

Baker, Lieutenant George: joined the 16th on 6 July 1809 as a Cornet straight from the Royal Military College. He obtained his lieutenancy by purchase on 15 August 1811.[2] He became a captain in 1820 after which his name disappears from the regimental history.[3] Dalton records him as a colonel on half-pay from 1846, dying in 1859.

Barra, Lieutenant and Adjutant, Joseph: Tomkinson lists Barra as joining the regiment on 27 August 1807 and receiving his lieutenancy on 4 October 1808.[4] Dalton says he was promoted to captain 29 July 1815, and went onto half-pay 25 March 1816. He was appointed Adjutant of the Chester Yeomanry, which post he held until his death, 13 July 1839. He was buried at Knutsford with military honours. At his funeral a sword was placed on his coffin, which bore the inscription 'To Lieut. And Adjt. Barra, 16th or Queen's Lt. Dgns., this sword was presented by the officers of his regt. as a token of their high esteem and approbation of his services both at home and abroad, 30th March 1815.'

Beauchamp, Lieutenant Richard: joined as a cornet on 14 March 1811, obtaining his lieutenancy on 19 February 1812.[5] He disappears from the regimental history after 1820.[6] He subsequently served in the Grenadier Guards, retired as a colonel in 1832 and died in 1850.

Beckwith, Cornet William: joined the 16th on 7 January 1813.[7] He disappears from the regiment's list after 1815, but Dalton records him as a major in the 14th Light Dragoons in 1831, when he distinguished himself in suppressing riots in Bristol. At his death in 1871 he was a general and Colonel-in-Chief of the 14th Light Dragoons.

1 Charles Dalton, *The Waterloo Roll Call* (2nd edition) (London: Eyre and Spottiswood, 1904), pp.86–89.
2 Tomkinson (ed.), *Diary of a Cavalry Officer*, Appendix 1.
3 Graham, *History of the 16th*, pp.284–88.
4 Tomkinson (ed.), *Diary of a Cavalry Officer*, Appendix 1.
5 Tomkinson (ed.), *Diary of a Cavalry Officer*, Appendix 1.
6 Graham, *History of the 16th*, pp.284–87.
7 Tomkinson (ed.), *Diary of a Cavalry Officer*, Appendix 1.

Belli, Captain John Henry: joined the regiment on 29 January 1807 as a captain, appointed major 10 October 1816 and brevet lieutenant colonel 21 January 1819. On the unattached half-pay list in from 1826.

Blood, Regimental Sergeant Major Thomas: enlisted in the 16th in March 1793 and on 17 April 1794 was with the regiment at Landrécies and on the 26th was at the Battle of Beaumont. By 1798 he was a sergeant and a rough rider. Serving with the regiment throughout the Peninsular War, he became the Regimental Sergeant Major in 1813 and was present at Talavera, Fuentes D'Oñoro, Salamanca, Vittoria, and the Nive. In 1812 he was employed in carrying dispatches to the Spanish General Castaños on the Douro. He found that the general had left seven days before, followed by the French. He managed to deliver the dispatches and return, passing through the French army. For this act he was given 100 dollars and offered a commission. He went to India with the regiment and was commissioned as cornet and riding master in 1822 and as a lieutenant in 1826. He was present at the Battle of Bhurtpore. He transferred to the 1st Royal Dragoons in 1833 and was on half-pay in 1834.[8] He died at Cheadle in 1840.[9]

Buchanan, Captain John Phillips: joined the regiment as a captain by purchase on 28 May 1812. Killed at Waterloo.

Crichton, Lieutenant Nathaniel Day: joined the 16th as a cornet on 29 May 1811, and obtained his lieutenancy on 20 February 1812.[10] In 1822 he joined the 5th Dragoon Guards as a captain, becoming a major in the 5th in 1826. He died in 1833. He was wounded at Waterloo.

Harris, Lieutenant William: joined the regiment from half-pay on 30 March 1815.[11] Captain from 2 June 1826, retired on half-pay in June 1830.

Harrison, Quartermaster J.: Dalton records his lieutenancy on 25 January 1816, and his going on half-pay on 25 March 1815. His youngest son Charles John Harrison (born 16 July 1815 – conceived when his father was sent home from the continent on leave prior to the Battle of Waterloo) migrated to New Zealand *circa* 1845, arriving aboard the Pudsley Dawson and bringing with him his father's portrait and writing box.[12]

Hay, Cornet Alexander: had joined the 16th as a cornet on 11 November 1811. At Waterloo he was in Captain Swetenham's Troop of the Centre Squadron. He was killed in action towards the end of the day, aged 18.[13]

8 The Queen's Royal Lancers and Nottinghamshire Yeomanry Museum, copy of the service record of Thomas Blood.

9 Allan Blood, 'Lieutenant Thomas Blood of the 16th Light Dragoons (Lancers): Captain J.H. Belle's Troop', http://www.theonlinebookcompany.com/OnlineBooks/Waterloo/Celebrations/DescendantsStories/76 (accessed 6 January 2019).

10 Tomkinson (ed.), *Diary of a Cavalry Officer*, Appendix 1.

11 Tomkinson (ed.), *Diary of a Cavalry Officer*, Appendix 1.

12 Auckland Museum, 'Portrait of a soldier in uniform [Lieutenant Charles John Harrison, Queen's 16th Regiment Light Dragoons, Waterloo]', http://www.aucklandmuseum.com/collections-research/collections/record/am_library-paintinganddrawings-1753?k=john%20harrison&ordinal=7 (accessed 19 December 2018).

13 Tomkinson (ed.), *Diary of a Cavalry Officer*, Appendix 1.

Quartermaster John Harrison. (Auckland War Memorial Museum)

Hay, Lieutenant Colonel James: joined the regiment in 1795 as cornet, and became a lieutenant in 1798.[14] Hay is listed in Tomkinson as a captain in the regiment from 28 February 1805. He was promoted to major on 2 January 1812, replacing the Honourable Lincoln Stanhope, who became a lieutenant colonel in the 17th Light Dragoons. He became a lieutenant colonel on 18 February 1812, without purchase.[15] Hay was so badly wounded at Waterloo that he was not expected to survive, and could not be moved for eight days. On 22 June 1815, on the recommendation of Wellington, he was appointed a Companion of the Most Honourable Order of the Bath (CB) for his services at Quatre Bras and Waterloo.[16] He is listed by Graham as a lieutenant colonel 1819, but not 1820.[17] He subsequently reached the rank of lieutenant general and was Colonel in Chief of the 79th Highlanders. He died 25 February 1854, at his home near Kilburn, County Longford.

Jones, Veterinary Surgeon John: joined the regiment on 25 November 1813;[18] out of the regiment in 1822.

King, Captain Charles: joined the regiment as a captain from the 11th Light Dragoons on 18 February 1813. He had joined the 11th as a cornet in 1810 and as a lieutenant lost his right arm at the battle of El Bodon on 25 September 1811. His promotion into the 16th was the result of the Duke of Wellington's recommendation. He served with distinction in the Bhurtpore campaign where, with Captain Luard, he captured a *rajah*. In 1827 he

14 Graham, *History of the 16th*, pp.281–86.
15 Tomkinson (ed.), *Diary of a Cavalry Officer*, Appendix 1.
16 John Booth, *The Battle of Waterloo, also of Ligny and Quatre Bras* (London: T. Egerton, 1817), p.280.
17 Graham, *History of the 16th*, pp.281–86.
18 Tomkinson (ed.), *Diary of a Cavalry Officer*, Appendix 1.

was made a lieutenant colonel and in 1830 became the Inspecting Field Officer at Cork. Ill health forced his retirement in 1835 and he died in Dublin in July 1844.[19]

Lloyd, Lieutenant Edward B.: joined as a cornet from the Royal Military College on 30 May 1811, and obtained his lieutenancy on 12 March 1812.[20]

Luard, Lieutenant John: joined the 16th from half-pay on 2 March 1815. He had previously served in the Peninsula with the 4th Dragoons. His brother, George, who had also been in the 4th Dragoons, had gained a captaincy in the 18th Hussars in 1813; thus both brothers were at Waterloo. When the 16th were converted to lancers, John Luard was one of the officers sent to London to learn how to use the lance so he could train the regiment. He obtained his captaincy in 1821 and served with the regiment in India, including the Bhurtpore campaign. He returned home in 1830, leaving the 16th in 1832, and by 1835 was a major and ADC to his uncle, Charles Dalbiac, Inspector General of Cavalry. He returned to India in 1838 as military secretary to Sir Jasper Nicolls, Commander-in-Chief, Madras. He returned home in 1844, and retired from the Army in 1848. He died in 1875.[21]

Macdougall, Lieutenant Alexander: is listed as a cornet in the 16th from 24 December 1812, and went on half-pay in 1814. He re-joined the regiment from half-pay as a lieutenant on 30 March 1815. He appears to have left the 16th in 1816.[22]

Mallock, Assistant Surgeon John M'Gr.: joined the regiment on 16 April 1812.[23] He was surgeon to the 46th foot in 1826 and still serving in 1830.

Monckton, Lieutenant Hon. Carleton T.: joined from half-pay on 30 March 1815, having previously served with the 16th. He joined on 17 September 1812 as a cornet and obtained his lieutenancy on 8 July 1813 and went on half-pay at the end of the war in 1814.[24] He disappears from the regimental history after 1815, and Dalton records him as a captain in the Cape Corps in 1823. He exchanged into the 24th Foot in 1824 and died in 1830.

Murray, Assistant Surgeon Dennis: he was appointed Surgeon's Mate on the hospital staff, unattached, on 9 November 1812. From May 1813, he was Hospital Assistant to the Forces. He was gazetted Assistant Surgeon to the 16th Dragoons on June 22 1815, and was present at Waterloo; to the 31st Foot on 10 November 1831; surgeon to the 46th Foot on 23 November 1832; to the 13th Foot by exchange on 2 June 1833; transferred to the 10th Hussars on 14 December 1841; to the 44th Foot on 20 March 1846, and promoted to the Staff (1st Class) on 18 September 1846. He retired on half-pay on 10 September 1847, and died at Enniscorthy Lodge, County Wicklow, on 17 March 1860.[25]

19 *The Gentleman's Magazine*, vol. 22 (June to December 1844) (London: John Bowyer Nichol and Son, 1844), p.320.
20 Tomkinson (ed.), *Diary of a Cavalry Officer*, Appendix 1.
21 Cohen, 'Brothers in war', pp.9–92.
22 Graham, *History of the 16th*, pp.285–86.
23 Tomkinson (ed.), *Diary of a Cavalry Officer*, Appendix 1.
24 Tomkinson (ed.), *Diary of a Cavalry Officer*, Appendix 1; Graham, *History of the 16th*, pp.285–86.
25 Royal College of Surgeons, 'Murray, Denis, 1793-1860', *Plarr's Lives of the Fellows* [online], accessed through the search box at https://livesonline.rcseng.ac.uk/client/en_GB/lives (accessed 8 July 2019).

Murray, Major George Home: first listed as a lieutenant in the regiment in 1800, a captain in 1807 and major without purchase from 18 February 1813 following Hay's promotion.[26] He held the rank of lieutenant colonel in the Army from 1815, but continued as a major to the regiment. He became one of the regiment's lieutenant colonels in 1822, achieving the rank of major general in 1825, and lieutenant general in 1826. He died at Cawnpore in 1833 while in command of the regiment.

Nepean, Lieutenant William: joined as a cornet from the Royal Military college on 11 July 1811, and purchased his lieutenancy on 2 April 1812.[27] He last appears in the regimental history as a lieutenant in 1821. Dalton records that he subsequently reached the rank of major general and died in 1864.

Neyland, Pay Master George: listed as paymaster from 10 September 1812.[28] He appears to have left the regiment in 1824.[29]

Nugent, Cornet George: joined the 16th on 7 October 1813.[30] He gained his lieutenancy on 14 December 1815. He disappears from the regimental list after 1816. Dalton records him as a lieutenant in the 7th Dragoon Guards in 1821, and a captain in 1824. He was still serving in 1830.

Osten, Lieutenant Wilhelm, Baron: joined the 16th from the King's German Legion in 1808. He obtained his captaincy in the 16th in 1817, became a major in 1827 and retired from the British Army in 1834.[31] He subsequently became a general in the Hanoverian Army and died in 1852. He was wounded at Waterloo.

Polhill, Cornet William: joined the regiment on 1 July 1813, and obtained his lieutenancy on 14 December 1815. He exchanged into the 1st Life Guards on 26 October 1816, and was on half-pay with the 23rd Light Dragoons from 23 January 1819. His dress uniform is preserved in the National Army Museum.

Richardson, Lieutenant Jas. Arch.: joined as a lieutenant, without purchase, from the 10th Hussars on 12 November 1814, but left the regiment in 1816. Dalton lists him as on half-pay from 25 January 1816.

Robinson, Surgeon Isaac: joined the 16th on 21 April 1804, and served with the regiment until 1830.[32] He then became a Deputy Inspector General of Hospitals,[33] but was on half-pay by 1846.

Swetenham, Captain Clement: joined the regiment as a cornet in 1803, lieutenant in 1805, captain from 1 June 1807.[34] He left the Army with the rank of major in 1817. In his letter of 19 June Swetenham refers to the death of Captain Buchanan and Buchanan's poor mother. In 1816 the 16th were posted to Ireland and Swetenham took the opportunity

26 Tomkinson (ed.), *Diary of a Cavalry Officer*, Appendix 1; Graham, *History of the 16th*, pp.281–86.
27 Tomkinson (ed.), *Diary of a Cavalry Officer*, Appendix 1.
28 Tomkinson (ed.), *Diary of a Cavalry Officer*, Appendix 1.
29 Graham, *History of the 16th*, pp.285–88.
30 Tomkinson (ed.), *Diary of a Cavalry Officer*, Appendix 1.
31 Tomkinson (ed.), *Diary of a Cavalry Officer*, Appendix 1; Graham, *History of the 16th*, pp.284–91.
32 Tomkinson (ed.), *Diary of a Cavalry Officer*, Appendix 1; Graham, *History of the 16th*, pp.283–89.
33 *The Edinburgh Gazette*, 28 September 1830.
34 Tomkinson (ed.), *Diary of a Cavalry Officer*, Appendix 1; Graham, *History of the 16th*, pp.281–86.

to visit Mrs Buchanan. There he met Captain Buchanan's sister, Eleanor, and two years later they were married.[35]

Swinfen, Lieutenant Francis: joined the 16th as a cornet on 15 December 1808 and obtained his lieutenancy on 1 August 1811.[36] He was placed on half-pay on 25 May 1817, and died in 1839.

Tomkinson, Captain William: joined the 16th as a cornet in December 1807, is listed as a lieutenant in 1808, and got his captaincy on 12 March 1812 in the 60th Foot.[37] News of his commission in the 60th reached him on 14 April. On 26 April he 'arranged with Lord Clinton for his troop in the 16th.' He went to the army's headquarters to do this, as Captain Lord Clinton was serving as an ADC to Wellington and not with the regiment.[38] He was a major in 1819, but did not go to India with the regiment. He retired as a lieutenant colonel in 1821. He died in 1872.[39]

Weyland, Captain Richard: joined the regiment 26 March 1807 as a lieutenant; captain from 5 September 1811, a promotion that seems to have involved a temporary exchange into the 99th Foot, his rank in the Army as a captain dating from 18 July 1811.[40] He left the Army in 1820 as a major.

Wheeler, Lieutenant Trevor: a cornet in the regiment from 17 November 1808, he obtained his lieutenancy on 11 July 1811.[41] He appears to have left the 16th in 1817, and Dalton subsequently records him as a major in the 5th Dragoon Guards in 1829. He died in 1869.

35 Private email, 12 November 2017.
36 Tomkinson (ed.), *Diary of a Cavalry Officer*, Appendix 1.
37 Tomkinson (ed.), *Diary of a Cavalry Officer*, p.ix, Appendix 1.
38 Tomkinson (ed.), *Diary of a Cavalry Officer*, pp.153, 156.
39 Tomkinson (ed.), *Diary of a Cavalry Officer*, p.ix.
40 Tomkinson (ed.), *Diary of a Cavalry Officer*, Appendix 1; Graham, *History of the 16th*, pp.281–86.
41 Tomkinson (ed.), *Diary of a Cavalry Officer*, Appendix 1.

Appendix III

The Waterloo Roll of the 16th (Queen's) Light Dragoons

[(k) – killed
(w) – wounded]

Lt Col James Hay
Major G.H. Murray[1]
Lt & Adjt J. Barra[2]
Qr Mr J. Harrison
RSM Thomas Blood
Pay Mr G. Neyland

Right Squadron

G Troop
Capt. Buchanan (k)[3]
Lt G. Baker[4]
Cornet G. Nugent[5]
Cornet W. Polhill
Trp Sjt Maj. Thos Wildman
Serjt Robt Kearney
Serjt John Maloney
Serjt Issac Hay (k)[6]
Serjt John Wortley
Cpl Cornelius Coward[7]
Cpl Harry McNamara
Cpl Patk Mount[8]
Cpl George Young
Trumpeter John Deardon
John Astley
Wm Baume
James Beard
Jos. Bethell
Joshua Brooks

1 'Head Quarters 3rd August, List of Promotions and Appointments, To be Lieut. Colonel in ye Army, Major G H Murray 16th Lt Dragoons', Cheshire Archives and Local Studies, DTM/72, Order Book of William Tomkinson, 8 August 1815. Date 18 June 1815.
2 'Lt Barra [will take] the Command of the late Capt. Buchanans Troop', Order Book, 24 July 1815.
3 Command of the troop passed to Lieutenant Osten: Order Book, 20 June 1815.
4 'Lt Osten is to proceed to Chantilly to take charge of cavalry [?] depo he will receive his instruction from Colonel Sligh [?] previous to marching – Lt Baker will take the Command of the late Captain Buchanans Troop'. Order Book, 1 July 1815.
5 'Cornet Nugent will proceed tomorrow morning to Chantilly & relieve Lieut. Osten on duty at that place'. Order Book, 22 July 1815.
6 This must be 'Corpl Hayes of Majr Bellis troop to be Serjt in Capts Weylands troop *vice* Rey killed in action', Order Book, 21 June 1815, as no Corporal. Hayes appears on the Medal Roll (presumably he subsequently transferred to Buchanan's troop).
7 'Corpl Coward of Capt. Buchanans Troop is reduced to the Ranks', Order Book, 23 June 1815.
8 Killed at Waterloo.

Wm Cavanagh
John Courts
George Daintry
John Davenport
Saml Davenport
Thos Dent
John Duggan
Wm Eardley
Edwd Edwards
Richd Faircloth
W. Fergusson (w)
John Fia [or Fid ?]
Wm Foxhall
Chas Goodman
Wm Gordon (k)
Philip Green
Benjn Gregg
John Hall
John Hasketh
Thos Hayes
Wm Hayes
James Heap
Josh Haythorpe
Jonathan Howard
George Hulme
Zach. Hulme
Edwd Hunt
Calib Jones[9]
John Jones
Robt Lake
Francis Lambert
James Lawrent
Josh Lawton
Thos Maddox
John Madmont
Jas. Maides
Harvey Manwaring
Arthur Martin
Morris McGuire
Wm Montgomery
Richd Moon
Thos Morgan
Edwd Nuttall
John Perkins
Mattw Plowman
James Riggs
George Stanfield
Thos Steel
Robt Street
Peter Summer
Wm Thomas
James Walton
Chas Williams
Thos Williams
John Woods
Thos Wooldridge
Richd Wynn

H Troop
Capt. Weyland (w)
Lt R. Beauchamp
Lt J. Richardson
Trp Sjt Maj. James Biggs
Serjt Josh Caunock
Serjt Thos Dally
Serjt Thomas Floyd
Serjt James Hicklington
Serjt Jonathan Reay (k)
Serjt William Tweed
Cpl Lot Cox
Cpl Joshua Gwyllam
Cpl Thos Lincoln
Cpl Wm Mitchell
Trumpeter Jonathan Wild
Edwd Baker
Wm Ball
Robt Barlow
Francis Baylis
Strettle Brearley
Wm Bridgman
John Burns
Jonathan Cannons

9 'Private Caleb James of G Troop is appointed Corpl in the same untill further orders, Nick Mowbury reduced for drunkenness & unsoldierlike conduct from the 25 July 1815 inclusive'. Order Book, 8 August 1815.

Thos Chadwick
Issac Chambers[10]
Robt Chapman
Philip Chitwood
Thos Clarke
Thos Connolly
Robt Cooper
George Davies
Patk Drum
John Daggett
Wm Dunn
Wm Field
Mark Greensmith
Joseph Horobin
Jas. Hawkinson
Richd House
Richd Howe
Thos Laurence
John Lewis
James Lord
Saml Loxton
John Lygo
Saml Massey
Wm Mitchell
George Moore
James Moreton
Thos Norman
James Oats
James Pemberton
Richd Pendleton
John Percival
Thos Pitman
Wm Price
James Reed
Cornelius Riley
Robt Roberts
John Rothwell
Thos Scott
Anthony Rosthorne
Saml Smith
Thos Smith
Saml Stafford
Joshua Storer
Samuel Stubbs
Jas. Tomkins
Charles Webb (k)
John Webb
Henry Wilman
John Wilson
Samuel Wingfield
John Wolton
John Woodward

Centre Squadron

D Troop
Capt. Swetenham[11]
Lt W. Osten (w)[12]
Lt W. Harris
Cornet A. Hay (k)
Trp Sjt Maj. Stephen Baxter (k)[13]
Serjt John Barrow
Serjt Abram Blythe
Serjt James Gripton
Serjt Wm Whitaker[14]
Cpl Peter Collins

10 'Private Chambers of H Troop is appointed Corpl in the same *vice* Pat Riding [not on medal roll] by the sentence of a regimental Cort Martial'. Order Book, 16 July 1815.
11 'Lt Swinfen to take Command of Capn Swetenhams Troop': Order Book 3 July 1815. There is no apparent reason for this, but, presumably, Swetenham was absent from the regiment.
12 'Lt Osten will take the Command of the late Capt. Buchanans Troop', Order Book, 20 June 1815. On 2 July, however, 'Lt Osten is to proceed to Chantilly to take charge of cavalry [?] depo he will receive his instruction from Colonel Sligh [?] previous to marching' Order Book, 1 July 1815. 'Lieut. Osten will do duty in Major Bellis', Order Book, 24 July 1815, having been relieved by Cornet Nugent.
13 Replaced by Sergeant Payne, Order Book, 21 June 1815.
14 'Serjt Whitaker of Capt. Swetenhams Troop exchanges with Serjt Pain of Capt. Kings Troop from this Troop', Order Book, 23 June 1815.

Cpl Danl Fitzpatrick[15]
Cpl Alexr Mckee
Cpl Thos Tongue
Trumpeter Jas. Loring
Thomas Ashworth
Wm Barrett
Henry Barry
Wm Bedder
James Berry
Henry Bolton
Richd Bowker
Wm Bradley
Thos Brown
Edwd Buckley
Robt Bulpot
Jns Byrom
William Caston[16]
Thos Caffrey
Henry Coles
James Dean
Richd Derbyshire
Samuel Frost
George Gilbody
Wm Griffiths
Jos. Hall
Thos Herbert
Zach. Holland
Edwd Holt
John Horrick
John Howard
Thos Hulme
John Humphries
Robt Jackson
Danl Johnson
Thos Jones
John Killer
Alexr Lowder
Wm Lay
Caleb Lodge
John Looby
Thos Lowe
Issac Marston
Andrew Mcall
Wm McBride
John Moore
Pickering Moscrop
John Prince
Robert Rolph
Thos Ratcliffe
Thos Royle
Wm Russell
Dennis Ryan
John Salisbury
John Smith
Thos Stevens
Jonathan Taylor
Wm Vincent
James Welch
Saml Whitehead
Joseph Whitehurst
James Wilkinson
John Williams
Robt Williamson
Richd Wooderson

F Troop
Capt. King[17]
Lt E.B. Lloyd[18]
Lt C.T. Monckton[19]
Lt W. Nepean
Trp Sjt Maj. Ben Smith
Sgt George Bedford

15 'Corpl Fitzpatrick of Captain Swetenhams troop is reduced to y[e] ranks for drunkenness & unsoldierlike conduct – from this day inclusive', Order Book, 1 September 1815.
16 'Wm Castens [Caston] of Capt. Swetenhams Troop & Robt Needham of Major Bellis are appointed Corpls to the late Capt. Buchanans Troop', Order Book, 23 June 1815.
17 'Capt[n] Ch King of the 16th L[t] Dragoons is appointed Maj[r] of Brigade to the Forth Brigade of Cavalry', Order Book, 25 June 1815.
18 'Lieut. Lloyd to do duty in Major Bellis *vice* Swinfen removed', Order Book, 3 July 1815.
19 'Lt Monkton is appointed to Capt. Weylands Troop', Order Book, 20 June 1815.

Serjt Thomas Green
Serjt James Wm Payne[20]
Serjt James Robt Sayers
Cpl James Greenfield (w)
Cpl John Lewis[21]
Cpl John Marshall
Cpl John Trotter
Cpl George Turner
Trumpeter Henry Rosthorne
Robert Aitkenhead
Richd Alliard
Thomas Armstrong
Geo Arnold[22]
Joseph Baker
Wm Bayley
Neil Baggan
Thos Bradley
Thos Bradshaw (w)
John Brown
Thos Butler
David Coopey
Thos Daniels
Enoch Davis
Wm Douglass
Wm Eadis
Jos. Faulkner
Anthony Fitzpatrick
John Forrester
Thos Golding
Chas Gould
Jas. Green[23]
Wm Griffiths
John Grindred
Wm Horton
John Hudson
James Hurst
Saml Hydon
Henry Jenkinson
William Kay
William Lewis
Sampson Lord
Thomas Matthews
John McCord
Peter Millington
William Moore (w)[24]
Patk Nunery (w)
James Osbourne
James Pashley
Wm Percival
James Pennington
Henry Price
Richd Savap
Henry Sergeant
William Slater
John Tate
John Taylor
Thos Thomas
Ridford Upton
John Warburton
Wm Ward
Thos Watkins
Wm Webb
Richard West
James Willis
Richd Wilson
John Wilson
James Wright
John Yates

20 'Serjt Whitaker of Capt. Swetenhams Troop exchanges with Serjt Pain of Capt. Kings Troop from this Troop', Order Book, 23 June 1815.
21 'Private Thos Rytes [not on medal roll] of F Troop is appointed Corpl in the same *vice* Lewis reduced for drunkenness & unsoldierlike [conduct]', Order Book, 16 July 1815.
22 Born 1799, and joined the 16th in Bedford on 1 March 1800. Served throughout the Peninsular War. Registered as a Chelsea Pensioner in 1822, and died 1869. Battle Honours, 'George Arnold', http://www.battle-honours.eu/george-arnold (accessed 18 December 2018).
23 'Jno Leakin [Lakin] of Capt. Tomkinsons Troop & Jas. Green of Capt. Kings Troop are appointed Corpls in Major Bellis Troop', Order Book, 23 June 1815.
24 Discharged, 'loss of a leg': E. Dwelly, *Muster Roll of the British Non-Commissioned Officers and Men Present at the Battle of Waterloo, Section 1: Cavalry* (Fleet: privately published, 1934).

Thos Yates

Left Squadron

A Troop
Capt. Tomkinson
Lt John Luard
Lt F. Swinfen[25]
Cornet W. Beckwith
Trp Sjt Maj. George Greave
Serjt John Flesh
Serjt Timothy Hill
Serjt Jas. Moon
Serjt Saml Williams
Cpl Key Grindred
Cpl Wm Hodgson[26]
Cpl Josh Pecker
Cpl John Smith
Trumpeter Josh Vince
Wm Baxter
Richd Birch
Joseph Collins
Thomas Cookson
Wm Cross
Wm Croaty
George Delaney
John Duffield
John Dimbar
Frances Emberton
Thomas Filton[27]
Hugh Flesh
Samuel Gardner
John Hall[28]
Francis Halliwell
Edwd Hammond
John Hanson (k)
John Harrison
John Hardiman
Charles Hooley
Robert Jamison
John Jolly
William Jones
John Laken[29]
Thomas Long
John Mainwaring
James Malkomb
Joseph Massey
Robt McGrath
Richd McGrain
James Moore
John Murray
Peter Maddan
James Ogden
Thomas Ogden
James Oldham
Thos Parsons
Wm Parsons
Thos Payne
James Pickett
Benjn Price
Henry Reynolds
Josh Richards
John Rosthorne
James Shelmerdine
Thos Siddle
Richd Seinester
Richd Skinner
Robt Sloane
John Smith
Chas Stacey
John Taylor
John Thornbarry

25 'Lt Swinfen to take Command of Capn Swetenhams Troop', Order Book, 3 July 1815.
26 'Corpl Hodgson of A Troop is reduced to the ranks for repeated neglect of duty from this day inclusive', Order Book, 6 July 1815.
27 'Fitton [Filton] of Captn Tomkinsons Troop is appointed Farrier Majr from this date', Order Book, 1 July 1815.
28 'Private Jno Hall of A Troop is appointed Corpl in the same *vice* Hodgson reduced for repeated neglect of duty' Order Book, 16 July 1815.
29 'Jno Leakin [Lakin] of Capt. Tomkinsons Troop & Jas. Green of Capt. Kings Troop are appointed Corpls in Major Bellis Troop', Order Book, 23 June 1815.

Joseph Tibler
Key Turner
Wm Venables
Wm Waddle
John Wain
Peter Warberton
John Weedon
J.B. Wilson
Saml Wilson
John Worthington

C Troop
Major Belli
Lt N.D. Crichton (w)[30]
Lt E. Mcdougall
Lt T. Wheeler
Trp Sjt Maj. John Clues
Pay Mr Sjt Jns Hodgson
Arm. Sjt Thos Meacham
Sad. Sjt Joseph White
Serjt Jos. Matthews
Serjt Wm Norton
Serjt James Platt
Cpl George Ashworth[31]
Cpl Thomas Lloyd
Cpl Thomas Shooter[32]
Trumpeter Wm Wilkinson
Henry Arthurs
Wm Aston
John Braithwaite
Thos Brooks
Chas Carter
Philip Childs
Michl Cockerane
Jas. Compton
Benjn Coomley
Danl Dailey
Patk Dailey
Chas Davies
Josh Fellows
John Fenton
Owen Ferrol
John Fielder
Seth Fletcroft
George Gibson[33]
Richd Gibson
George Goodwin
Joseph Gregory
John Henderson
John Heywood (w)
Thos Hilton
Richd Hitchcock
Joseph Hobbs[34]
Robt Hornfield
John Houghton
John Jeynes
James Kenworthy
James Lang
George Lawton
Saml Lee
John Lees
John Masser
Henry May
Alexr McFarland (w)
Wm Melville
Wm Morris

30 'Lieut. Crichton [will do duty] in Capt. Tomkinsons Troop', Order Book, 24 July 1815.
31 Promoted to sergeant *vice* 'St Stewart of Maj. Belli's troop is reduced to the Ranks for misconduct on the 18th Inst for being absent without leave', Order Book, 21 June 1815. No Sergeant Stewart is listed under Belli's Troop on the Medal Roll, but is possibly the Private Stewart listed in that troop.
32 'Corpl Thos Shooter of Major Bellis Troop is reduced to the ranks for unsoldierlike conduct from this day inclusive', Order Book, 29 July 1815.
33 'Gibson of C Troop is appointed assistant Farrier in G Troop & Farrier Coates [not on medal roll] to H', Order Book, 1 July 1815. Unfortunately the Order Book does not specify which Gibson.
34 'Private Joseph Hobbs of Major Bellis Troop is appointed Corpl in the same untill further orders *vice* Shouter reduced for unsoldierlike conduct the above apt to date from the 30th July 1815 inclusive', Order Book, 19 August 1815.

Jas. Nankeville (w)
Robt Needham[35]
Richd Newton
Jas. Parker
Wm Peake
Thos Pears
Walter Pendergarst
Thos Ridsdale
Jas. Rogerson
John Silcock
Richd Smith
Richd Smithhurst
Wm Steinwell
Jas. Stewart
John Sumner
George Thistlewood
Wm Tiley
Peter Travis
Henry Walker
Jas. Walker
Thos Westfold
Benjn White
Wm Wignall
Josh Wooten
Wm Wooten

In addition Dwelly lists a John Hackersley as killed, but no other mention of him has been found.

Siborne gives a total of 18 non-commissioned officers and privates as wounded, but Dwelly names only five: Privates John Haywood, Alexander McFarland, William Moore, Jas. Namkeville, and Patrick Nunery. Tomkinson records the wounding of Sergeant Flesh, but he is not listed as wounded by Dwelly.[36]

35 'Wm Castens [Caston] of Capt. Swetenhams Troop & Robt Needham of Major Bellis are appointed Corpls to the late Capt. Buchanans Troop', Order Book, 23 June 1815.

36 Dwelly, *Muster Roll*; Captain W. Siborne, *History of the Waterloo Campaign* (London: Greenhill Books, 990), p.564.

Bibliography

Archives

Cheshire Archives and Local Studies, DTM/67, Diary of William Tomkinson.
Cheshire Archives and Local Studies, DTM/72, Order Book of William Tomkinson.
Luard Family Archive, Diary, Journal, and Letters of John Luard.
The National Archives, MINT/16/112, Waterloo Medal Roll, 16th or Queen's Light Dragoons.
The Queen's Royal Lancers and Nottinghamshire Yeomanry Museum, letter of Cornet William Beckwith, 19 June 1815.
The Queen's Royal Lancers and Nottinghamshire Yeomanry Museum, copy of the service record of Thomas Blood.
Private collection, Geneva, letter of Lieutenant William Harris to his father, 19 June 1815.
Private collection, letter of Captain Clement Swetenham to his mother, 19 June 1815.

Published Primary Sources

Anon., *Instructions and Regulations for the Formations and Movements of the Cavalry* (London: War Office, 1796).
Anon., *Instructions and Regulations for the Formations and Movements of the Cavalry* (3rd edition) (London: War Office, 1799).
Anon., *Regulation for the Provision of Clothing, Necessaries, and Appointments, for Corps of Cavalry, dated 17th August 1812* (London: War Office, 1812).
Browne, Major General Robert, *Regulations and Orders Observed in His Majesty's 12th or Prince of Wales's Regiment of Light Dragoons* (London: W. Clowes, 1813).
Dalton, Charles, *The Waterloo Roll Call* (2nd edition) (London: Eyre and Spottiswood, 1904).
Dwelly, E., *Muster Roll of the British Non-Commissioned Officers and Men Present at the Battle of Waterloo, Section 1: Cavalry* (Fleet: privately published, 1934).
The Gentleman's Magazine, vol. 22 (June to December 1844) (London: John Bowyer Nichol and Son, 1844).
Gurwood, Lieutenant Colonel John (ed.), *The General Orders of Field Marshal the Duke of Wellington, KG* (London: W. Clowes, 1832).
Horse Guards General Order, 24 December 1811, 'Regulations relative to the Dress of Officers'.
Page, Julia V., *Intelligence Officer in the Peninsula* (Tunbridge Wells: Spellmount, 1986).
Siborne, Major General H.T., *Waterloo Letters* (London: Greenhill Books, 1993).
Siborne, Captain W., *History of the Waterloo Campaign* (London: Greenhill Books, 1990).
The Edinburgh Gazette, 28 September 1830.

Tomkinson, James (ed.) and Tomkinson, Lieutenant Colonel, *The Diary of a Cavalry Officer in the Peninsular War and Waterloo Campaign, 1809–1815* (London: Frederick Muller, 1971).

Secondary Sources

Bamford, Andrew, *Gallantry and Discipline: the 12th Light Dragoons at War with Wellington* (Barnsley: Frontline, 2014).
Bamford, Andrew, *With Wellington's Outposts* (Barnsley: Frontline, 2015).
Booth, John, *The Battle of Waterloo, also of Ligny and Quatre Bras* (London: T. Egerton, 1817).
Brennan, Godfrey, 'Uniform, 16th Light Dragoons, Waterloo', *Journal of the Society for Army Historical Research*, 18:72 (1939), p.242.
Cohen, Clive, 'Brothers in war: George (1778–1847) and John (1790–1875) Luard – paths to Waterloo', in Andrew Cormack (ed.), '*... a damned nice thing ... the nearest run thing you ever saw in your life ...*' (London: Society for Army Historical Research, Special Publication No. 17, 2015).
Fletcher, Ian, *Galloping at Everything* (Staplehurst: Spellmount, 1988).
Glover, Gareth (ed.), *Letters from the Battle of Waterloo* (London: Greenhill Books, 2004).
Glover, Gareth (ed.), *The Waterloo Archive, Volume 1: British Sources* (Barnsley: Frontline, 2010).
Graham, Colonel Henry, *History of the 16th, the Queen's, Light Dragoons (Lancers), 1759 to 1912* (Devizes: privately published, 1912).
Leslie, N.B., *The Succession of Colonels of the British Army* (London: Society for Army Historical Research, 1974).
Luard, John, *A History of the Dress of the British Soldier* (London: W. Clowes, 1852).
Oman, Sir Charles, *A History of the Peninsular War*, 7 vols. (London: Greenhill Books, 1996).

Electronic Sources

Auckland Museum, 'Portrait of a soldier in uniform [Lieutenant Charles John Harrison, Queen's 16th Regiment Light Dragoons, Waterloo]', http://www.aucklandmuseum.com/collections-research/collections/record/am_library-paintinganddrawings-1753?k=john%20harrison&ordinal=7 (accessed 19 December 2018).
Battle Honours, 'George Arnold', http://www.battle-honours.eu/george-arnold (accessed 18 December 2018).
Blood, Allan, 'Lieutenant Thomas Blood of 16th Light Dragoons (Lancers): Captain J.H. Belle's Troop', http://www.theonlinebookcompany.com/OnlineBooks/Waterloo/Celebrations/DescendantsStories/76 (accessed 6 January 2019).
Royal Collection Trust, 'Henry Beauchamp Lygon, 4th Earl of Beauchamp; Lieutenant General, Colonel of 10th Hussars, After John Luard (1790–1875)', RCIN 658287, https://www.royalcollection.org.uk/collection/search#/3/collection/658287/henry-beauchamp-lygon-4th-earl-of-beauchamp-lieutenant-general-colonel-of-tenth (accessed 12 February 2019).
Royal College of Surgeons, 'Murray, Denis, 1793–1860', *Plarr's Lives of the Fellows* [online], accessed through the search box at https://livesonline.rcseng.ac.uk/client/en_GB/lives (accessed 8 July 2019).

Index

From Reason to Revolution – Warfare 1721-1815

http://www.helion.co.uk/published-by-helion/reason-to-revolution-1721-1815.html

The 'From Reason to Revolution' series covers the period of military history 1721–1815, an era in which fortress-based strategy and linear battles gave way to the nation-in-arms and the beginnings of total war.

This era saw the evolution and growth of light troops of all arms, and of increasingly flexible command systems to cope with the growing armies fielded by nations able to mobilise far greater proportions of their manpower than ever before. Many of these developments were fired by the great political upheavals of the era, with revolutions in America and France bringing about social change which in turn fed back into the military sphere as whole nations readied themselves for war. Only in the closing years of the period, as the reactionary powers began to regain the upper hand, did a military synthesis of the best of the old and the new become possible.

The series will examine the military and naval history of the period in a greater degree of detail than has hitherto been attempted, and has a very wide brief, with the intention of covering all aspects from the battles, campaigns, logistics, and tactics, to the personalities, armies, uniforms, and equipment.

Submissions

The publishers would be pleased to receive submissions for this series. Please contact series editor Andrew Bamford via email (andrewbamford18@gmail.com), or in writing to Helion & Company Limited, Unit 8 Amherst Business Centre, Budbrooke Road, Warwick, CV34 5WE

Titles

No 1 *Lobositz to Leuthen. Horace St Paul and the Campaigns of the Austrian Army in the Seven Years War 1756-57* Translated with additional materials by Neil Cogswell (ISBN 978-1-911096-67-2)

No 2 *Glories to Useless Heroism. The Seven Years War in North America from the French journals of Comte Maurés de Malartic, 1755-1760* William Raffle (ISBN 978-1-1911512-19-6) (paperback)

No 3 *Reminiscences 1808-1815 Under Wellington. The Peninsular and Waterloo Memoirs of William Hay* William Hay, with notes and commentary by Andrew Bamford (ISBN 978-1-1911512-32-5)

No 4 *Far Distant Ships. The Royal Navy and the Blockade of Brest 1793-1815* Quintin Barry (ISBN 978-1-1911512-14-1)

No 5 *Godoy's Army. Spanish Regiments and Uniforms from the Estado Militar of 1800* Charles Esdaile and Alan Perry (ISBN 978-1-911512-65-3) (paperback)

No 6 *On Gladsmuir Shall the Battle Be! The Battle of Prestonpans 1745* Arran Johnston (ISBN 978-1-911512-83-7)

No 7 *The French Army of the Orient 1798-1801. Napoleon's Beloved 'Egyptians'* Yves Martin (ISBN 978-1-911512-71-4)*

No 8 *The Autobiography, or Narrative of a Soldier. The Peninsular War Memoirs of William Brown of the 45th Foot* William Brown, with notes and commentary by Steve Brown (ISBN 978-1-911512-94-3) (paperback)

No 9 *Recollections from the Ranks. Three Russian Soldiers' Autobiographies from the Napoleonic Wars* Translated and annotated by Darrin Boland (ISBN 978-1-912174-18-8) (paperback)

No 10 *By Fire and Bayonet. Grey's West Indies Campaign of 1794* Steve Brown (ISBN 978-1-911512-60-8)

No 11 *Olmütz to Torgau. Horace St Paul and the Campaigns of the Austrian Army in the Seven Years War 1758-60* Translated with additional materials by Neil Cogswell (ISBN 978-1-911512-72-1)

No 12 *Murat's Army. The Army of the Kingdom of Naples 1806-1815* Digby Smith (ISBN 978-1-912390-09-0) (paperback)

No 13 *The Veteran or 40 Years' Service in the British Army. The Scurrilous Recollections of Paymaster John Harley 47th Foot – 1798-1838* John Harley, with notes and commentary by Gareth Glover (ISBN 978-1-912390-25-0) (paperback)

No 14 *Narrative of the Eventful Life of Thomas Jackson. Militiaman and Coldstream Sergeant, 1803-15* Thomas Jackson, with notes and commentary by Eamonn O'Keeffe (ISBN 978-1-912390-12-0) (paperback)

No 15 *For Orange and the States! The Army of the Dutch Republic 1713-1772. Part I: Infantry* Marc Geerdinck-Schaftenaar (ISBN 978-1-911512-15-8)*

No.16 *'Men who are Determined to be Free': The American Assault on Stony Point 15 July 1779* David Bonk (ISBN 978-1-912174-84-3)*

No 17 *Next to Wellington. General Sir George Murray. The Story of a Scottish Soldier and Statesman, Wellington's Quartermaster General* John Harding-Edgar (ISBN 978-1-912390-13-7)

No 18 *Between Scylla and Charybdis: The Army of Friedrich August II of Saxony, 1733-1763. Part I: Staff and Cavalry* Marco Pagan (ISBN 978-1-912174-89-8)*

No 19 *The Secret Expedition: The Anglo-Russian Invasion of Holland 1799* Geert van Uythoven (ISBN 978-1-912390-20-5)

No 20 *'We Are Accustomed to do our Duty' German Auxiliaries with the British Army 1793-95* Paul Demet (ISBN 978-1-912174-96-6)

No 21 *With the Guards in Flanders. The Diary of Captain Roger Morris 1793-95* Peter Harington (ISBN 978-1-911628-15-6) (paperback)

No 22 *The British Army in Egypt 1801. An Underrated Army Comes of Age* Carole Divall (ISBN 978-1-911628-17-0)*

No 23 *Better is the Proud Plaid. The Clothing, Weapons, and Accoutrements of the Jacobites in 1745* Jenn Scott (ISBN 978-1-911628-16-3)*

No 24 *The Lilies and the Thistle. French Troops in the Jacobite '45* Andrew Bamford (ISBN 978-1-911628-17-0)*

No 25 *A Light Infantryman With Wellington* Gareth Glover (ed.) (ISBN 978-1-911628-10-1) (paperback)

No 26 *Swiss Regiments in the Service of France 1798-1815. Uniforms, Organisation, Campaigns* Stephen Ede-Borrett (ISBN 978-1-911628-12-5)*

No 27 *For Orange and the States! The Army of the Dutch Republic 1713-1772. Part II: Cavalry and Specialist Troops* Marc Geerdinck-Schaftenaar (ISBN 978-1-911628-13-2)*

No 28 *Fashioning Regulation, Regulating Fashion. Uniforms and Dress of the British Army 1800-1815 Volume I* Ben Townsend (ISBN 978-1-911628-09-5)

No 29 *Riflemen. The History of the 5th Battalion 60th (Royal American) Regiment, 1797-1818* Robert Griffith (ISBN 978-1-911628-46-0)

No 30 *The Key to Lisbon. The Third French Invasion of Portugal, 1810-11* Kenton White (ISBN 978-1-911628-52-1)

No 31 *Command and Leadership. Proceedings of the 2018 Helion & Company 'From Reason to Revolution' Conference* Andrew Bamford (ed.) (ISBN 978-1-911628-53-8)

No 32 *Waterloo After the Glory. Hospital Sketches and Reports on the Wounded After the Battle* Michael Crumplin and Gareth Glover (ISBN 978-1-911628-48-4)

No 33 *Fluxes, Fevers, and Fighting Men. War and Disease in Ancien Regime Europe 1648-1789* Pádraig Lenihan (ISBN 978-1-911628-51-4)

No 34 *'They Were Good Soldiers'. African-Americans Serving in the Continental Army, 1775-1783* John U. Rees (ISBN 978-1-911628-54-5)*

No 35 *A Redcoat in America. The Diaries of Lieutenant William Bamford, 1757-1765 and 1776* Edited and Annotated by John B. Hattendorf (ISBN 978-1-911628-47-7) (paperback)

No 36 *Between Scylla and Charybdis: The Army of Friedrich August II of Saxony, 1733-1763. Part II: Infantry and Artillery* Marco Pagan (ISBN 978-1-911628-08-8)*

No 37 *Québec Under Siege: French Eye-Witness Accounts from the Campaign of 1759* Translated and Annotated by Charles A. Mayhood (ISBN 978-1-912866-73-1) (paperback)

No 38 *King George's Hangman: Henry Hawley and the Battle of Falkirk 1746* Jonathan D. Oates (ISBN 978-1-912866-64-9)

No 39 *Zweybrücken in Command: The Reichsarmee in the Campaign of 1758* Translated with additional materials by Neil Cogswell (ISBN 978-1-911628-55-2)*

No 40 *So Bloody a Day: The 16th Light Dragoons in the Waterloo Campaign* David J. Blackmore (ISBN 978-1-912866-66-3)

* indicates 'Falconet' format paperbacks, page size 248mm x 180 mm, with high visual content including colour plates; other titles are hardback monographs unless otherwise noted.